Empty the Cave:

Awaken the Spark

Second Edition

Howdie Mickoski

Empty the Cave: Awaken the Spark
Second Edition (Dec 2024 edition)
book 2 of Exit the Cave series
Copyright ©2024 Howdie Mickoski
All Rights Reserved

ISBN: 978-82-94094-03-5

Font: Baskerville Old Face 12pt
Cover Design by V. Ettlin
Cover Photo by: Pexels.com, Horacio Lander

This book is dedicated to all seekers, who wholeheartedly have had the Intent to first see what the Cave is, secondly find if there is a way to Exit, then are committed to act on what they found.

Table of Contents

THIS BOOK

Everything in this book, as with all of my books, is my personal opinion coming from 30+ years of experiences and research. This is not medical or psychological advice, just philosophical opinions on how I see reality. I don't have all the answers, and this writing is to allow readers the possibility to think deeply on a variety of subjects, so that you can locate answers within that you feel are honest and truthful for you. I don't want you to agree with my answers, only that you spiral within yourself to locate your own.

I mention several times a calm and stable mind is required to come to material such as this. If you feel that this is not where you currently are, it would be wise to have that as your current focus, then come to this work at a later time.

While with a book like this I could keep re-writing, editing and revising for the next twenty years, there comes a time when you feel it is able to do the job it was intended. Finally, after almost a year of work, I feel the work has reached that state. Any errors that remain in the text are from late additions prior to printing, and not the part of the excellent editing team.

A reminder from a famous Asian text to find your own speed and method upon one's path,

"The faster they hurry, the slower they go."[1]

– Faith Mind Sutra

---

[1] Bart Marshall, *The Perennial Way* pg148, Stanza 12

Chapter 1

THE CORE INTENT

"The whole planet is a fiction, a picture show. Sometimes it can be a rather engrossing picture show, but that doesn't make it real. We get programmed with all sorts of infatuations and obsessions. Some of them use up years and decades of our lives. Entire lives pass this way, from one petty obsession to another...Yet some come to realize that life is at best a dream, and at worst, a nightmare."[2] (Richard Rose)

Hi Everyone.

So, you want to Exit Plato's Cave/the Matrix?[3] It is a very grand quest to take on. However, it might not be what you think it is. Such a quest cannot be defined in words, so nothing in this book can possibly describe it. That is because Exiting the Matrix has nothing to do with "you," as it is an Exit of yourself as much as the Cave.

Being someone who chooses to Exit the Cave is a rare and monumental decision. Looking into this type of material usually

---

2   Gold, Dave and Marshall, Bart *After the Absolute* pg 13; Also found in Kent, John *"Pathway to Reality Through the Self"*

3   The Cave refers to the idea of the allegory Plato's Cave, discussed in chapter 2 of my first *Exit* book, while the Matrix refers to the ideas of a trapping simulation as presented in the movie of the same name.

comes after a life that includes personal trauma, an empathy for the suffering of other beings of the world, anger against all the lies presented, and a deep resolution to attain a state of real Truth and Liberation. As I say often, I do not have all the answers, I just share my opinions on what I have found in my 30+ years of searching as a suggestion for you to explore and come to your own understandings. The good news is that others have Exited the Matrix, so it can be done. The problem is that the pathway is not forward, but 180 degrees in the opposite direction. We do not move forward to a searched for end goal, we actually fall backwards into what we Are.[4] The way out is via the way in. The confusion starts because as one has to clearly see that this reality is a trap for one's essence, yet paradoxically, there is no trap, because there is No-thing to be trapped.

This book is the combined progression of two of my previous books, *Falling For Truth* and *Exit the Cave Book 1*. *Exit* presented that this reality is a type of AI-based simulated Matrix, created by an evil deity, for the sole purpose of harvesting energy to keep the simulation running. *Falling For Truth* was a summary of my eight year test on the solidity of the world that led to seeing it as an illusion, and my fall into a canyon which led me to see that I was also an illusion. A key chapter of each of these books can be found at the following footnote[5]. And probably like you I have read hundreds of books, yet none I have read can compare to the live and in person experiences and practice done at the home of Korean monk Byung Chul Park, and in the sweat lodges of three Native Medicine Men: Bruce Starlight, Clayton Bunn and Dennis McKay. This book is also a progression of what they shared with me.

With that, we can begin.

*

---

4   I discussed some of my first "falling backwards" experience with Emptiness in my book Power of Then when testing and falling backwards into various false doors in Ancient Egyptian mastabas at Giza and Sakkara.

5   A key chapter from each book can be found at the following links on my website https://howdiemickoski..com

"Wait, you are now saying there is no trap," asks my editor Anders. "But you wrote in your last book all about how this is a trap and a suffering pit of hell."

"Correct."

"So which is it? A trap or not a trap?"

"Both. The trap had to be laid out in the previous book to shake people from their normal seeing of reality, but now I have to circle back and present a much wider range of information."

Anders, my editor with *Falling For Truth,* has returned to work on this project. He chose not to edit the first *Exit the Cave,* so I had to find another editor for that book, and she did a great job. But after reading the first *Exit,* Anders decided to return and help. I can see he is confused because even though this book is the second book of the Cave series, it is a very different book from the first one.

"Firstly, I no longer refer to this realm as only a 'suffering pit of hell,' it is, but that concept is too limiting to describe this nuthouse. I am now referring to the Matrix as a 'giant pit of distortion and insanity' of which the suffering/pain part is the most noticeable. But as I mention in my chapter on *The Good Place,* actually it is the smaller distortions and manipulations that are more entrapping."

"Multiple small distortions would be harder to track, and would feel overwhelming to figure out."

I nod. "That is why a key antidote to this realm is clarity and sanity (to overcome distortion). Secondly, the whole realm is a paradox. The biggest problem to Exiting the Matrix is not the archons, the Fallen Creator[6], the government, or what you need to

---

6   As discussed in my previous book, I have now come to understand that this reality
     was not created by a loving and caring God, but rather by a creator that is
     sometimes referred to as the Demiurge (after the use of the term by Plato). I no
     longer use the word Demiurge, as I have no trust in the message that Plato was
     delivering. The term that I now use is Fallen Creator (a being of false light). The

fix about yourself. The problem is the projection of you, with all of its hopes, fears, wants, beliefs, and struggles. That is why it is claimed that you already have the key to unlock the prison of the Matrix. One needs to see the totality of the trap of the archons and the loosh energy harvesting, but if one also does not see through the illusion of the self, then the understandings of the Cave will do little. The doorway Home is through the realization of Emptiness. Yet that realization alone is not enough, or every Zen or Advaita master will Exit the Cave (likely they will not). Nor may a great traditional Medicine Person automatically be able to Exit the Cave, no matter how strong their abilities within it. That is because the Matrix must be equally seen, in all of its sick and insane complexity, yet also realized not to even exist. Both sides of the paradox must be seen through, and then one's Awareness finds the midpoint between them where one resides in a type of still, yet calm, tension."

"So in a place of what you wrote about as between-ness?"

"Exactly. One resides in the gap of everything and nothing, walks without walking, and moves while in stillness. One knows when it is time for action, and when it is time to stop."

*

*"The only way to deal with an unfree world
is to become so absolutely free
that your very existence is an act of rebellion."*[7]
- Albert Camus

Gnostics (writers of the Nag Hammadi codices discovered in Egypt between 1945-47 used the name Yaldabaoth (the lion headed serpent) or Saklas for this creator, while the Cathars of Southern France referred to it as Rex Mundi (king of the world). After creating this place, the Gnostics identified that this creator then manifested a series of helper beings (archons or demonic entities) to assist in the trapping of real beings from outside of it into this controlled reality. These demonic entities later became known as angels in many religious texts. The Gnostics saw another Being beyond the Matrix creator, which they called The Father, who resided in a pure realm called the Pleroma, a place I call Home.

7   Albert Camus "The Myth of Sisyphus"

8

The majority of people think this is a beautiful reality, or at least could be with just a few changes. Young children are conditioned to think that they should be grateful to their Creator for such a wonderful place for them to live. The masses ignore that this world is insane and generating suffering for everything within it on a staggering level. The last few years since 2020 should have revealed that. The majority are in denial about all of this because of worldly pushed beliefs like; "God is love," or "Earth is a school of learning." These ideas seem to override any examination of how things really are. Others might admit that while there is much suffering in the current reality, God will soon restore the paradise, and all we have to do is help him by being more loving. The "Golden Age" is coming they might say, or soon we will "ascend" to the greater world, but in each of these ideas are hoped for happy places in the future, not the examination of things as they are now. Examining the influence and manifestations of demonic beings (archons) tend not to be on most people's spiritual to-do list.

When someone has come to see that the world is insane (not loving), rather than re-examining the core belief (God is Love), a new belief is created that God needs our help to fix it (and themselves) back to the original perfection. What can be called self-help and the New Age Movement are ideas promising to find ways to fix things to make everything happy and wonderful. Few seem to consider that for all the billions of people who have tried to fix reality, and the perhaps trillions of prayers throughout history sent to God, reality never gets fixed. As time goes on, the world only seems to get worse.

Things start to make sense when this reality is realized to be constructed from the start to be insane, to create the maximum amount of distortion, misdirection, and suffering, all the while packaged in a beautiful presentation. Yes, this realm contains beauty and joy. This too is part of the grand deception. Love and hate will trap you equally. What is beyond both?

> *"As long as you think there's a solution,*
> *you're part of the problem."*[8]
> - George Carlin

---

8   George Carlin, *Brain Droppings*

A key understanding moving forward with this book is that this world will never get any better or improve. I will repeat that. This is a world of suffering that will never get any better or improve. The belief the realm will improve is one of its greatest tricks. If what I present about this world is true, then would not reality be doing exactly what it was designed to do? Moreover, that any attempt to "fix it" would be futile? Like trying to force a video game about cars to become a video game about golf. It is just not designed to be something different.

Granted, at the core of what we are there is a tremendous power, a power greater than the Matrix. If accessed, this power that can generate some major transformations, miracles even. However, if that power is projected outward to fix the Matrix to what "we want it to be," the energy becomes dispersed and lost. There seems to be great change possible when one stops projecting energy out to fix or save the world, turning it instead back towards oneself, which can then lead to transformation (for oneself, a small group of people, or a local environment). It is the small transformations that have great value. Thus you save the world by saving yourself. I repeat: you save the world by saving your Self.

When West Virginia teacher Richard Rose[9] was asked at a lecture in the 1970s why he was not out helping people or saving the world, he replied coldly, "There is no world, there are no people. You have to come to see that." Then he went on to take the next question, while the previous questioner sat in stunned silence for the rest of the talk.[10] That of course does not mean that even though Rose saw through the falseness of this realm and the people in it that he was not being helpful. Perhaps he just set his bar to the correct limit for his energy not to be wasted. He provided help, but only where it could really be of use. He also clearly stated that if one did gain the power to move mountains, you would leave them where they currently are, because they are exactly where they are supposed to be.

---

9 I consider Richard Rose to be one of the great spiritual teachers of this last century. His work can be found through the TAT Foundation

10 John Kent, *The Path to Reality Through the Self* chapter 4.

*

"Do not seek the footsteps of the wise,
seek what they sought."[11]
- Matsuo Basho

A few days ago, I did a bit of an Internet search to see what results I would get on the topic of "Exiting the Matrix." I was not surprised to see that all of the results were related to living differently in the material world, things such as: being more in tune with nature, getting rid of your TV and smartphone, having less fear, or perhaps fixing the government or financial system. Many of the results also related ideas such as: raising your vibration, loving more, being your best, and taking authority over your actions. Always something related to how the human form can become more comfortable in the material world, or that if a worldly problem gets fixed, everyone could live "happily ever after." The catch is that these suggestions all focus on the idea of "what's in it for me?"

Seeing beyond these hopes was clearly written many years ago by Gary Harmon's lecture notes from a visit to Rose, "*If you accept that all is an illusion without including yourself in that illusion, you have made the classic spiritual mistake.*"[12] It took the fall in the canyon for me to see through this error. The realization was that the physical-mental thing that I always thought I was is as false as all the rest of reality. However, the canyon experience revealed something that was much more real than I ever thought, And that Realness is what I had always been. It was just that the Howdie thing got in my way and got me to "forget" what I really was.

Standard reality is a deception played on the Ultimate Viewer to believe that it is what it perceives. The trap ends when one sees that what they are is No-thing. Since only some-thing can be trapped or contained, this realization begins to unravel the Matrix. Yet this No-thing is not nothing. That error has been made

---

11 https://english.stackexchange.com/questions/280014/do-not-seek-to-follow-in-the-footsteps-of-the-wise
12 "TAT Forum" April 2002

by many nihilists over the years. No-thing and some-thing are opposite sides of the same coin. One cannot understand this using the normal mind, only from a realization from beyond the regular mind. An important point I can make in this first chapter, as presented by my friend Norio Kushi is: *"Only that which is Real and True can Exit the Matrix, all that is false never leaves it."* False is changing while the Real is still. Thus we seek out that which is unchanging and not able to be trapped.

Many have the hope that Exiting the Matrix will mean the end of their suffering. However, Exiting has nothing to do with the material "you." The body-mind thing that you know is not asleep, it is a projection from a much deeper reality. It is this deeper reality, what Gnostics called a Divine Spark, which has been put in a coma and needs to awaken. Joe or Martina are characters in a stage play, actors in a movie and do not awaken. There is something that is behind them, and Awareness, which you might say borrows the actor. That is what needs to wake up.

In the movie *The Matrix,* Neo Anderson played by Keanu Reeves, is not asleep. Neo is a projection of the more real Neo, the one in the pod bubble. The movie is symbolizing awakening when the Neo in the bubble breaks all of the wires and cables that have him attached to and projecting the simulation. Ok, actually that is not awakening either; because the Neo in the bubble was also tricked (he never tested his new reality to see if the world of the hovercraft was as fake as the previous one).[13] Nevertheless you get the general idea.

There are many layers of deception in this reality, much like the Russian Nesting Dolls (one doll, inside another doll, inside of another doll). Every time you think you have figured something out, you open that layer only to find another layer/doll within. This is symbolized in Zen by the metaphor of the world being described as a turtle on the back of another turtle, and so on to infinity. To reach an Ultimate Answer, one has to work backwards through every one of these layered dolls/turtles. Seeing through any layer is important, but unless one sees that they must eventually move past

---

13 This came from the blue pill-red pill trick that was played on him, which I will explore in the additional material.

their current layer of study, they will become stuck there. This goes for any layer, no matter how important we think that it is. There is another Nesting Doll waiting for examination.

To work on this pathway one must fully define the Self (that which actually perceives), and you cannot do that after death in the astral realm. You have to do it now. As Christ responded, "The dead know nothing,"[14] or we could say they know no more there than they do here. The Near Death Experience is a trick presented by the archons to get people to believe that they can do all of their work after they die. The power to see through all the distortions is available now, not after one's death.

In my books and talks I have presented this world as a type of simulation. I want to suggest that it is not the correct word to give an idea as to what this Matrix is. A simulation is defined from Webster as, "the imitative representation of the functioning of one system or process," or "models to test problems and possible results," or "the imitation of the operation of a real-world process or system over time." And while our world can seem like it is one giant experiment, and might be, the word simulation can be a bit confining for one's examination of reality. A better word is simulacra, which can be defined as "copies that depict things that either had no original, or that no longer have an original."[15] This word is similar to how ancient texts refer to this realm, often as a copy, or mirror of a world beyond this one. What is interesting is that the definition suggests that there can be many simulacras in operation, and that it is possible that the original may no longer exist. To make a photo copy of a document is simply a copy of the original. To make the copy, but then destroy the original, would in fact make the copy the original. Thus this reality can be described as something that looks like a simulation, but may have no real function from the standpoint of "learning or testing anything" perhaps only exists as an inverted and distorted copy that is running perhaps only for the purpose of continuing to run.

---

14 Ecclesiastes 9:5
15 https://en.wikipedia.org/wiki/Simulacra_and_Simulation, https://www.merriam-webster.com/dictionary/simulation

We do have to pay attention to this physical reality, as it is providing clues as to who the projector is of this realm. One should not ignore their physical form, instead following an idea in which Richard Rose termed "getting your house in order" (which I will get to in an upcoming chapter). There is also value in what I may refer to as Schopenhauer ideology, gaining an empathy for the suffering of others and finding ways to reduce that suffering (be they persons, animals, plants, or yourself). Yet these ideas of maintaining order and reducing suffering have nothing to do with Exiting the Matrix/Cave. These are the foundational starting points for the long journey to define Self.

*

As for what exactly is "trapped," one of the earliest terms for this True part of us was found in certain Gnostic gospels (such as the *Apocryphon of John* and *Gospel of Judas*) which described people as having the goddess Sophia (wisdom) within. Over time, Sophia came to be known by the term Divine Spark.[16] It indicates that from the start, the Gnostics symbolized the Spark in feminine terms.

The words used to make up the term Divine Spark provide some indications of what this True component may be. Divine has three definitions which indicate either "of or like God," "very pleasing and delightful," or "to prophesize." Combing them it could be described as an all-wise stillness. Spark tends to be defined as "that which can start a fire," or "a small flash of light." The Spark reference is meant to infer Fire. It is my opinion that it was not several individual Divine Sparks that entered from the Pleroma (original Totality outside of the Matrix), but was a single Divine Fire. That original Fire is what, after being deceived, became fragmented into many Divine Sparks. Each Spark gained its own individualized presence and awareness.

This is the first great seeing. There are only two things within the Matrix, one is True (a fire not from the Matrix); the

---

16 In this context, the word God is referring to that which is Outside of the Matrix, which entered either via temptation or through wishing to give life to a non-alive creation.

other is false (water, which is the reflective projection of the entire Matrix and everything within it). This leads to there being two different types of oneness, which I will present in chapter 7. This is the reason that the Cathars claimed that John could not be a legitimate baptizer, as he did so with water. Only Christ could be legitimate because he baptized with fire. A water baptism focuses on reincarnation back into the Matrix, symbolized by the metaphor of the drop of water returning to the ocean. This water idea is also referenced in the myth of Narcissus, who becomes trapped by looking at his own reflection in the water. Water is a symbol for the cycle of reincarnation, and the image he falls in love with (himself) is a metaphor of how we project out a false reality and then become mesmerized by the hologram we create. In other words, the human form we observe in a mirror and on top of still water are tricks to get us to believe that the projection is what we are.[17] Once fragmented from the Fire, each of these Sparks was tricked to project the astral and material experience of the Matrix. It is the Creator of the Matrix that these water metaphors in early creation myths are pointing towards.

The Divine Fire links outside to the Pleroma, thus a baptism of fire would be the method of return of the individual Spark to the greater Fire. Water soothes and comforts, fire burns. Water is the comfort all seek, fire is the Truth that few do. Information of the Divine Spark found its way into many ancient myths such as Prometheus, fairy tales like Sleeping Beauty (especially the old Norse tale of Sigrdrifumal), and even with the idea referred to as the Holy Grail. When the realization that the Spark is Sleeping Beauty, and we (as a form) must become like the prince of the story and awaken her, the pathway has been defined. This is what spiritual work is attempting to do.

The metaphor of a Spark also indicates light. This is another misconception that has been transferred over to the spiritual path. The Cathars claimed that to end the reincarnation cycle, one had to generate a body of light. This is taken to mean that someone has to become holy and perfect so that they will shine beauty to the world. A number of gurus have learned this

---

17 See the additional material for more detail on the myth of Narcissus.

trick and made millions from it by claiming this radiance is enlightenment. However, there is far more meaning to the word enlightenment, which to me relates to the connection of the Spark back to the Divine Fire. It has nothing to do with being "holy" but of being "whole-y."

Those I know who have experienced a connection with their Divine Spark refer to the experience as a heat within their chest that creates no sweating. And the heat is safe, calming and clear. They knew it was the more real deeper "them," as opposed to what they had thought themselves to be previously. That warmth is the first sign the coma is being broken. This is not the same as a kundalini release, which can share certain similarities, but will often feel much more intense. Kundalini is another link to the Matrix, and thus mimics the feeling of connecting with the Spark. The Spark is not intense, overwhelming or linked to any new powers, but is a warm, clear, knowing of what we have always been. Some might ask if this is similar to the feeling of opening the heart. The answer is yes. There is a connection between the two. What is called an open heart, tends to be felt as a warmth in the chest, but this warmth tends to be directed outwards towards the world of objects (or to a deity).[18] With an open heart if one would just turn their attention of Awareness back upon themselves, to see their True Self, which is a pathway towards the Divine Spark. Yet the outer world of objects and experiences and wishes are very tantalizing and it takes great work to make that 180-degree turn to put the focus on Self and not "out there."

*

Anders has been just somewhat casually looking out my window at the mountains across the fjord. The section on the Divine Spark has got to him somewhat, and he has been thinking it over. He turns to ask me clearly, "So this Divine Spark. I don't think I have ever felt it. But others have?"

---

18 There is a second heart within us, that is not in our chest that the famous alchemic texts are alluding to. Our modern spiritual world has put the focus on the heart in the chest, which has value, but by doing so excludes the knowledge of an even more deeper heart.

"Oh yes, about half of the people I was with on an intensive recently had an experience of it."

"Is there something wrong with me because I have not felt it?"

"No. Only there must be certain walls that are up for you. The Matrix walls are not built to keep you in, but to keep the Divine Spark out. Or better said, keep Sleeping Beauty asleep. When the interior belief walls go down, it happens. Simple as that. The work is to remove the walls, not find the Spark. The walls have to open for that to occur."

Anders takes a moment contemplating the depth that I revealed in the previous paragraphs. "As for the water reference that you make. What is wrong with water?"

"Nothing is wrong with water. I like water. It is good to swim in, to drink, to wash with, to sit beside. I enjoy streams and lakes and rivers and oceans and even swimming pools. Normally water in myths and tales tends to be claimed to symbolize ideas such as meditation, reflective thought, even femininity. Yet, there seems to be another symbolic message that appears in certain older myths water is used as a different symbol. In those since water is reflective (thus a projection screen) it can be used as a symbol for the projected Matrix. Fire however, seems to just appear from nothing. Water is always here, but fire has to be "ignited." There is a bunch of twigs and then a spark from somewhere ignites the twigs, and the fire appears."

"What of Christian baptism?"

"The Western Christian culture has taken the baptism of water to be the key to just about everything. If you see in this case (from the standpoint of the archons) this type of baptism means an immersion in the Matrix. But the baptism of Christ, of fire, is different. That no longer appears in church services, only in their texts, though very few understand even what those ideas are referring to. That says something."

"Did you get baptized?"

"By water? No."

"How about fire? Have you been baptized by fire?"

I keep staring at the fjord for a moment, before turning my head and shoulders slightly to face Anders. With a stern, yet soft look in my eye, I slowly nod in the affirmative.

I sense his mind go still. He just nods back.

*

I know many want to ask me when exactly the concepts that became Exit the Cave began. That is difficult to say. It could have been when my ex-girlfriend was murdered, or maybe in my depression when I saw the Egyptian TV documentary that introduced my study of Egyptian Pyramids, or perhaps it was when I first met Mr. Park. All were likely stepping stones, but my current feeling is that this thesis really began to become formulated on June 11, 2005, three weeks after I fell in the canyon.

On that afternoon I went for a walk along the river, just taking in an enjoyable warm day and contemplating the experience of Emptiness and No Self in the canyon. I noticed a small plane fly directly over me heading towards downtown. I chalked it up as an odd co-incidence, and was ready to keep walking, when I observed that just a short distance away it was banking and turning. It then flew directly over my head again. Now I was getting irritated. I watched it, and it again banked, and then flew directly over my head once again. I knew that this was some sort of message being thrown at me by this reality. It was not a co-incidence, this plane specifically wanted my attention. I do not want to say that Matrix was targeting me, or thought that I was special. Just for some reason in that moment (likely due to the clarity from the canyon experience), it was you might say, "checking me out." Still seeing that I was being in some way monitored by reality annoyed me to no end. When I got back to my apartment I quickly wrote the following journal entry which very clearly captured my mood at that time:

> *"I'm tired of this shit. I'm tired of the matrix keeping us in a prison reality. I'm tired of the illusion, all of it. I didn't come back to be in the same shit again. I want to open the bubble and then open everyone else's bubble."*

That is about as clear as it could be looking back now. In that entry I used the words "Matrix" and "a prison reality." I am not sure I ever made such a statement prior. I wrote I wanted to not only open up my bubble, but also everyone else's bubble, and perhaps that has been the underlying intensity to write these books. The intensity of the time was because both sides of the reality coin were flipped within two weeks of each other. I was still just beginning the process of integrating the first (Emptiness) when I got hit with the second (trap).

In time these two realizations created a problem, as they seemed to be the opposites of each other. That created confusion for me. How does a prison reality of demonic beings match a reality of Emptiness and complete freedom? I still had some "black-white" thinking that was claiming only one of these revelations could be true. I spent time just trying to figure out which one it was. Eventually I chose Emptiness, but as you saw in *Falling For Truth,* entities, forces of adversity and mind confusion were part of my presentation in that book. So I made a choice that I felt was "supposed" to be made, like most teachers seemed to suggest.

I did not realize until much later how lucky I had been. By only getting one of the sides of the coin, it can become very challenging to even imagine that there could be a completely opposite realization also be as true. I went through a ten-year illness in the midst of all that, because my mind was trying to understand each side of these realizations separately...but internally my deeper Awareness wanted both sides understood and integrated together. I was blocking what Awareness wanted, focusing on one or the other, so I was operating like grandfather clock, swinging from one side to the other. That did not start to change until the clock came to rest in between (which is what the most intense part of the illness did) so that I had nowhere else to "go" and could finally see and accept both revelations equally. It is why I had to present Exit the Cave material as I did in the previous book (without the Self Definition material that appears in this one) as it was hard for me to discuss both halves of this work at once, so I chose the trap-reincarnation side first to shake people out of their "Earth is a place of love" thinking. But now in this book, I can return both sides to their rightful place of understanding.

*

"The great path has no gates,
thousands of roads enter it.
When you pass through the gateless gate,
you will walk the universe alone ."[19]
- Mumon

I also want to be clear that just because I am describing this reality as an illusion does not make the experiences that take place in this simulation to be meaningless. They have meaning from the standpoint of the character we know ourselves to be and to the movie called Life on Earth. The joys are enjoyable, the pains and suffering can be horrible. One must see that the sufferings that have occurred in our lives are not some sort of random freak occurrences, or happened because there is something wrong with us. That is the concept the Matrix tries to guilt us with, that the suffering of our lives happen because we are some sort of bad person, or we have terrible karma from a past life. Many traumas, especially early in one's life, happen because they have been written into our life script by the very beings who later try to guilt us for their occurrence. The problem is the entire system in which we are residing in. The guilt should be felt by the archons and the

____

19 "The Gateless Gate," written in 1228,
    https://en.wikisource.org/wiki/The_Gateless_Gate

system, not us. From seeing this can come a great compassion for oneself, the journey we have lived, and can create the formation of real empathy for others who had to suffer similar "scripted" traumas.

Trauma is something that is at the core of all beings who exist within this Matrix. All the relative traumas we go through in life (no matter how horrible) are just a fraction of the feeling of the original trauma, which occurred when the Fire that we are first entered into this Matrix reality. That is the original sin. It has nothing to do with two people having sex or eating an apple in a garden. It is the same deep wound all have here, the wound of leaving Home (Absolute) and entering this reality (the false light dual world). That is the deep trauma to be healed.

I will repeat this idea many times in this book: only that What Is True can Exit the Matrix. Everything false will have to be left behind. Even energy cannot Exit the Matrix, because energy is the core of the Matrix, the power for the computer. Energy (as we have come to understand it) has nothing to do with the Divine Spark, so raising your vibration or having a loving open heart is not Exiting the Matrix, because both are based on energy. Awakening the Spark from the coma has similarities to these ideas, but it is not the same. When one has the utmost of intention to locate Absolute Reality, Liberation is close at hand.

You may notice that I have not used the word "freedom" in this first chapter to describe the direction or intent of this work. That is because the understanding of language is important, for it is one of the main building blocks of the trap itself. English is a designed language that has many built in synonyms and homonyms so that the same word (or sounding word) are conveying multiple messages. A greeting like "hello" is actually putting the word "hell" into the subconscious of the one been greeted.

The word "freedom" indicates a state of being "free." However, what does the word "free" mean? Free from shackles? Free in the English language also means goods or services "that can be taken without payment." Why would we want to use a word which indicates that we could be in a state that allows us being taken "without payment?" As such, the best English word to use for our goal should be "liberated." Because the word "liberate" means to eliminate beings from imprisonment, slavery, enemy occupation or oppression. We want that.

*

*"If you do not fast from the world,
you will not find the Father's kingdom ."*[20]
- Gospel of Thomas

Exiting the Matrix should be one's Core Intent. We become like St. Anthony the Hermit (who will be explored in an upcoming chapter), resisting all temptations and fears, because he was rooted in Self.

The place I call Home resides at the core of our being, as a memory of something greater than the simulacra. It is the feeling that this reality is not where one belongs or originated, that there is a somewhere else, a true origin. It haunts us constantly with wisps of nostalgia, but we cannot exactly place where this is. Most may think this nostalgia must be a memory of how good this Earth was at one time in the past, so they work hard to try to fix it. Some take this to feel that they want to relive their childhood (to a time when things were simpler). When one finally figures out that this nostalgia is not pointing to this realm, one begins walking backwards towards that which never changes, away from the false projections, to the one thing Not False. The understanding is that Home can not be found in the Matrix.

We must see that there is a trap, and yet at the same time, these archons cannot trap what we really are; No-thing (Emptiness). We learn how to navigate the Matrix as opposed to fighting it, seeing it clearly rather than trying to fix it, and act within it while operating from stillness, as opposed to attempting to

---

20 Gospel of Thomas 27

achieve excessive material world goals. We want to end the reincarnation cycle completely. All other goals become secondary. We do that via Self Definition, Awareness and clarity

I will end this introductory chapter with some words from the *Ashtavakra Gita,* a text I will return to in the final chapters. At the beginning, the text states that a focus for stepping out to be free is to, "*shun the experiences of the senses like poison. Turn your attention to forgiveness, sincerity, kindness, simplicity, and truth...Liberation is to know yourself as Awareness alone – the witness of all. Abide in Awareness with no illusion of person. You will be instantly feel free and at peace.*"[21]

Awareness is the stepping stone, for it is the seat of the clear seeing required, not only to view the Matrix as it honesty is, but also to see the depth of our being as it honestly is. Sleeping Beauty is waiting to be woken from her coma. Once that happens, and this Divine Spark gets back its unlimited power, everything changes. That is when one can really begin to chart a pathway Home.

---

21 *Ashtavakra Gita* 1.2-1.4 found in Marshall, Bart *The Perennial Way* pg103

Chapter 2

THE GOOD PLACE:
Awakening in the Dream

I had been sitting on a couch in a waiting room for some time, wondering exactly where I was and why I was there. Across from me was a wall that was bare other than the odd words "Welcome! It's all good." Then a door to my left opened and an older gentlemen invited me into his office.

I sat in a semi-comfortable chair across the desk from him. He seemed to be a man in his late 60s, with gray hair, glasses, and wore a grey suit with an odd bow tie. For some reason, I felt the urge to ask for a beer, but then that urge faded.

"I want to let you know that you, Howdie Mickoski, are dead. You are now moving on in existence. There is a crap place or a super place you can go. You are here, in the Super Place."

"This can't be the Super Place," I responded

"Of course it is, I designed and created it personally. I am the architect of it," said the man.

"As philosopher Emil Cioran pointed out, 'good can never create. Only evil can create."

The man: "Don't say that. You too are a creator, a wonderful creator being."

"That's a saying used over and over again by New Agers hoping to make themselves feel important. I am not a creator, just a projector, projecting illusionary objects and ideas to help the Fallen Evil Creator continue to make a simulated prison reality. Good is something else entirely, and found somewhere else. So if this is a place that was created, then it is quite obviously evil, and thus you too must be evil." I then stood up to say, "I am done with all of this."

The man was obviously terribly upset with me, and replied: "Get out! You are going to ruin everything here! Get out of this reality and never come back!"

Walking to the door I turned and smiled to him. "Exactly! Cheers."

The above was a personal adaptation where I was the participant in the 2016-2020 Television program *The Good Place*.[22] Now I will explain the show as a metaphor to understand our reality.

*

THE SYSTEM

In the last fifty years, standard mythology has pretty much been forgotten in the Western world. Old myths used to be common stories, and it seems humans on some level need them. With the old myths no longer taught in schools, they have been replaced in the modern era by movies and television shows. These have become the common stories for the general population. Far more people can discuss the plot of a *Seinfeld* or *House* episode than they could the trials of Hercules. Probably myself included. Thus it seems that many of the clues that used to placed into myths in the past, are now inserted into modern entertainment. Where the origin of these insertions are from is not certain, only that they

---

22 I am not suggesting that the creators of this show consciously created the clues that I will be sharing in this chapter, but whatever the co-incidence, many of the show's key themes help to, in my opinion, reveal key workings of the Matrix reality.

occur. Recall that what is aired on TV is not called "programming" by mistake.

There are many tricks being presented with *The Good Place,* one to the characters in the show, and another to the viewing audience. The first season offered an insight into the nature of our reality. It also had an ending of the series that very few understood, which on the surface seemed to be a happy ending for Eleanor and the humans. Actually it was anything but that. This is my thesis on how our reality is set up, using the TV show as a metaphorical guide of explaining it.[23]

The TV series had an "architect" named Michael (the name of a key angel of many Western religions), played by Ted Danson. Danson also played Sam Malone (bar owner and bartender) from the popular TV series *Cheers* in the 1980's and 90's. *Cheers* might share a similar allegory of hell, which I will cover later. In *The Good Place*, at the end of season one, we find that Michael is in fact a demonic being, who has created a complete town in an after-life hell designed for only four humans: Eleanor, Chidi, Tahani, and Jason. Hell has been presented to them as heaven, so to keep the trick going, the tortures presented to the four had to be subtle or the humans would have noticed where they were. Thus *The Good Place* was not actually a good place, but a disguised hell. This mirrors our standard reality in the Earth world, where a hellish material realm is made to seem "not all that bad" at times, to get us to not see the many layers of what is taking place in reality.

The rest of the several hundred characters that reside in the town were all demons in disguise, pretending to be other humans who also made it to the "wonderful heaven." Actually the sole purpose for the townsfolk/demons was to make this a private hell for the human foursome. And since things cannot be too obvious, the chosen method of torture was psychological. The townsfolk were going to get the humans to torture themselves.

---

23 Another to display insights about our reality is the 1993 movie *Groundhog Day* , with Ned Ryerson likely portraying the Devil, and the time loop that Phil is caught in symbolizing the reincarnation trap. I discuss this in a blog post https://howdiemickoski.com

The Good Place townsfolk could be seen as high level NPC's (a reference to non player characters in video games). They are there to set up the very situations that would create constant annoyance. The first twist showing this comes early in the first season when it gets revealed that the characters Eleanor and Jason understood that they were not the "correct persons" that were sent to *The Good Place*, as they were somehow switched for a similar named person after each of them died. How a perfected Heaven could make such a mistake was never really considered by either of them, and the "not in the right place scenario" set up a ton of interactions in the upcoming episodes that would be used to create the guilt, shame, and regret that all the four human would go through.

This similar premise was used as the central idea of Jean-Paul Sartre's 1944 play "No Exit," where three recently deceased people, are forced to spend eternity in a featureless room where they torture each other based on each other's character flaws continually. The most well known phrase of the play is, "Hell is other people."

I believe this show is presenting a template of our current Earth-realm: A carefully designed and manufactured reality that is meant to induce the maximum suffering for the few human souls that exist here. Our main suffering is not what we have come to think it is from; conflicts, wars, illnesses, injuries and natural disasters, which are just a small part of the package. The real torture setup uses what humans do to each other psychologically. This is what makes the system so sick yet ingenious. In *The Good Place*, Michael and the demons staged scenarios they thought would have the biggest psychological effect on the four humans. Then the humans would continue repeating these inner problems internally with themselves, and with each other.

While some researchers today suggest this reality is a type of manufactured AI hell, tend to miss the various detailed layers of how this reality is structured. It works more similar to *The Good*

Place, with the main suffering being originated internally, while other humans unknowingly put more pressure on each other. The external pain (war, trauma, injury, disaster) are not only additional suffering tools, but a distraction big enough that no one notices the real damage going on, one small bite at a time. These smaller avenues are setups the archons are constantly creating, to produce a result of humans to torture each other day after day. The false belief is that our world is a wonderful one of love and joy, something like the cities in the movies *Pleasantville* or *Truman Show,* or the believed *Good Place.* Yet when any of these towns were looked at more closely, there is a trap built into the supposed happy exterior.

One significant possibility for me is that there are very few real humans in our reality (by that I mean those who have a connection to a Divine Spark). My current take is that perhaps only 5% of the population have this Spark connection. Thus in a world of 8 billion human shells, there may only between 400 million "humans with Divine Sparks." The remaining 95% would be what tend to be described as NPC's (non player characters), of which maybe 0.5% might actually be demonic beings (archons), often situated in high places of decision making to control the direction of the entire material realm. However, I am not a fan of the term NPC, and will use a new term going forward that may explain this phenomena in better detail, but first I must present how the system is set up.

A big way Divine Spark humans are being manipulated is by being paired in various friendships and relationships where they don't really match. These allow more natural friction to be created, even though the people involved are tricked into believing they do match. This is usually set up via co-incidental meetings that make each of them receptive for a friendship. Granted, I think that there tends to be a natural draw between humans with a Divine Spark, so there tend to be more connections within a community. The challenge is that within those possible Divine Spark relationships, the Matrix system tends to push the more challenging pairings into close connections, while finding ways to keep those with excellent matches apart. I have noticed this often. With those I really wanted to have a close connection with, these tended to have a lot of challenges to be able to stay connected over time (as examples, one might be pushed to move to a new city, or a rumour about one is spread to get them to lose interest etc.). Our life is definitely manipulated by archons from the outside, using what are called life scripts. Rather than these scripts being set in stone, they tend to be ever changing manipulations by the system (as presented in the 2013 movie *the Adjustment Bureau*), which force us towards people and situations that the system wants us to be with for its own benefit, not ours.

Many have come to question just why this reality is set up with so much built in pain, where everything needs to eat something else just to keep living. This is a world where a few people own yachts, planes, helicopters and multiple houses, while a majority of the world's population is starving. Such an unjust and sick society could only have been programmed. It could not have occurred "naturally."

A great trick that the TV show reveals is that within the Good Place framework, evil is playing both sides. Michael was never a good guy, on the side of the humans. He pretended goodness and caring as a trick to human sentiments. That is one of Lucifer's original tricks, which was not just to create a dual reality, but to divide his presence into two: a good god (that most people pray to for help) and Satan-Devil (an evil force that people ask the good god to get help with). Both sides are one and the same, evil using the mask of evil, and evil using the mask of goodness, as required. Anyone praying to this supposed goodness is really praying to the "nice" face of Lucifer. So much of what may be called the prayers and ceremonies fall into this distortion. Everyone means well, but few check to see where their prayers are really being directed. Granted, it could be that prayers being directed to nature itself may have a higher chance of being received with no "energy demands" placed on them, because one is asking for help from other beings that are also within the Matrix trap system. But then we have to be ready to answer the calls of help from nature to keep this two-way street of help strong and clear.

The majority of big prayers, no matter the tradition, all go to something that they call the Great Spirit or Creator. This is the good side of Lucifer. So when help comes from such prayers, as it certainly can (which is why they keep doing them) they likely do not realize that there is a "tax'" placed on the help by this "good god." You might say this good god adds some fine print that says, here is some energy to help with the problem that you prayed to me for, but you owe me energy back, either later in life or after-death. As I mentioned in *Exit the Cave 1*, the best prayers are payers that are directed to what is true within us (our Divine Spark), because it is linked to the power which is outside of the Matrix. Outside of the Matrix is where the only Real Good exists, to a location considered "Non Dual," thus existing in a place without distortion or manipulation. This is the place we wish to obtain our energy from, not from the distorted Matrix.

Again, it is not really the big obvious stuff that causes the most problems for us, it is the small stuff. Like little pin pricks over and over that cumulatively lead to massive energy loss and psychological confusion. The problem of course is the parasitic ego that each human obtains while still a child, which creates the conflict. A Divine Spark has no conflict with another Divine Spark. Conflict is ego to ego, and as long as egos are in place, *The Good Place* trap can be put forth. This is the reason to work with Self Definition. The more we find what is True about what we are, also means the more false has been dropped.

This is not the first world or simulation that exists here. There were several previous to this one. Perhaps in the original this realm was not a place of psychological torture, but rather only a place of physical torture, via volcanoes, tidal waves, wild animals, and other natural calamities. In the struggle, as humans learned to band together and reach great elements of empathy for each to deal with these situations, the system made a switch. A new "world" simulacra was created where suffering was lessening due to the increase of empathy and compassion that were seen. In its place, humans were given a non-physical ego, and then setting up a system to torment that new ego constantly. Some outer suffering still happens here, but the main set up is to have humans torture each other, so that we will lose our empathy, integrity and courage.

I suspect that in this most recent simulacra, in order to keep humans confused, the archons set up "systems of control" (presented as ways to help us) within the Matrix, so that they could be in direct "hands on" control of the societal structures and keep people divided from each other. This includes systems such as government, financial, spiritual, educational, even religion or spirituality. All are designed to present distortion, control and manipulation as some type of assistance.

It is my belief that this realm today is built on trauma and suffering (with inter spaced moments of peace and calmness to act like a battery charger for the next trauma). Thus, the traumas are not there to "teach us" anything. Beings are placed in a series of "life script traumas," starting in childhood, to act as a foundation for the future. Original childhood traumas are codes built into one's personal system. From that point forward, depending on how we have shaped our sense of self, the ego takes these first traumas and structures them in such as way that we continue to manifest similar occurrences as our life continues. The life scripts put in place (usually by tricking our soul to agree with them) set the foundation for what comes after. Without such foundations, we would not be creating continuing guilt, shame and regret, which are the building blocks of the archon reincarnation trap.

Through deep Awareness and introspection, one can ask the right questions and start to see through traumas. To see that these original traumas of one's life were not caused by "bad luck," or because we are somehow an "unworthy person," but rather were scripted into our lives by demonic beings before we were born. These scripts can then become unraveled and end their influence on our day to day life.

*

AUTOMATONS

The discussion of the NPC has been one of the areas of strongest resistance in the Exit the Cave message. It is important to know that I do not see NPC's as some type of robot, nor do I call them non-human. They are human, they have souls[24], can be a good friend, repair a car, help a child with an illness, offer good advice or be a terrific sex partner. They are just missing a connection to a Divine Spark. Without that, they loose depth. They will not have the driving curiosity to look into philosophy, nor the need to understand what reality, the self or death is. They may have a passing interest in these subjects, read a few books, or join some retreats. However, spiraling inward will never happen. Even though they may have been on a 20-year spiritual journey, to those who knew them when they began, it may seem like they have not taken a single step forward.

I have to admit, the term non-player character is one that I really do not like to use, and after long consideration I came across the word automaton. The specific definitions for this word are: "a moving mechanical device made in imitation of a human being," or "a machine which performs a range of functions according to a predetermined set of coded instructions." The word has its origin from the Greek automatos, meaning acting of itself. That is a perfect description for these types of people, they simply react to the cues of their environment. There is little deliberation. This is not just animal based functioning, there is thought and consideration involved, but 99% of the time those considerations will only be about goals in the material world. That which is more lofty than the material tends to be disregarded, or simply falls into a simple belief that never again gets questioned.[25]

A closely related English word "autonomous" has an entirely different meaning. When presented for a country, region, or person, it means having the freedom to govern itself or control its own affairs independently. So what is interesting is that the way

---

24 All beings have a soul, which is a connector point in reality between the high
    energetic realms and the material.
25 Definitions in this paragraph come from various Wikipedia pages

to Liberation is through being autonomous for oneself, yet surrounding us are various humans who only act in automatic ways. Thus no longer will I use the term NPC but automatic humans (AHs), for that term gives the indication of how the person is in operation now (automatic), but it also suggests that a shift is possible. They could go from automatic to autonomous. Perhaps a younger version of myself might have been classified as operating in automatic mode from the viewpoint of today. AH's can not exactly gain a Divine Spark, but if they have an inner "shake up" and start to examine beyond the programming, they can Exit the Matrix. It is just it that few will choose that possibility, tending to happy to follow their programming.

So what of the automatic humans in our midst that surround us? Often someone who is tremendously good looking or in great physical shape might be an AH. Not always, but it there seems to be a compensation that many AHs make, to try to make itself seem to have an outer perfection. Divine Spark humans will come across as more beautiful on the inside (which should make them more appealing) because they offer the possibility of depth. In the earlier simulations there were few AHs. The rise in population to our time is only the increase of the number is not due to any increase of Divine Sparks (which I feel never grows, only lessens, as one's Exit). The excess population are AH's, which allow (in Westworld thinking), bigger storylines.

The danger for us is though their antenna. We all have an antenna within, a type of radio link that was implanted as part of the parasitic ego that is meant to pick up frequency messages from the AI source. The AH has very little filter with this. Whatever frequency comes in, gets absorbed and then "projected" as their own thoughts. This is happening to us as well, but the Divine Spark acts like a blocker to this frequency. The stronger the Divine Spark, the stronger the block. That is why it is so easy for the masses to go along with anything the system wants them too, as there is little filter to the "radio broadcasts." If the AI wants Jim to bring up a subject with you that happened ten years ago that the system knows will make you uncomfortable, it can trigger Jim to bring it up. If you ask Jim why he is talking about "that" he might honestly say "I have no idea, just now came to mind." An AH are not demons (as in *The Good Place*), but they can hurt you by producing situations designed to trigger something within. One must be hyper vigilant at all times. All might be fine and smooth for two hours, then for no reason, one small commentary occurs with the potential to create upsetting feelings within us.

These external triggers and events with others however are just the base layer to the challenge. When we are alone, our parasitic mind will continue the attacks within ourselves. External situations are not continuously needed, as the mind parasite has built-in means to keep remembering these events and words over and over. All of it is designed to get us to feel guilt, shame and regret (over everything we have ever done or did not do), in a realm where we are placed in situations to send us into inner torment again and again. This is the Earth experience the New Age community considers to be full of wonderful love.

Many who do not want to contemplate if the AH idea is true, will just claim that I am looking down on people and de-humanizing them. I am just presenting things as I have come to see them. In *The Good Place,* the others in the town were all actual demons. If I was one of the humans who resided there and discovered the hidden secret of the village, it would have been a good thing to let the other humans know about. If something like that were true here, wouldn't you want to know? I don't believe that the majority of human shells in our reality are demons, evil, or even zombies like some try to portray them. They are just have direct frequency antennas with little to stop the message that comes in. That is all. I know several AHs of course, and have friendships with them, but I also know there is a very clearly defined limit as to how deep I can ever go in any conversation with them. They have no interest in a journey to know the Totality of Reality and the Self. They really can't even contemplate what that is. This helps us to know who we can share the depth of our journey with, and who we have to stick with talking about the weather and our new deck.

*

LIFE CONNECTIONS

Now let's move onto what we call two people who become life partners, and even bigger, the idea of soul mates. This was one of the tricks played on the characters in the TV series, that the after-life was all about spending continuous time with their soul mate. That sounds like heaven does it not? But what if the whole soul mate idea is another trick, one that gets woven into us at a very young age, especially via modern version fairy tales where the prince and princess get married and live "happily ever after." Do you know of anyone who has lived "happily ever after?" Of course few understand that the original tales were not about a coupling of two people in the material realm, but were discussing work for an inner marriage of the male and female halves of the Divine Spark.

Why do our modern ideas of marriage also come with terms such as "wed-lock" (meaning that you are locked in) or to call your partner a "ball and chain." One standard definition for marriage is the "legal union of two people." The use of the term legal is indicating that some authority has the power to allow or disallow two people to spend their life together. In our current world, a marriage is a type of a contract, a way for two people to come together and share expenses and chores. Yet, just like the way the characters of *The Good Place who* were manipulated with ideas of a "soul mate," people today take this idea as if they must find this "divine half" which will create unending happiness, and a "sense of completion."

At our core, we are all feel incomplete. What follows is my opinion after reading the various Gnostic scriptures. It seems to me that upon entering the Matrix, the Divine Fire was split into many Sparks. But it went further. Each individual Spark was again split into two (a male and female gender). The male part entered the Matrix (and became either a male or female form) while the female half stayed at the doorway. The female half is what was put in the coma, and thus relates to the tale of Sleeping Beauty. Thus half of our Spark is active in our day to day life, while the other half is in the coma and cut off from a completeness. This split was ingenious for Lucifer, for it produced a guaranteed partner-seeking mechanism within every manifested form in creation. The Spark within us feels "incomplete," which it is, and as such has a natural tendency to find that which will complete itself. The Matrix has built in the idea that this incompleteness can be remedied by obtaining an object in the material realm. This search for completeness is generally presented through a relationship (especially finding what is called a soul mate). However, there is no relationship or object that can be obtained in the material world that can heal the inner feeling of being incomplete (because it is not a material issue), so the outer seeking continues.

When one realizes that the feeling to seek wholeness originates at one's core, that it is a "core split" of one's being not a lack of something in the world, then a shift can finally begin to occur to find the only thing that has ever needed to be found. The female half (Sleeping Beauty) in a coma at the Exit door. This split, first by the Fire into Sparks, and then by the Sparks into male-female halves is the original trauma. Every being in reality with a Divine Spark feels this wound, and it can only be healed by first strengthening the Divine Spark half we have within, and then giving it the power to magnetically connect back to its other half. This would make the two Sparks whole again, and thus able to reconnect with the Divine Fire. This is what the Christ baptism of fire is all about. Granted there is a way where two people can speed this process up, symbolized by what the Holy Grail was pointing towards, but that is something very unique and usually not what couples are doing. I will explain some of this in an upcoming book on Southern France

That does not mean that excellent "marriage matches" within the material realm do not exist. They do. One of the first indications that two people might have this deep connection is to see how hard the Matrix tries to be sure the two people can not be together. This happened to me when I was 19 years old, and met what would have been an outstanding connection, but beyond being good friends, she was never interested in dating. Eventually I got the hint and sadly moved on. About ten years later we met again, and she told me she had said no to a date because she never felt she could be good enough for me. She claimed a voice in her head kept telling her over and over not to spend time with me. Eventually she just believed it. Of course this voice would be the voice of the archons, pushing to life scripts of their choosing. It was during our last meeting (she died shortly afterwards) when she shared this information with me. During that meeting she also revealed that she then understood that the voice in her head had been mistaken, and she shared that she acknowledged that we both lost a good life together. Saddest day of my life when I said good bye to her that day, but I am thankful that at least we were able to both know this deeper truth about how this Matrix world is structured to constantly deceive.

I can not consider her some sort of "soul mate," or that a loving deity was arranging some sort of positive destiny for my life. If there had been any such life script, it would have been part of the archon world. We were just two people that matched well, simple as that. I share this story because good matches for friends and lovers exist in this reality. The archons like to derail peace, clarity and happiness any way they can. Be aware of this as you go forward with your pathway, and watch how events transpire after you meet someone or begin a friendship. How the Matrix responds, or does not respond, will give you a lot of clues as to the possible depth of the underlying connection.

One of the big problems that we face is that while we are immersed in our life, it is a life that we don't really understand. We have no real context for it. A question so many ask is, how did I wind up at this point in my life? Because generally, people don't know. The decisions that caused us to turn left over right, which led us to where are are, are unknown as to their origin. Why did I turn left instead of right, take one job but not another, move to one city but not another? Who made these decisions? The more we examine such things, the more we might begin to speculate that something "not the normal day to day us" was making these decisions.

Philosopher Arthur Schopenhauer would likely claim that the majority of the decisions that get made for a human comes from an underlying unconscious force that he labeled Will. This Will has its main purpose to make sure we stay relatively healthy so that we can receive doses of romantic love, have sex with someone and make babies, stay healthy enough to look after those babies, until they grow up and can get their dose of romantic love and continue the cycle. This force Freud would label the Id and Rose the Umpire. It is a type of mind that is not really going to help us spirituality, but will look after us (keep us safe enough to follow its bidding). That so many decisions are tied to this feature, and there is no doubt that the archons (demonic beings controlling reality behind the scenes) are manipulating us via the Will. Part of our job to is see that this is happening, and a huge amount of what can be called "spiritual work" is designed to help us get a good viewing of this Will so that it is no longer pushing us along like a puppet or robot. But this will take much more work to do than is normally presented.

*

HOW IT ENDED

In *The Good Place,* Chidi and Tahani never figured out that they were actually in hell, because they saw themselves as special and deserving humans. They believed they were terrific, so expected heaven as their reward. They had no belief system in place to question their believed specialness. Eleanor and Jason both knew that they were in the village by a mistake, thus were not special, and so they were in a different state of awareness, making them able to explore and analyze their environment differently. The point is, if one feels special, evolved, deserving, or above others, it will be nearly impossible to see reality clearly, because their belief structure demands them to be in heaven to prove their specialness. Also recall that in *The Good Place,* after every memory wipe, Michael snaps his fingers and what is shown is a white light. This is an indicator of what is really going on with this show. The reincarnation trap is presented over and over with the memory wipes, but the complete recycling comes in the very misunderstood series ending.

That takes us to Michael, the architect of *The Good Place.* In religious terms, Michael is known as one of the arch-angels. Arch being a short term for archon. The arch-angles are the chief archons of this realm. What are called angels are archons in disguise, as Michael was in *The Good Place* (his Ted Danson character was wearing a suit covering the demon that he really was). An angel named Michael is one of the few common elements to all three western religions, which is odd in itself. Why is this name one of the few things that permeates all of them?

At the beginning of season two, once the demons realize they cannot stop the humans from figuring out they are in hell every time the experiment is reset, they switch their tactics. Michael now decides to promise the humans that he can get them into the real Good Place. All the demons suddenly become nice and helpful. Does this make any sense? Archons are archons, demons are demons. They are built only to lie and deceive. It is what they do. Why do these humans believe all of these demons have now magically changed their ways? Was it because he happened to be the fun loving bar owner in *Cheers?* Weren't all of the Cheers patrons sort of trapped in the bar, never being able to leave? Doesn't *Cheers* also seem to be a similar allegory for hell? Even *Frasier,* who spun off into a new series of that name, seemed to stay in hell even though he moved as he had to live with his father, always failed with women, never really received recognition for helping people, and was constantly battling with his brother Niles for status. Another television series with an allegory representing hell was *Gilligan's Island.* Gilligan, as the Devil in a red shirt, assured that the others could never get off Hell Island as he thwarted every escape attempt. Interestingly one had Gilligan in the red shirt, and the Skipper in a blue shirt (an original Matrix movie red pill-blue pill choice). Duality was also later connected with the show as a question men have been given over the years is who would you choose, Ginger or Mary Ann? This continued to shows such as *WKRP in Cincinnati* making the question Jennifer or Bailey? A third choice is never given.

Back to *The Good Place.* What was really going on with this supposed demon alteration? My sense is that once Michael saw that the humans were thwarting his Good Place village plan, he decided at that point to trick them to go into the white light. The final two years of the show were all about this final trick played on the humans. However, Michael cannot force the humans to go into the white light, they must do so willingly, similar to the attempts made by the demon being on Commander Janeway in the *Star Trek: Voyageur* episode "Coda." The walking through the door that will happen in *the Good Place* is not a walking into Heaven, the void, Home, or anything else. It is walking into reincarnation. It is why nothing happened for Michael when he walked through the door, as he was an archon and does not get recycled back through the reincarnation system.

The main trick of the final season is being played on Eleanor. There is even a suggestion that perhaps the other three humans were also demons in disguise, all to trick her into believing that she somehow converted the main demon architect into a good guy that wants to help her get to the actual good place/heaven. Believing all this, at some point she would consent to her essence to be reused again as a battery in a reincarnated mind-wiped limited experience. She walks through this door on her own accord, trusting what Michael has told her was going to happen.

In *The Good Place*, rather than presenting someone's close relative as a person in the after-life that they should trust, here in this world they are using Janet (an AI) to whom the humans have come to (mistakenly) trust. If you notice, none of the four humans had any real religious or spiritual backgrounds, and they were all rather materialistic. Even Chidi's philosophy was only focused on ethics and behaviour, and never to answer questions of who and what this universe actually is. As such, this group would have had no trust from any religious figure, thus it made sense to give them a type of somewhat fun but misunderstood female robot who could answer their wishes to trust. She was there to give the humans a "seeming" friend that they would trust and believe in. However AI can never be our friend, for it is a connection point to the Matrix not to which is beyond it. Thus for the humans in the town, Janet was just always data collecting on them.

Eleanor was the last to go through the door. She didn't walk through until she felt completely alone. One part of the many tricks to get her to make this decision was to get her to believe that the eternal afterlife they were presented was boring, with very limited freedom and creative abilities (oddly this is similar to how the afterlife was presented to Robert Monroe, which I discuss in an Additional Material chapter). The humans were not really given an eternal afterlife where one can create their own reality and do anything they want, but one full of boring parties, DJ contests, and endless video games. Eleanor never questioned such a stupid afterlife. That lack of critical questioning became her downfall.

We see in this final "heavenly" season that the humans are being tortured in subtle ways, even when it seems the demons are being helpful, claiming to be finding new ways to help other humans grow and learn. For example, Vicky's test for Tahani is just another way to torture her, under the pretense of finding ways to "challenge her." She is being tricked into receiving more psychological torture.

The ending of the entire series is not presently fully understood. After Eleanor goes through the door, a letter seemingly in the wrong mailbox appears to a man on Earth. He decides to take it to its rightful recipient, who turns out to be Michael, who has taken a human form. The letter seems to be a point reward card to a shopping location known as "Coyote Joe's Marketplace." Michael is listed as Michael Realman. Section 1 of that letter states "In addition we will be collecting data on everything you buy and making sure that ads are targeted directly to you for all your needs. Fun!" So the letter is discussing the AI and data control slave system imposed on the humans in this realm, something of course a demon like Michael would love. And the name of the market was the coyote, the famous trickster of Native American mythology.

This is not really a letter telling Michael he joined some grocery points club. Viewers saw this ending as some sort of wonderful news for him about being a real human in the material world of the mundane. My guess is that this was a message he set up for himself to receive when all four humans (or at least Eleanor) finally on their OWN accord go through the door and get reincarnated. This letter would be his verification of the success of his plan. That is why he was so happy on seeing it, his plan had succeeded. His response to end the show was "keep it sleazy," which pretty much describes his behavior from the first moment he appeared in episode one. He is the archon architect, and his only goal is the suffering of humans. He was tricking Eleanor every moment since her arrival in the after-death state. I even wonder if the man delivering the letter was the reincarnated Eleanor? It would be even more of a sadder twist if that were true?

The show is actually a continuous four-season mind fuck, which likely none of the millions of viewers who watched each week ever figured out. They thought Michael became a nice guy, and what luck that he got to get to Earth and live a human slave data mined life, while Eleanor got to go to some unseen heaven. Everything happening was a lie, all meant to deceive the characters in the show, thinking that the demonic archons might care about them, that the slave control material world is fun, and that the white light is their friend. No wonder less than 1% of 1% ever truly Exit the Matrix.

> *"I took my stand in the midst of the world , and in flesh I appeared to them. I found them all drunk, and I did not find any of them thirsty. My soul ached for the children of humanity, for they are blind in their hearts...when they have vomited their wine, they will change their ways."*[26] - Gospel of Thomas

---

26 *Gospel of Thomas* 28, slightly restated from
    http://www.gnosis.org/naghamm/gosthom.html

Chapter 3

AFTER-DEATH REALMS
Awakening From the Dream

I was excited when I recently started reading *The Divine Comedy* by Dante. I had thought this famous work was going to have pointers for Exiting the Matrix. I based that idea on a key phrase that Dante placed over the gates of Hell (Inferno); *"Abandon all hope ye who enter here."* I thought he was claiming that the hell of his story was our material realm, and thus his story would be a Cathar-Gnostic metaphor.

I began to read the text, but it did not take long to realize that my idea of what he was writing about was incorrect. He was not writing about Exiting the Cave. I believe he was writing about a standard Near Death Experience (NDE). This because the book contains all of the normally presented NDE elements: the white light, love, peace, dead relatives or religious figures, life review, pressure to return to life, and at times seeing hell-like images of people who were not "good enough" during their lives. Albeit it is presented in an experience presented in a very poetic and beautiful way. Dante must have had a rather long NDE, as he needed almost 800 pages to describe it all.

Still, Dante's famous Canto 3 phrase; "Abandon all hope ye who enter here" should be seen as a rallying cry if we use it properly. Hope is one of the key trapping mechanisms of the Matrix. Changing systems is another example for trying to "fix the world," because of the belief that the only reason negative things are happening is because of all the "bad people" who are in charge of the system. If we just get some "good people," then everything will be OK. Few see that the systems themselves are the issue. That is why nothing ever changes. People are working to fix the last layer of the material reality without realizing the totality which includes various higher levels of interconnected deceptions. As such, "hope" becomes one of the most insidious traps.

*

I am sitting in the kitchen of Anders and Liv as we slowly eat a simple lunch they created, a salad of vegetables from their home garden. Anders has been editing this chapter, and it has caused him a small dose of concern. He has obviously shared at least the overview of this chapter with his wife, because she too is also showing signs of apprehension.

"So Howdie," Anders begins, "this chapter on what happens after you die. Do really know for sure this is the way it is going to be?"

"Of course not, I don't think anyone can be sure specifically what will happen. Even those with a Near Death Experience, because it was near-death, they came back to the material realm. However, I feel confident that what I am presenting in this chapter, the sources I have used as my guides, have a high likelihood of being correct."

Liv speaks for the first time on these subjects, "But it all seems so horrible. Isn't there anything good about the after-death realms? Don't we get some knowledge there, or the ability to create our experiences, meet all of our dead loved ones? Don't we get any of that?"

"Sure, you could. There are many traps the archons have set up for the after-death realms, they let the hopes, wishes and fears of the now-dead soul have all sorts of, lets call them projections, to play with. But they are just toys in a kindergarten. Because if one has not found their True Essence and bypassed all of the lies, then the projections will be believed to be real, awareness will move towards and grasp onto them, and the cycle continues."

I explain to them in more detail how I consider the entire set of experience possibilities one can have in the after-death state to be nothing more than a giant projection. A type of programming codes to make experiences for the soul that are built out of the soul's wishes and fears. The might be schools, and reunions with family members or getting to hit that home run when in the real world you struck out. They could be experiences that seem to last months or years or even centuries. Yet all that is really happening is a personalized magic trick is getting played on the soul. It might seem like one has gone through a "lifetime" of experiences, but from the standpoint of time, it was all in an instant. Just like if we have a dream at night for thirty real-time minutes, but dream twenty hours, it is similar in the after-death world. A whole lot of story can be placed over a very tiny slice of "time." All to make the soul believe that 'something' has happened. It doesn't even matter so much what that is, as long as it was believed to be 'real.' No matter what gets generated, the end result is that the soul will have all of it's energy eaten, and then be recycled into another material world. That's all."

"But do you really think it is all as horrible as you are pointing out at the end of your chapter?" Liv asks sincerely.

"Yes. The standard NDE, that I discussed in the first book, is a unique set of coding given to some who will be brought there for a quick look around, then sent back to the material realm as if they are scouts of the unknown. Since the majority have not had a death experience, they have to trust the scouts, especially given that all of the various messages are amazingly similar. That right away should be clue to question them. No set of witnesses to anything tend to be uniform in their presentation, just see a set of police witness reports of any car accident to verify that. The main message of those who return from a NDE tends to be of love, light, Jesus, Buddha, and dead grandma. That message gives living humans comfort. And that is what people are really seeking. Some say they are seeking happiness, the end of their suffering, or to have power or importance. But at the core, the majority of people just want to feel comfort; feel that some supernatural deity or force is looking out for them, so all is safe and they are cared for. The NDE does that magnificently, so people no longer think about death. They think, 'its all good.' And on one level it is, just not the way the NDE has conditioned them."

*

In my eyes the whole after-death realm we get presented is a manipulated projection, no different than the false realm presented to humans in *The Good Place* . That is really why this chapter is so challenging, because it can take away the wished for comfort around death. But really this chapter is about power. There is someone looking out for you, but that of course is your Divine Spark. However, she can not really be looking out for you because she is in a coma. Awaken her, and there is no longer a need for anything in the archon after-death realm. You will have You. What more would you ever need?"

What one really seems to face when they die for good is less like a comforting NDE and more like what happened to the food in the movie *Sausage Party* , after the humans (gods) take it from the supermarket back to their apartments to eat it. Yet again even that is a projected experience, another trick in a finer dimension. As long as you are taking the realm to be real, and you (as a person, identity or a soul), believe you need a savior, believe you need to navigate archons, believe you have to discuss a life review or karma, or believe that you have entered a wonderful place of bliss and learning...the trap has you.

*

Anders wants me to continue my little lecture at the kitchen table and asks, "So are many of these people correct, that there is some sort of blocking device or shield placed in the astral realm, and our job is to learn how to in a sense swim around it to find the cracks or breaks in it. Sort of like being in a sinking ship, and navigating our way through the ship and up to get above the water line?"

"If I can simplify this. At the moment of death, if you have not realized your Totality and have complete Awareness, the after-death game will play out. And there may be all sorts of possible experiences such as: a life review, karmic committees, white light, going to schools of comic learning, being in a calming heaven or void, or having demons coming after you. It is all possible, but there is nothing real in the astral. Thus there is nothing that must be navigated, no net to maneuver past, no doorway to find. Before you die you have to first find Yourself, Become the Divine Spark and release all that is false. Since the Matrix and the archons and the after-death realms are false, they would all be released. Yet, as I have said, you must know that the Matrix and archons exist within this simulacra or they can not be released. You have to know the after-death game that wants to be projected so that it can be rejected, not after-death, but before you die. In a sense you dissolve it now, in the current moment."

Anders look up from this chapter notes and asks, "So right now? You are saying the Exit door gets built now, not after we die?"

"The reunification of the Divine Spark and the realization of Emptiness, are in my opinion, two of the key elements required to Exit past this entire projection. Liberation does not happen from dealing with archons and navigating mazes, or following what Jesus or Krishna tell you to do. Liberation comes from bypassing all of it. You either created your own doorway via the work you did in a body or not. Granted you can still do a navigation-like journey after-death if you realize that you are still caught up in that projection, and this is what texts like the *Tibetan Book of the Dead* and the Ancient Egyptian *Book of What is in the Duat* were describing. If you didn't finish the work before death, then find yourself in the astral with all of its traps. It can be navigated there, but that requires a ton of clarity. Best to complete all of this work now while in a body, so that after-death we head immediately for our Home, not theirs."

Liv has been slowly running her hand through her hair. Normally this would be a sign of "preening" (making oneself look better for a potential partner), but that is not the case here. This small external act is related to a deep introspection that is going on within her from this conversation, or one could say that she is "preening" for her Divine Spark. Things are quiet as I sip some of the tea in my cup when she looks at me and clearly states, "This chapter of yours is not really horrible or scary is it?" I smile. "Its really about great possibility and about the power to, how do you say it in your title, creating your own doorway. That is really what this is about. Gathering your own power and knowledge into one package."

"Yes Liv. But like always, one has to see and break through the walls that cover over any next steps. One can not jump to the creation of a doorway as long as they still think the after-death world has gifts for you, a dead relative is there waiting for you, or that any beings you might come across have some help for you. One has to see it is a simple choice of either the insane Matrix or Home. But that choice can not be made until one has seen the Matrix clearly. Most take that to mean one has to see the way government or the education system work, or see how programming is being put into TV shows and movies. That is one step, but it is a multi-layered Matrix of control and demonic deception. The deception layers keep going deeper than we ever thought, and extends to the entire after-death realm as well."

"I feel somewhat calm about it all. Like it all seems do-able, even for me," Liv smiles.

"Of course it's do-able. For everyone. Just very few seem able to do enough of the doing it requires." We laugh.

"Die before you die.
And be absolutely dead.
Then do whatever you want.
It's all good." [27]
- Bunan, Zen master

____

27   Suggested to have lived between 1602-1676
     https://terebess.hu/zen/mesterek/bunan.html

In this short statement by 17th century Zen master Bunan is a lot of coded information. The first part of the presentation is that the work he is describing (reaching of Emptiness/No Self) has to happen "before we die." He does not say to be dead, but absolutely dead. This means to be dead to the Matrix, but alive to the Absolute. When he states then do what you want, that does not mean to follow all the wants and wishes of his character in the dream, but what the real (Divine Spark) wishes to experience. Thus he is pointing towards a touch of controlled folly, discussed in chapter 7. The actions get labeled as good as his actions will no longer be focused by trying to get anything from the Matrix for oneself any longer, only that the actions are now driven by something True. His message is not a call to kill oneself (the physical body). The death here is not of the body, it is of the belief in the Matrix on all levels. The body will still go on in the material realm, just one becomes dead to all we thought we would "achieve" and "do" and "be" here. He is discussing the revolutionary 180 degree turn.

*

THE STANDARD NDE

I discussed in some detail what might be termed the standard NDE (white light, grandma, Jesus, love, helper beings) in *Exit the Cave 1.* As such this will be a quick presentation. I liken the standard NDE to like being in the dentist's waiting room, but never actually seeing the dentist. Due to the waiting room only-type experience, the belief afterwards becomes going to the dentist isn't so bad. Yet those who have been to see the dentist knows that it can mean pain from drilling, numbness from needles, and prods that have nothing to do with reading magazines in the waiting room.

First off I will say that the majority of those sharing their NDE are sharing an honest experience. And I give everyone a thanks for doing so, otherwise we would not have the plethora of stories to go through so as to find commonalities and differences. I want to thank Mark at "Forever Conscious Research"[28] for going over hundreds of these and providing expert analysis of what is being presented, while Wayne Bush on his excellent website[29] provides snippets of thousands of NDE for examination. Given that over 95% of NDEs are pleasant, it is this enjoyable message gets passed on to the masses, and today their message is passed on stronger than ever. Internet channels that present NDE's often now get one millions views. People are drawn to them, because the end result of most of them is comforting: death is fine, God loves you, Jesus or dead grandma will be there to protect you. But every once in a while a different type of NDE comes about, from someone who actually got called to the dentist's chair. Their story is so unbelievable that they are either ignored or shamed.

You could liken the after-death realm as a movie projected on a hospital wall for someone going through a non-anesthetic surgery. It is giving the mind something to focus on so it is not paying attention to what is really happening. Even back in Dante's time, the NDE was tailor made for the newly deceased. The Matrix seems to have a standard experience that gets slightly adjusted for each new soul. No matter, as long the soul believes in it enough to move towards the projected experience, the Matrix wins.

When a soul in the standard NDE is not overwhelmed by the combination of love, light and dead relatives, the beings switch to authority games, tricks and threats. The main purpose of the NDE for the beings encountered is to get the soul to return to their life on Earth, and present a "positive" package of what occurred. One way or another, the archons have to get the soul to believe that all that goes on in the Earth realm has all for the soul's benefit, growth and the creation of unbounded love, and that all that goes on in the after-death realm is the opportunity to present yourself to be judged. All deceptions on every level.

*

---

28 https://www.youtube.com/@ForeverConsciousResearch/streams
29 Trickedbythelight.com

At first I had seven pages digging through and denouncing all of the basic aspects of the NDE, and then wondered, why am I writing this? All of it is just a deception so why even write about it here in detail? A fully awakened Divine Spark connected to the Celestial Fire has no need for karmic committees, life reviews, dead relatives, religious figures, false love, white light, universities of endless knowledge, or anything else. If one has Become its True Nature, what more is needed?

Well, nothing actually.

You do the work to "die before you die" to avoid the after-death realm completely. Because if you have not "dissolved" the entire Matrix instantly on death, and have wound up in any of the scenarios usually expected, you are now on to plan B (following the advice of ancient texts and navigating the death realm). My book is about plan A, the direct Exit of the Matrix via the Realization and Becoming of one's Totality. What follows in the rest of this section is a few preparation reminders in case plan B is called for should you wind up in the after-death projection. You can do more study in these areas if you feel that will be valuable to you.

Most souls during their time on Earth have dealt with feelings of aloneness and being misunderstood. When Rodney Dangerfield claimed, "I get no respect," he was tapping into the deep feelings of his entire audience. Everyone feels they get no respect. The white light of the NDE, is a "shiny thing" that is getting all of the attention, while hiding the fact that it contains no real substance beneath it. It is just blasting people with a dose of feeling good, and the majority have felt lacking for so long, they can not resist it. This is likely why Julian Johnson in his book *Path of the Masters* presented that when it comes to using the senses in the latter part of the spiritual work, one must turn away from the main focus of the eyes and instead learn how to hear the Cosmic Sound (something Mr. Park also spoke to us about).

One of the things most claim to have experienced in their NDEs is a life review. This is really not about going over one's life so the person can see how they lived, and thus learn and grow.

What this review is really about is that the beings the soul will meet (archons in some kind of disguise as a karmic council, beings of light, or something projecting authority) scanning through one's human life to highlight all the moments of guilt and shame they can. Even young children receive a life review. Think of the Akashic Records as a Universal database which will be scoured through to find exactly the kind of manipulation, pressure, or goodies to be used to get the soul to "agree" to what the archons want you to agree with. It is one of the many reasons for performing a complete recapitulation prior to one's death, so that should such a life review be pushed on you, you know that you have already completed such a task, and completed it for your own total knowing not for some deceptive purposes of the archons.

One of the things many NDEs present is that the beings we encounter claim to have some sort of an authority over us, and that one should be in both fear and awe of them. This is likely the main reason one is programmed since birth to "respect authority" and to never question it. You don't discuss or deal with these entities (if you wind up in this predicament) you must be rooted in your Divine Spark. You go past them, by dissolving them, and as such seeing that everything they are and present are manipulated lies, that they have no authority over anything that comes from outside of the Matrix.

Another concept the beings try to push on the newly deceased soul is of the validity of karma, that one's previous life was based on previous life experiences as a way of improving oneself. It is then this council of light beings that judge the now deceased soul's "goodness," and experience mirrored in the *Egyptian Book of the Dead* where the heart must weigh less than a feather. Thus this judgment program has been going on for a long while. But this is not a judgment to help the soul, but the beings doing the judging. Those who allow such judgment to take place are abdicating their own authority. We have to drop the idea that anyone or anything is above us or has the authority to judge us. Only the Divine Spark within can do that, and the Divine Spark never judges.

Any judgment that should be happening is upon the beings who created this insane reality to begin with. It could have been created differently, but they made this place the "suffering pit of hell" that it is, they created the bodies being used, and the lies and deceptions presented. They are the ones needed to be judged, not the souls in the Matrix. In the after-death realm everything is backwards and upside down to what is truthful (as shown in images in the Egyptian Funerary Texts). There can be no karma the way we have been told because we were given genetics, instincts, and desires by THEM. Secondly, no "owner's manual" was provided upon entering. We are supposed to figure everything out on our own and to trust our parents, who we find out as we get older actually know very little themselves. On top of that, if we study our recapitulation carefully, we will find that many times we have been directly manipulated by these beings, moved us away from people and experiences that would have been helpful and positive for us, and then made us think that our shortcomings are our own fault.

People here are doing the best they can, given the set of insane circumstances we were all provided. Granted, there is some level of responsibility that must be taken the more one comes to understand the true nature of this realm and who they really are. This idea is mirrored in the Cathar Consolamentum. After taking this ceremony, one was expected to no longer "commit sins." Sin is a very confusing word, but in this context it refers to acting in opposition to what yo u have realized to be true. After the ceremony one would act in a truthful manner from that moment forward, not perfect or holy but truthful.

Some unique NDEs have discussed seeing symbolic rooms that held billions of soul contracts. Of course, like any valid contract, they must have been signed in good faith and without manipulation or deception. And that is what must be seen about these so-called soul contracts; no matter how these beings try to enforce these agreements, they are not valid due to the many layers of deception, lies, and pressure put into them. As such, they are all null and void. It is all just a Westworld type "backstory" that is placed in the soul's unconscious to explain the pain and suffering one will experience in life. The contracts are as fictional as everything else in the Matrix, they will only exist because we have been tricked to "believe them."

I see many people today suggesting that all one has to do is write out on a piece of paper affirmations such as, "I do not accept contracts" or "I demand my energy back," or "I am sovereign and the archons can not touch me" and then say them each day. This is the same as *Saturday Night Live's* Stuart Smalley constantly saying in the mirror, "I'm good enough, I'm smart enough, and doggonit, people like me!" And while there is no harm in this (it is better than sitting around watching TV), I feel that this will have very little real impact on regaining the Truth of one's being because the "I" that is the base of these affirmations is not being defined. One is hoping they can make a wish come true, rather than find and define their Total Self, which would reveal their Ultimate Power and thus have no need for such affirmations. Yet this "trap" will still be in operation unless one also sees the makeup of the trap.

Such a Becoming of what We Are, indicates that there can be no trap in the astral or other realms, as there is No-thing to be trapped. That is why the deceased soul becomes easy to manipulate, they fully believe they were Laura from Tuscon. Then by presenting dead relatives, pets, or past lovers, these beings get one to adhere to their previous life and physical world persona in the after-death realm. The external projections in the after-death state are designed to keep the soul projecting the same "me" that they were projecting in the physical, sometimes even making another similar body in the astral to really "play the part" of me. If one sees through the soul trap, but still believes their Matrix self to be real, they will be fooled. If one has seen through the lie of the individual self, but thinks the Matrix is just a fun game and all they have to do here is drink their tea and not study the horror of it, they will also be fooled. All of the various seemingly opposing layers must be clearly seen, and then joined together like in a jigsaw puzzle.

I guess the bigger question that is being asked is, if the standard NDE is just a trick being played in the dentist's waiting room, what happens when the soul actually goes in to see the dentist?

*

AFTER-DEATH LOOSH

This section of the chapter has gone through a recent revision. The problem stemmed from the fact that originally I wrote this book solely as a tool for myself, to dig deeply into various areas where uncertainty remained, to sort out once and for all layers where I was hanging on false or truth. One of these areas, after dismissing standard versions of what occurs to one's soul after death, was to find what might be the most likely scenario of what would occur. To this end there appeared to be only one source that gave a likely presentation of that process, that being Angeliki Anagnostou, author of the excellent 2012 book *Can You Stand the Truth.* It might be the best out there at explaining the make up of the Matrix itself. In two chapters of her book, "The After Death Worlds" and "Release From Karma," she outlines the more likely scenario While she did not provide any personal reference or experience for this message, something instantly seemed true in this thesis.

When I made the decision in the summer of 2024 that what I had been writing for myself was in fact useful for others to read, I had a big job. That was to take a massive 500 page text (written for only my eyes) and turn it into something that would be a functioning book for others. With the text you are reading, I first had to pare it down a 500 pages series of notes in half (to the 250-60 pages you now have).

This chapter was one of the hardest for me to make the change from just for me, to for everyone else. That is because it just happened that those two specific chapters being discussed here, also included some ideas of a Christ ransom, the Rapture, chakras, and a twist to dealing with the Demiurge. So I have altered this small section to reflect a focus more on my view of what Exiting means. All the basic ideas are still there, just now I leave it to the reader to go into Ms. Anagnostou's book if they wish to, and read Ms. Anagnostou's book, and these specific chapters for yourself. Use the discussion there as a pointer to spiral inward to obtain your own answers on these subjects. The main questioned to ask yourself is, do I really need a saviour? And if so, who or what is there to be saved?

*

When we look into what the ancient world had to present about the death experience, they were not putting the layers of love and joy on it that have become common in the last 100 years. They presented an underworld full of demonic beings, traps, guards, tests and tricks. That dangerous underworld is common for most cultures including: The Egyptians with the Duat, the Greeks with Hades, the Norse with Hel, in India it was Naraka, in China Diyu, in Japan Jigoku, with the Maya Xibalba, and by various names in various Native American mythology. Many of these cultures presented that this underworld was a real place that existed within the Earth, accessed via various tunnels and caves. The after-death world was still presented as one of demons prior to the mid 1800s, then (as just about every origin of our modern world) ideas get changed, and new loving ideology gets formed around death, with no real explanation why. It is the new 19th century idea around death that has carried through to our modern world.

Yet the ancient world did not live in fear of these horrific after-death worlds, for they also had myths that presented hero-like actions of those going into these hell realms to find or rescue someone or something. This of course is symbolic of the rescue of the Divine Spark. In one Greek myth it is Hermes who rescues Persephone, another has Hercules who rescues Theseus, while Odysseus travels to the Underworld. Cultures all across the world share similar hero stories of descents and returns from underworld hell realms. There is one unique Greek myth, that being the story of Psyche (soul) who went on her fourth test in the Underworld to win the love of Cupid. While she manages to navigate the underworld and bring back the box of beauty she had been told to bring back, her egoic nature caused her to open the box to try and obtain the beauty for herself. Doing so puts her into a deep sleep. Cupid (seeker of the Spark) finds Psyche asleep and takes the sleep from her face and replaces it into the box. They are thus able to fly to Venus and be married.[30] Psyche in a deep sleep is the Divine Spark. Thus to the ancients the Underworld was a place to test oneself, and by transforming themselves in some way, no test (trap) could hinder them.

The first question on this whole examination is, given the ancients were not presenting the after-death world as one full of love and light, what might this realm be?[31] Many have asked why souls in the standard NDE are sent back to the Earth experience, for of this is a realm just for loosh energy harvesting, then the archons should be eating the souls as soon as they arrive in the NDE? Why send them back to the material at all? Ms. Anagnostou gives a suggestion that is real "food for thought" in these two chapters as she claims souls are sent back into a body because their energy is not "tasty" enough. Just as we wait until a piece of fruit is ripe to take it off a tree, they do the same with us. *"(The soul's) astral body needs more desires, passions, sacrifice, or more of the nice and happy energy for the "upper classes" of entities."*[32] She presents that there are two types of astral archon beings, keeping duality intact even in the non material realms. The lower (demonic looking) entities want dark and dangerous desires, while the upper astral entities want nice loving energy. Generally it is these upper entities sending souls back in the standard NDE. That is so the soul can create and store more of the specific energy

---

30 https://en.wikipedia.org/wiki/Cupid_and_Psyche

31 Anagnostou, *Can You* p.430, One issue Ms. Anagnostou discusses in her chapters is the problem of the astral realm being one of emotion, thus normal logical knowledge is not accessible there. In the material realm we have access to what she calls the lower mental body, a logical mind that gets built the moment we get born, but stops being added to at the moment of death. This logical mind is available after we die, but only what we managed to store there while alive. In the astral world of emotion, this lower mental body is quite limited in how it can interact. There is no "knowing everything" in that realm as is commonly presented. We have access only to that which we have built, which in this case tends to be very inefficient for any navigation of the after-death realm

32 Anagnostou *Can You* p.427

that these archons like to eat after the person dies. These upper entities help set up a loving experiences when the person returns to their physical body. It is not about helping someone grow, it is about the quality of the energy feeding the beings will get after the complete death. This insight was very important for me, that being two types of astral archon beings, built as eaters of opposite sides of the energy battery. This relates as well to messages that Mr. Park shared with us that I will discuss later in this chapter.

When one passes from the waiting room to the main dental treatment room, this is when she claims that the final eating of the loosh begins. The standard NDE does not include the horror of being eaten, which only occurs when there is no going back to Earth as "Joe Smith." That can be one of the main reasons people have an intrinsic fear of death. It has nothing to do with the ending of one's material existence, or the loss of one's egoic self. The fear of death well could be the residual memory of all that happened to us (soul energy part) in the after-death realms previously. We get eaten. This is the main reason for the memory wipe, not to erase what happened in the previous material existence, but to erase what happened in the astral realm. The archons don't really care if a few "past life" memories survive, but they want to be sure that nothing of the times we were eaten in the after-death worlds remain. This idea that the astral realm is a type of hell can be found in Gnostic texts such as *The Gospel of Phillip*, "*Beyond this world, there is something that is really evil: it is the intermediate world, the world of the dead.*"[33]

The Tibetan Book of the Dead also discussed the demons that one can encounter in the after-death world,

> "*Yama (Lord of death) will tie a rope around your neck and lead you away. He will cut off your head, rip out your heart, pull out your guts, lick your brains, drink your blood, tear your flesh and gnaw your bones. But you won't die, even though your*

---

33 *Gospel of Philip* 62, Can you p. 430, 435

> *body is cut to pieces. Being cut up again and again,*
> *you will suffer immense pain .*"[34]

In chapter 125 of Ancient Egypt's *Book of the Dead,* the eating of the soul and its energy was done by Ammit (Devourer of the Dead). Even if the soul could by bypass Ammit at the heart weighing, they still had to navigate the Lake of Fire in chapter 126. This lake was surrounded by four baboons who required specific answers to questions for the Lake to be avoided. Otherwise the soul would burn in it.

No one really wants to hear what these quotes are pointing towards, but denial is not the best way of dealing with the upcoming possibilities. These quotations sum up what is likely waiting the traveler in the after-death state if they have not fully reunited the two halves of their Divine Spark. This has nothing to do with whether one gets into heaven after death, the heaven myth being another trick played on the human soul. Hell is not something you experience after death based on a judgment of how naughty or nice you have been. It is the experience that all will be going through if they do not Exit the Matrix and return Home. If someone gives over their authority and allows this "judgment" to take place, then the soul will enter the White Light, be eaten, and then reincarnated again into the material part of the Matrix.

These demons have been just out of our material sight, but influencing our thoughts none the less. Now they do not need to say hidden and fully reveal themselves and, *"now demand ALL of the energy payment they think they are owned."* Ms. Anagnostou claims that the lower (nasty) astral beings will be the first to eat the energy, and *"The more unfulfilled desires such as lust, gluttony, or jealousy remain, the longer the soul will stay in the eating area."*[35]

She then describes in her chapters that once the lower beings have eaten the negative emotions, there is no rest for the soul even though the positive angelic beings appear. This is not the positive love experience that the soul hopes, but she reminds that

---

34 *Tibetan Book the Dead* translated by Robert AF Thurman pg 197
35 *Can you* p 439, 441

these higher beings are the ones that everyone had worshiped, prayed to, had ceremonies for, and who in turn dished out help and healing when called upon. But now they will demand their "praying tax," which is to eat the "positive emotions," (especially love) generated and stored by the person while alive.[36]

She makes a powerful reminder that the emotions known as love, is just energy. And all energy is part of the Matrix. It is not a message that most want to hear. The emotion known as love will also be eaten by these beings, because love is energy, and all energy is from the Matrix. I had already mostly dismissed the idea of the importance of the emotion of love after my canyon experience, but a few talks with Karl Renz helped to clarify the trapping element that it entails. Both Karl and Ms. Anagnostou reminded that there is a type of Divine Love, but that only exists in a place that Karl reminded me where their is "no time or space, where there is no other to be an object of this so-called love." Love only really exists when there is No-thing that required a second to project love upon. This is not what people are experiencing on Earth, in which love is a chemical reaction. Schopenhauer was very clear in his concept of the Will (underlying force in humans) that we will become attracted to another person and get a strong emotional feeling, have sexual relations to make babies, which will cause us to feel attached to so that we will then take care for those babies, so that they will safely grow up, to have sex and make new babies and keep the slave circuit running. I know everyone wishes this love thing to be more since it feels so nice, but it is part of the energy loosh system. That does not mean one has to get rid of it, but to see it for what it is, and don't add importance upon something that is another part of the Matrix as a whole.

The spiritual community often pushes the idea that what must be done to make any sort of advancement is to stop generating negative energy, thus avoid interference from these lower negative astral beings. And that part of it is true, stop having lower vibration thoughts, and you will stop attracting low vibration entities. Yet the spiritual community have been misguided in believing that if they fill themselves up instead with only positive

---

36 *Can you* p.443

energy, they can somehow bypass the astral eating. What they fail to see is that the "loving beings" in the astral are still archon demons, just with a nice face. They are Michael in *The Good Place.* This love "program" is something that they created, granted a mirrored copy of something greater from Home. It is why on one level everyone senses something important with this love feeling, but because they are still stuck in the material level of world and self, they can never go beyond the confines of the material trick.

This means Ms. Anagnostou has a different concept of karma than most. She describes in her book that when reincarnated, the previous good souls wind up with good lives, while the bad ones get bad lives. This has nothing to do with karma as it is normally thought, it is more just that certain groups of archon entities have gotten used to eating a particular energy from that particular soul, and so they set up the system to keep their energy "catch" in their clutches. That is all karma really is, the continual wheel to determine which side of the astral archons will be the eaters of the soul's energy. Now of course if once can begin to swing to a better and more kinder life, it tends to free up more available energy which (if there is an intent to Exit the Cave) can be used to seek out the Truth of this realm and reconnect to their inner Divine Spark. But that is just a short term requirement of the actor in the material realm.

In *The Gospel of Thomas* Jesus presents the idea that one must free themselves from their father and mother, which symbolically means all emotional ties to the material realm.[37] Granted, positive and loving actions are better than negative ones from the standpoint of our energy in the Earth simulation, for it makes our interactions with other people, animals and nature much easier. Also, these positive entities are more likely to give out energy to people for healing or life quests if they are generating the "nice" energy that the entities like to have. But there is always a payback after death demanded since the archons see them as "loans." Whether the energy is positive or negative at its core, it is

---

37 This was the idea that Ben and Elaine had at the end of the movie *The Graduate*, just they never planned anything beyond the break. Hence, they sit staring at the front of the bus with a "now what do we do" look.

still part of the dual loosh battery system. Thus love, while a useful pathway to more enjoyable life moments, does not liberate anyone from the Matrix. All energy is going to be eaten and recycled, no matter how nice and loving to the world people are. The same goes for for evil and hatred. Salvation is not to be found anywhere in the material world or its objects, but in the Divine Spark and its original Home outside of Plato's Cave.

> *"Fear not the flesh nor love it. If you fear it, it will gain mastery over you. If you love it, it will swallow and paralyze you."*[38] - Gospel of Phillip

A huge part of the step to leaving the Matrix is seeing that the entire universe is in an evil trap, even the nice parts of it. Thus one has to pretty much disown oneself from the Matrix, astral after-death heaven included. The negative actions are an obvious trap that most can see, due to the guilt, shame and remorse these actions generate. Few discusses how to act within reality from a place of complete between-ness, where neither negative nor positive energy is being generated, where the energy component of any action stays neutral. Thus we act from a place Carlos Castaneda referred to as the Controlled Folly (chapter 7), which can only happen after the personal realization of Emptiness (No Self). All of the attachments of this realm, are mistakenly placed upon the objects. It is not the objects of the material world that are the problem, it is the personal self that is taking ownership of the objects or experiences. This idea of detachment is another subject I dig into in chapter 7, but for now I leave this clue: detachment is from the person, not of the person.

We have been programmed to get all of our energy from the Matrix, but this is not the only power source that is available. If energy is used from the Matrix itself, the archons will claim ownership over everything done with it. A shift has to happen to allow the use of the power that exists outside of the Cave (which the Divine Spark links to) to become the driver. Then one has tapped into a much more complete and never-ending source. This is what Jesus was referring to in the *Gospel of John, "I am the*

---

38 *Gospel of Phillip* 66

bread of life. He who comes to me shall never hunger, and he who believes in me shall never thirst."[39] This is not Jesus, or a being that is this bread. It is the Absolute Reality this message is pointing towards. But this can not happen as long as we keep thinking we are in a world set up for our benefit as a school of cosmic learning. The Divine can never be found while still surrounded by a wall of false.

Mr. Park told us something similar about the pathway to knowing our True Nature, which he claimed was a three-stage process. He described the first stage as Kwang, a word that he said meant Sun. When I looked up the word Kwang in Korean dictionaries, it was more a word that meant explosion or eruption. But then in the Sino-Korean language, it is the word for light. He said this first stage was to remove the darkness that was within, and to wind up with a heart that was light. He called the end of this stage an experience of "delight happy." This first stage is what has become modern spirituality.

The second stage was more difficult, which was what he called Myung (moon). This stage was about learning to reflect. It took me a long time to understand what he was referring to about this stage. It was not only about learning how to reflect what the material world was projecting at us, but also to see that what we believe to be ourself is also a projection. Thus, here we were supposed to learn how to reflect and reject all projections, which also includes our material self.

The third stage he rarely spoke of, but looking back now it is obviously the process of firing up the Divine Spark and Exiting the Matrix. He spoke of how the healing work that he was doing with us was to "purify our DNA" as he called it. My understanding became that he viewed our DNA as a type of computer code, and part of the pathway to freedom was to remove every bit of coding that had come into that DNA after its original creation (our creation). To get back to working only with what we had at the start, and not all the rest of the "refinements" that the system overwrote in us after coming into the material realm.

---

39 *Gospel of John* 6:35

I want to talk a bit about help, because several people who have listened to my various Exit the Cave interviews have come away thinking that if this is an entirely evil reality, then one is alone and helpless in this process. There is help for those moving towards Ultimate Truth (as I got some help from the *Nova Egypt TV* documentary that came on the night of my birthday in 1997 for example), but that help is not coming from the places we normally think of (spirit guides, angels, helpers, or guardians). Generally, if something is providing "direct" information, it is from the realm of archons. That does not mean some of these messages or energy assistance might be helpful, just that it comes with the "energy tax" they expect one to pay after death. The Pleroma does have a "connection" this reality, through our Divine Spark. This means that the saying "all the help we ever need is within" is accurate.

When one gets a vision of the Divine Spark, it can appear very angelic. It is revealing itself visually in a most appealing way. The archons take this vision, and appropriate and repackage it for its own deception. That is why it is difficult for one to tell who or what they are dealing with when they meet beings in the astral realm. People are in such pain and confusion that the image of an angelic being is simply ran towards, as the hope over-rides any critical examination. But sometimes the view of an angelic being is really that, the Divine Spark as a vision, is revealing itself to itself. I have noticed that help that is coming from a True Inner Source is not as direct as we thought it might be. It is more like a tufting of breeze that suddenly occurs on an otherwise still day. Subtle, yet there if one cares to notice it. One has to know it could come to us, as when it does, we have an inner stillness where we "feel" out the world in these particular moments.

*

That was where my original overview of her two chapters was meant to cover. How the actual death experience will likely differ from the Near-Death-Experience. Again what was presented above is a thesis, but my intuition informs me that it is the most likely scenario (as it has the most commonality found in early ancient texts on the subjects of death and the underworld). But in reading those two chapters, I realized that there were some other very big topics about Exiting that were being presented.

It was valuable for me to examine, firstly as an attempt to see if they can fit within the framework with the realization of Emptiness presented in the following chapter. I found none of them could. The only saviour one ever needs is themselves. Outside religious saviours can be useful for a time to act as a type of template of questioning and inner seeking, and feel like they have something looking after them while they do, but at some point there will have to be a break of the idea that I need something outside of myself to Define Oneself completely. That intention of complete Self Definition in itself changes the entire dynamic of what Exiting the Cave means.

One area from those chapters that I will discuss here in my book is that Ms. Anagnostou claimed that what she calls "holy souls" that will *"bypass the astral realms altogether, by piercing though them like shooting stars in the night, and straight to the higher mental plane which is located in the neutral zone."* I too agree with this idea. I would present it differently, but the underlying idea is similar. However she claims a key part of the spirit's "Exit" at death must be via the 7th head chakra. She discusses (and I agree) of how the other six chakras are archonic plants in the energy field used for loosh harvesting purposes. Why would the 7th be any different? These seven chakras are always portrayed together in every spiritual treatise as a complete group. In my view, there is no helpful chakra. They are all part of the larger trap. Another standard chakra trap of the last 50 years has put the focus on the heart chakra. This has led to standard spiritual calls to open the heart, be more loving, more connecting." More something anyway. This is currently the most insidious part of the current trap, pushing everyone towards the one thing that an in-pain egoic self is looking for (love, connection and happiness). Various ancient alchemic texts discuss another heart within the body, not in the chest, and it is this heart that gets used for the pathway to Ultimate Liberation.

An early Christian text known as the *Gospel of Mary Magdalene*, discusses a conversation that the soul is having after death with what it calls the seven atmosphere's (or levels) that the soul is ascending through. Given there are seven of these indicates that it is a trip through the chakras. Part of this Gospel is missing (much of the papyrus sheets destroyed), but in the existing version it picks up with the question-and-answer session happening with the second force Desire (the second chakra).

The Gospel is presenting how the soul in the text (representing the direction the soul of the reader should follow) is rejecting each of these chakra levels, along with the tricks they are trying to play. The seven "manifestations" that the text claims are to be rejected are: darkness, desire, ignorance, jealousy, carnal inebriation, intoxicating wisdom, and devious wisdom. There are seven manifestations, and we have seven chakras, so this text would be placing one "trick" for each chakra. But Ms. Anagnostou in her in her book suggested that the 7th chakra is positive, and she combines the final two manifestations (intoxicating wisdom and devious wisdom) together into the 6th chakra, leaving the 7th free. Why would this be assumed? Intoxicating wisdom is a good indication of the dangers of chakra six (third eye power and magic), and it would seem that devious wisdom would then be chakra seven, which would be the last major trick to hold a soul to this realm. So it seems clear to me that one seeking Ultimate Liberation must avoid all the chakras, as each are part of the Matrix energy control system. None of them at their core are there for our benefit.[40]

What we do generate while alive is not through any chakra, but to make a direct link to the total wisdom of the Pleroma.[41] For me this body mentioned is the Awareness of Emptiness, which we can not so much develop, but can develop a pathway that can allow Grace to reveal Emptiness in all of its Totality.

---

40   There has been discussions from various healers lately that someone should remove their chakras. I don't suggest that, for in my opinion there is no need. We reject what they stand for and the tricks they try to play, we take away the power that we give them, not the need to remove them from the level of the material trap.

41   Anagnostou *Can you* p.452-53

The challenge with all presentations about the material or astral realm, and they ways they must be navigated, is that each is still a projected experience in a a projected reality. One needs to see through the illusion of everything, and that includes body, chakras, world, dimensions, and even personal identity. So too the ideas of archons, karmic committees, white lights, or questions we have to answer. Why would you need to present any information, about any experience or wishes of a saviour in a fictional reality, to fictional entities, in a fictional astral world? You don't need the archon's answers, explanations, or acceptance about anything. They are parts of creators of the insane Matrix. At worst they should simply be ignored and stepped around, or at best bypassed instantly due to have reconnected with the Celestial Fire. Granted some ancient texts (such as the above mentioned *Gospel of Mary Magdalene*), *The Apocalypse of James* and the *Egyptian Papyrus of Ani* do present a type of Question and Answer session with beings in the after-life. I get the sense that it is less of a preparation for a real Q and A but instead a literary device (as many Hermetic texts of the day were presented as discussions between teacher and student).[42]

More importantly, these astral realities and beings don't even exist, only as an appearance, a trick and deception. They exist only because that which perceives believes they exist or have authority. Neither does the you thing supposedly being judged. Again this is why complete Self Definition is the critical foundation to all of this. As long as one is still in the belief they are some-thing, they can be drawn into interacting as a projection, with other projections. All realms occur on the stage, and we want to shift Awareness from the things on the stage, to the No-thing in the

---

42 These texts are not about answers one must memorize like a high school test. These texts rather point to a deep Knowing that we must have. One such "answer" in *The Nag Hammadi* "First Apocalypse of James" is, "*I am a son, and I am from the Father...I will go to the place from which I have come, there I shall return.*" This was in response to "where is one from?" A similar exchange in the "Gospel of Thomas 50" has the response, "*If they ask you where you come, say, we were born of the Light, There, where Light is born on Light. It holds true and is revealed within their image. If they ask you who you are, say, 'We are its children, and we are the beloved of the Father.'*" The underlying message of these answers indicates that one knows, and has Become that Which They Are, thus awakened the Divine Spark, so answers to such questions are automatic.

audience that is Observing the production. This stepping out of all false projections can not occur unless ALL layers of the Matrix are seen through prior to death, thus no matter the experience, it is seen as a projected false experience happening to a projected false actor, in a stage play of no real significance. At that particular level of realization is where I feel Lucifer begins to be very nervous about one who has come to see No-thing, in the middle of his false AI projected some-thing. The push from him then tends to be to get such a "person" to believe either they have to fix the world, or to deny the suffering elements of the Matrix instead suggesting to just drink tea and smile. As I discuss in the next chapter, there are as many traps after a realization as there is prior.

There is key question that is bound to come up around this reality being one of distortion and suffering. That being if this original Father is omnipotent and all powerful, then why would he allow such a terrible universe to be created in the first place? Why would he allow Divine Sparks to be trapped, and why would he need to send this Christ figure into this Matrix to suffer pain to pay off a ransom to Lucifer? The likelihood is that this Father cannot directly fix it, as based on the ideas of Emil Cioran in his essay "The Evil Demiurge." Cioran claimed that the real Father cannot create nor is omnipotent. He presented that Good, being perfect and Absolute, has no interest in creating. Only evil has the urge to create, and thus the creator of such an insane realm must be evil. This message is important from Cioran, for the underlying message is that the Great Father (if one does exist) is not going to save us. We have to save ourselves. A Christ figure (whoever and whatever that may have been) came here to show that an Exit is possible and what is needed to be done. They are but a pointer to lead us to see that we are our own true saviours. These famous religious figures are more like coaches to show us how we can go past our limits. We save ourselves.

I have mentioned that in my opinion Divine Sparks are the shattered elements of the One Celestial Fire. The entire Fire Exits not each Spark individually. Though once a Spark is reunited with the overall Fire, it is reunited and will not be split again. It may seem like it is "waiting" at that point, but that would be a sensation of the Matrix and time. Once the Spark is with the Fire, they have already Exited, even though there is the appearance of time for the entity of the Fire to be reunited.

My feeling, from my own experience following the fall into the canyon river, is that if a realization of Emptiness (or awakening of the Divine Spark) happens, the Spark gives the character (form/me) a task. Something rather difficult, that one must go through all the way with and complete. This is not the idea of having a mission, fixing the world, saving anything, or even necessarily having the task be anything seemingly that important. It is just something the Spark/Emptiness deems that the actor in the dream-state must complete in order for the "slate to be cleaned."

It takes a while to firstly even see there is a task given to us from our more deeper Truth, then to figure out how to complete it, and then put in the required time (often many years to see it through). Once completed, the last vestiges of the gripping of the Matrix are let go of, and now the Matrix has nothing to grab onto. Ultimate Liberation is now at hand. These *Exit the Cave* books have been a part of my task, a task that is soon coming to its conclusion. It took me many years to understand this, so in once sense I could have completed these works many years ago. Or perhaps the timing indicated that this was the best time. Who knows for sure? It is just a feeling I have about the interaction between Emptiness and the form once it has been realized. It has played out this way for me anyway, it might be different for others.

*

I do want to share that the two suggested chapters of *Can You Stand the Truth* ends with what I consider an excellent clue, built on a metaphor that the Divine Spark (which she calls Celestial Man) became trapped in the Matrix when he entered and wound up being poisoned by the Fallen Creator in serpent form. This poison put the Divine into a type of hallucination-hypnosis, as the Man was symbolically swallowed by the Serpent.[43] The snake then

____

43 This metaphor might relate to the story of Jonah being swallowed by the Great Fish in the *Old Testament*.

commanded Man in the coma to dream and create via projection. This projecting became the material world simulation, which acts like a continuing hypnotic spell.[44] In a sense, Lucifer or whatever you want to call the Creator, only set up the parameters of this creation. To give it life, he needed Divine Sparks to project the simulation. To do that he wanted them in a coma so as to not notice that the experience they are having is only a false projected dream, a dream reality they themselves are projecting. This mirrors the idea that the chains we have are unlocked, as we are the one's who have placed them on ourselves by believing our own projections. As such, Lucifer must now be vigilant, the ever-watching eye, not watching the simulation per se but rather watching for signs of the Divine Spark in its hypnotic coma coming out of its slumber. Our current world of mass surveillance is likely just a mirror of a much greater surveillance at the level of the soul, to be sure it remains in a coma.

Ms. Anagnostou then makes one of the most important statements in her book, "*What we must do is to realize that Truth is the anti dote to the* poison." She explains that to overcome the coma, one must gain some Truth, and in doing so, the paralyzed (Spark) can begin to wiggle. More Truth then causes the slumbering Spark to move more, making the serpent more uncomfortable, eventually forcing the snake to "throw him up."[45]

Two very important elements are being presented here. The first is that Truth (the total knowing of the Matrix, Divine Spark, and the Pleroma) is the antidote to the hypnotic poison, which causes the coma to be dispelled and the wiggling movement to begin. Truth is symbolically the kiss given by the prince to Sleeping Beauty to awaken. As this Truth grows, and the Spark becomes more awake (and thus more powerful) she now becomes dangerous for the "system." There is a reason that Lucifer set things up for the Sparks to be in a coma, because if no longer in the deep sleep, they might become like a poison itself to the system. The result is that symbolically the Fallen Creator vomits us

---

44 This need for the Divine Sparks to create life to the Matrix is a key part of the "Apocryphon of John." This is echoed in the conversation about New York City in the movie *My Dinner With Andre*.

45 Anagnostou *Can You* p.457

back out. This is why I have come to say that the task is not to EXIT the Matrix, for the pathway is not really a physical one, nor is it some labyrinth that gets navigated in the astral. What we do is to become like a poison to the Matrix by Becoming complete Truth, that even though the Matrix "needs us" for power, once we access the True Power from the Pleroma again, it has no other choice but to EXPELL US. And by using the word expel, I am also symbolically saying "ex-spell" as in removing the spells that put us in the original coma. We Become that which Albert Camus was pointing towards in his essay "The Myth of Sisyphus, "*The only way to deal with an unfree world is to become so absolutely free that your very existence is an act of rebellion.*" The end result will create a being that will be impossible for the Matrix to keep. THE MATRIX GETS SICK AND TIRED OF HAVING YOU AROUND.

That is why wishing to go Home will not accomplish the end of the reincarnation cycle. Nor will concepts like "standing in your authority," "not going to the white light," "raising your vibration," or "living off grid." Exiting requires a complete overhaul of everything we have come to believe, everything we think of as real, and everything we are fearful of or joyous about. Exiting is not about the character we are playing, nor how awake the person in the dream is. It is about how awake the Divine Spark is. But an Awake Divine Spark means the end of the character one has believed they were all along.

This deep realization of what we really are automatically begins to cause one to lose interest in many of the physical activities we once used to such as: gaining possessions, experiencing new adventures, seeking importance, even seeking love and happiness. Everything here, everything positive, and negative, originates from the same AI cesspool. Perhaps no better overview of the spiritual path, the intensity of work and focus it requires, and of the deep power over the matrix we actually hold is in the following quotation from Richard Rose which indicates the great challenge of the work, and the great power found in fully walking it:

"How do we do it (awaken)? We do it by carrying water on both shoulders, but not allowing it to touch either shoulder. We stagger soberly between the blades of the gauntlet with recklessness and conviction, but we pick our way through the tulips with fear and trepidation, because the trap of the latter is sweet. We charge the gates of Heaven by urinating our way through hell, all the while sitting for forty years on the banks of the Ganges, going nothing. We sit on the banks of the Ganges, not from laziness, but from an anger at angriness, a fury against our inner fury for wasted activity. And we pull back a terrible arrow...but never let it go. And by so holding, with the universe as our target, the universe is filled with terror at our threat."[46]

We bypass the White Light trick by never even making it to the White Light. And that does not happen by wishful thinking, faith in a savior, becoming a really nice boy or girl, or even learning every possible yoga posture. It comes through a realization of Emptiness. You stop needing a saviour when you realize that there is no one here to be saved. Lucifer gets tired of trying to keep forcing No-one to believe they are some-one. No-one is dangerous for a system designed on falsified projections believing the projections, and themselves, are very important. Thus oddly, after a long chapter all about what might be the most correct after-death experience, of course the correct answer is there will be none. No matter what it is, it will be a false projection. The white light, and Jesus, Karmic Committee and Life Review, is as false as the archons eating one's loosh in a horrible experience. Yes if a soul believes they really were Joe Smith, really lived on Earth, really have karma, really need a saviour, really anything...they are in the recycling of the Matrix.

I will say it again. Only that which is True can Exit the Cave. All that is false is part of the Cave, thus can not Exit. All of it

---

46 Found in Richard Rose *The Direct Mind Experience* p 286, and John Kent *Path* p 214

must be dropped, especially the very body-mind-identity that believes it can or has to drop anything.

Thus the real pathway Home comes in the direction through Emptiness. It is not the doorway, but the mat that Awareness will wipe its dirty feet on before going through the gateless gate. The next chapter will be challenging for many readers, and for a while it can only be taken as a mental understanding. But I wrote it for all as more than a preparation on the path, but also be a reference section should Emptiness occur for "you."

> *"Only if you reject all other paths, can you find your own path."*[47] UG Krisnamurti

---

47 UG Krishnamurti *Mind is a Myth*

Chapter 4

EMPTINESS
Awakening From Yourself

*"I'm Nobody!
Who are you?
Are you - Nobody – too ?"*[48]
- Emily Dickinson

The world is an illusion. This message is often reverberated in spiritual teachings. Yet to the average seeker who comes across this idea, there is little tangibility to it. I know when I first came across this concept thirty years ago, I took it as a type of metaphor. Granted, this idea never left my mind, even if I never took it seriously. After a couple of years there became an inner questioning: if all of these books say the world is an illusion, a type of dream, what do they mean? Is there a way I can test this out for myself directly? I soon found that there was.

This chapter can be thought of as a continuation of my earlier book *Falling For Truth,* which discussed my eight-year obsessive path of testing reality, and led to my fall in the canyon which revealed Emptiness or No Self (also described as Not Self in some Eastern traditions). If you are serious about Exiting the Cave, Emptiness is your springboard, and Self Definition is your ladder.

---

48 Emily Dickinson, short lyric poem first published in 1891

There are three parts to the work of Exiting the Cave. The first is the complete definition of the small s self, what we see in the mirror everyday. For most, examining their self is rarely ever thought of. One might say; "I'm me, what more needs to be discussed?" Or; "Sure I might have some things unknown about me, but I can just read some self-help books and fix them." A few might even go another step and respond that they know that they are "more than a material body," but when you ask them exactly what that "more" is, they usually reply that they are some sort of a spirit, soul, or consciousness. When you ask them to define what this spirit or consciousness is, all you usually get back is a confused stare.

The work begins when we decide that we can not really be sure who this person is we live as every day until we have examined "ourself" fully. What is this person, what does it like, not like, what fears does it have, what are its wishes and beliefs, what is the life it has really lived? A total understanding of who this thing that we walk around every day with is required. This is where work like Recapitulation, Inventory, or Not-Doing (all mentioned in *Falling For Truth)* becomes valuable in this examination.

The second area of study becomes an examination of the various levels of the world/Matrix. This involves not just examining how things are structured within this location (who runs what from the standpoint of systems) but also to test the solidity of reality itself. How do we know it is a table, chair or tree? How solid are they? I spent almost eight years testing the structure of what we call

---

49 Said by Richard Rose in one of his lectures

the material world, and at the end of that study, found that is nothing like we have been made to believe.

The third stage can happen when one has fully defined their small s self, and then begins to find clues that they may be something else than a person on planet Earth. That is where the work moves from small s self definition to large S Self Definition. Self Definition (of the Greater Self) is not a joyous experience of being in the now, practicing mindfulness or doing yoga; it is a focused effort of spiraling inwards to our core. Spiraling inwards is a great term for this as it intuits the labyrinth-like maze one must navigate, and that all of one's attention has to shift from "outside" to "inside." This will likely be a shattering process to everything we have always thought we were. It can only occur when there is a demand to know what exactly we are, and not stopping until one knows. As long as one chooses to believe that they are the thing they see in the mirror everyday, and there is no need to look into it any further, the process has ended before it can begin.

Many will say that they want to awaken (define their Greater Self), and that they are involved in some sort of spiritual practice to do so. However, examined closely, all they really want to do is to make the prison cell of the body-mind feel more comfortable. Most live a life totally oblivious to what is surrounding them. They believe what they have been told, and never question what they should be thinking or doing. Even those that do get a glimpse of something deeper within, it is so opposite to what they have been told they should believe, they tend to just cover it over with things like booze, sex, drugs or even travel to India.

Yet for some, all of their denial begins to get really irritating. There now is only one place to turn, and that is inwards. The "way out" is found from following the "way in."

HOUSE IN ORDER

As mentioned, this search begins with a full examination of the small s self we have come to know. We get to know the complete story of what the character is and has been. An important part of that process is what Rose called "getting one's house in order."

A key starting point is to overcome the misplaced idea that a path to knowing is about adding things. The belief is that "I don't know enough," so I need to go to another course, read another book, watch another video. Yet, we have all the answers we need within, it is just that they have been covered over with all sorts of belief walls. The majority of the early path is removing the walls that has covered over the link to inner answers. Richard Rose was the first to put this in easy to understand terms, describing the work as a path of finding false, then dropping it, then go looking for more false. We do not walk forward to Truth (since we do not know for sure what it is), but travel backwards as we drop false. Eventually we come to the one thing that no matter how much we try to declare it false and drop it, we can not. That is the Truth. And as everyone who has come to it has suggested, it is nothing like they ever expected it would be.

Foundational work begins with learning about the labels that are used constantly, me and I. Very few realize just how undefined this "me" or "I" thing is. When you start to examine yourself closely, you notice that you do not have one "I," but rather several. And these "I's" almost always tend to be in conflict. One "I" wants to go to the party, another one does not, another wants to eat a hamburger, while fourth is thinking about tennis shoes. And these "I's" can morph in and out literally in seconds, so the point of reference being used (this "I" thing) can change several times during a short conversation. That means totally different "I's" are presenting very different wants, that are changing over seconds. No wonder everyone is so confused! We like to think of ourself as one stable continuous person, but if the I (which is a type of barometer of perception and action) might be changing minute to minute, then we are not the continuous thing we have believed ourself to be.

Taken one step further is the concept from biology that every cell in the human body will have died and been replaced in seven years. This is a staggering concept, that there is nothing physical in the body that is more than seven years old. All events older than seven years have never been experienced by even one living cell in the current form. Every event older than seven years is just a memory, a *Westworld* type back story, that has not actually existed for anything material I call "me." And even if I try to say that memory resides in my brain, all of these brain cells are also no more than seven years old. "We" are changing at the cellular level year by year, week by week, and minute by minute. How do we figure out what we really are? How do we get ourselves to a place of stability where we can study who we are?

Grounding is a key part to the ability to follow a commitment vector. Much of the spiritual community is looking to be in denial of where they currently are, to pretend to be on the mountain top when they are still at ground level. Many are talking about how many hours they meditate, but when you look closely, their life is a mess. They have three divorces behind them, and they are in the process of marrying number four. Or they have no income but are spending money on new yoga mats, while you are thinking, just get some food for your fridge. Spirituality has become their attempt to jump out of material life into some sort of wished for happy place. But that is not being grounded.

Grounded understands that while this realm is not the main focus, we do not ignore it either. We find out what is the amount of time and energy that is required for our "house to be in order," so that we have available time and energy is for our Intention towards Truth. It was part of the reason Rose required students come out to his farm. They didn't just come to have some sort of retreat where they sat there quiet and alone (though he did recommend one of those personal alone periods per year). He had the students work building fences and repairing barns. He wanted them to have their hands in the soil. He was grounding them, to be sure they were not going to fly away from reality when the heavy spiritual stuff began. Those that were not serious didn't last with the group long. Hard physical work was not in their spiritual wishes. How are you grounding yourself? Are you doing some gardening or swimming daily in a lake?

Having one's "house in order," has as its main goal being one's mind. When the mind is calm and clear, the rest of our world follows. Yet while someone is working on that, they have to begin to bring their small s self into more balanced and healthy living. This tends to be ignored by most seekers because these ideas do not seem "spiritual." But this house in order is one of the most important understandings we can have for building a vehicle that has the "ability" to seek.

If one is not healthy in the body for example, then that will take up a lot of our energy just for healing, and that energy is then not available towards a deeper search. How can we find more health? Do we need to change our diet, to lose weight and gain muscle, to learn qi gong or yoga, or see an acupuncturist, herbalist or doctor? It's not Exiting the Cave stuff per se, but the more healthy the body becomes, the more energy we have available for putting towards our Ultimate Commitment. A "house in order" also means to have one's basic needs covered, or one will always be scrambling, full of anxiety about if they have food to eat or place to live. That would also take up much available energy. This is not a call to be rich or powerful, or even to have a long term address. It is knowing what "enough" is for you so not have anxiety around basic needs. We simplify our life but do not ignore the basics.

The eventual goal of a "house in order" is to create a balanced mind. An unbalanced mind is going make it hard to see anything clearly. If someone has unresolved traumas from their past still infringing on the mental form, any glimpse of something beyond the Matrix is not going to be handled well by this already confused mind. Actually, this might be one of the best elements of the ego. It won't let go of its mode of control if it is "psychologically injured." Even though ego is a distortion, oddly it has to be healed in order for it to be stepped beyond. When one has healed (or better said to have transformed) their traumas and balanced their mind, they will be in a place to operate with clarity, and apply their pathway in a rational healthy way. If you feel that your mind is not in a stable calm place, if traumas are still "infusing" your system, that is where you have to begin. You have to find qualified help to turn an unstable mind into one that can be clear and stable. A therapist, psychologist or energy healer is not going to take you to Exiting the Cave, but they might help you get through a wall that you need to see through in order to keep moving.

If a balanced mind gets a look at what is beyond the Matrix, it can let go of the steering wheel and see clearly. You don't kill the ego. This is a distortion of what is going on. It is not the ego nor the false self that is killed, but the part that identified with it gets revealed and stops believing most of what the ego presents. Ego has its uses in the material realm, and so this more aware part keeps the useful ego parts active. This concept is presented in the Ancient Egyptian story of Set (egoic mind) who gets tamed by Horus (the power of our commitment). At first Horus tried to win by fighting Set directly, but that only led to a stalemate and injury to both of them. Something changes in the story, and the Horus symbolically tames and then heals Set. We don't fight the mind, we see the mind from beyond it, shine a light on it and fully define it. Once that process is complete, Horus can allow Set to lead Ra's Solar Boat (Divine Light), to which Set will each night battle and spear Apop (Matrix archons). Such symbolism can also be found in religious images such as St. George slaying the dragon. The now healed mind is no longer a problem, but a valuable tool. When the mind, along with the body and one's life, has stabilized and harmonized, one can say their house is in order. Now one is ready for the final stages of the work.

Bart Marshal has a chapter "The Way of the Warrior" in his book *Becoming Vulnerable to Grace*, in which he presents eight foundational pathways which he lists as: Befriend death, Maintain vitality, Be self sufficient, Question everything, Know the terrain, Reconnect with nature, Embody Integrity, and Be a friend.

I suggest you read his recommendations chapter yourself. Here I will discuss one of these, that is to "have integrity."

When it comes to integrity, it is a word that is rarely used in our modern technological society. Integrity tends to have two usual definitions, "the quality of being honest and having strong moral principles," and "the state of being whole and undivided." The first part has the word honesty in it. Firstly this means to be honest to yourself and not do things that you know are not in your best interest. No level of external pressure or temptation will get one with integrity to act in ways they know are against their "principles."

I would add three other words that go into the idea of integrity, those being fairness, reliability and courage. If you ask a person with integrity to come and help you at 7PM, they will be there at 7PM. You don't even have to wonder if they will show up or if they will cancel. They will do what they have said they will. They will be fair with people. They will have boundaries and not allow others to push against them or be unreasonable, but they will take into account circumstances and look for solutions that offer value for all involved. They will also show courage to stand their ground for what they believe, or take actions that follow their principles. Just to be able to say no in some cases takes great courage. And integrity has a great amount of empathy. We learn to share what we can of it with other creatures in the world, not trying to save everyone or everything, just offering little bits of help and encouragement when we can. We can not save every suffering animal for instance, but can we help one? This is all linked to "in the world" integrity.

Sleeping Beauty (Divine Spark) only wants to be awakened by a prince with integrity, direction, honesty, clarity, and empathy, not any jackass who wandered by the castle. The trials that the prince in the story went through symbolizes his work to obtain inner integrity. Thus the entire discussion here of "getting your house in order" and the transformation of the small s self, is done so that one can become a man or woman of integrity and sanity that Sleeping Beauty will want to awaken for. Don't focus on finding the Divine Spark, focus on being the kind of self in the

Matrix that the Divine Spark can not help but to be magnetically drawn to.

When Sleeping Beauty begins to come out of her slumber, there will be a new type of experience that begins to come into one's reality. That is the taste of what Asian traditions refer to as Emptiness.

*

AUGUST 27, 2001

Along with several others, I am sitting on the floor of a small living room in the house we have all come to in order to spend time with the 80+ year old Korean monk Mr. Park. We are seeking a spiritual path, and we all were somehow lead to him. Of the group on the floor I am the youngest, most being in their 40s or early 50s. At 3PM the group was in the process of a half-hour sitting as was normally done at that time of the day.

There are five of us sitting today, even though there are also others staying in the house and paying money to the main renter. Mr. Park is taking none of the money for himself, and our donations are just making sure to get food for him and cover the costs of the house. During these hour sessions, my focus was simple, to just sit still and try to stop my mind from thinking. Which is what I thought we were supposed to be doing, given that being still and "not thinking" was the message of most of the standard spiritual books of the time.

On this day Mr. Park came out of his bedroom, something he rarely did, and gave us all a strange look over. I remember that I was in sort of a state of pretending disinterest upon his arrival, yet at the core I was looking for his praise. I was hoping that he would recognize that somehow I was meditating better than all the others. Looking back, it is strange seeing how many times I was trying to turn "being silent" into a competition.

Mr. Park walked over to the oldest member of our group, Roger, and whispered in his ear. Roger was the only one of us who understood some Korean. Then Mr. Park nodded at all of us, and shuffled back into his room. When the door was shut, Roger turned to us all to pass on Mr. Park's message, "He said that he wants us all to think of nothing but nothing."

"He wants us to think of nothing?" asked Sonja.

"No. He said nothing but nothing."

"What does that mean?" I asked

"I don't know. I thought you might know," Roger said back to me.

We all sort of just sat there for a moment, looking at each other. I am sure we all were having similar thoughts, "Is that not what we were doing? Making our mind quiet to have a silent mind?"

"So he wants us to have no thoughts?" Sylvain from Montreal queried.

"Well he didn't say that," Roger replied while slowly shaking his head. "He said to think of nothing but nothing. Not, not to think. He wants us thinking, but putting the thinking towards nothing."

"How do you think about nothing?" I asked.

"He didn't say nothing, he said nothing but nothing."

We were back to staring at each other and wondering, "What is this nothing that he wants us to think about?" Sylvain asked.

This went on for weeks, sitting still and trying to think of nothing but nothing, but failing. He reminded us a week later,

"Don't think about nothing, think about nothing but nothing," again disappearing into his room.

Then four years later, after a careless fall into a hard flowing river, I came to understand the nothing that Mr. Park was pointing towards.

*

CANYON TEACHINGS

Cue four years ahead. It is just after my fall into the river in front of the Upper Falls of Johnston Canyon in Alberta, and the subsequent shattering of the personal self in the death experience which occurred (see chapter one in *Falling For Truth).* This shattering created a new seeing whereby the body, mind, thoughts, feelings, emotions, experiences, hopes, and fears were all seen as projections. Figments in the imagination of a larger Awareness, an Awareness which I had always been but had "forgotten," until the moment of accepting my death. Some have tried to attack me by saying that I did not have a death experience in the canyon because my physical body did not die (thus generate the NDE they so much want to validate). Something better than that happened. My body didn't shatter, "I" did.

It finally began to make sense what Mr. Park was pointing to with his suggestion. The first was that he wanted us to "think," presenting that what we were doing was an active practice and not an attempt at being still. It was to think "of nothing" which on the surface seems to suggest a blank mind, but because there was more "but nothing," the initial nothing word was a directional pointer. The pointer was to have only one thought. He could have said the same opening as "only think about." He was directing us to put the focus on reaching Emptiness, which is more real than any segregated self could ever be.

About a year later, I found that Richard Rose had said something similar in a 1979 lecture, "*You can't think of nothing. What happens is, after you bombard yourself with possibilities, you blow the head. And, nothing is there. Your thinking becomes nothing. But you don't think of nothing. So this is the difference between what I call choosing the symptom–trying to imitate the symptom of no-mind–as opposed to just attacking the problem and attacking the problem, until the head just blows. Thought ends as the thinker ends.*"[50]

When I read the above paragraph it made perfect sense as to what Mr. Park was referring to, that the nothing was No-thing (from the standpoint of objects in the material reality) yet is also the All-pervasive Awareness that was revealed in the canyon. The last sentence by Rose was the most poignant, that thought will end when the thinker ends. The only reason that thought had been occurring in my life to that point is because there has been a thinker that I identified with as "me." I had been the thinker, the feeler, the experiencer, and the observer. In the canyon, the thinker (and seeker, do-er and anything else) dissolved. Thought no longer occurred. I could see what the point of all the work was to reach this very point point. Real work was not to still the mind or make a happy mind. The work is to overload the mind with intense questioning thought beyond its capacity to understand, and so doing, it just stops. Examining who is doing the thinking is something the mind can not actually do. It either gets you to forget the idea and do something else, or if you still continue, it cuts out. A hole then appears in the wall where mind lives, which creates the space for No-thing to come in.

Mr. Park's exercise was designed to try to force our rational egoic mind to contemplate Nothingness, which is impossible for it to do. He had skillfully with his exercise placed the end goal as the exercise itself. He even implanted the idea into the daily morning body-breath exercises that we did. So the idea of "nothing but nothing" was floating in my awareness in some capacity every day since 2001. But for sure, there is no preparation possible for a realization of Emptiness. A few suggestions and ideas of what it is like can be shared, but beyond that, it is one of those things someone has to "come and see for themselves."

---

50   John Kent *Path to Reality* chapter 16

*

Anders and I are picking up a few items at the local grocery store in the small Swedish town he and his wife live in. Liv has "directed" us to go and get a couple of extra things needed for dinner. Directed as in giving us a very detailed list so that even the two "males" would return with the items requested. As we walk around the aisles obtaining the items on the very neatly handwritten list, he asks me about Nothingness.

"You wrote a lot about this subject in *Falling For Truth,* so I was wondering, right now in this store, do you think there are people here who have also had an experience of Emptiness?"

"You mean the other shoppers? Could be. We would be unable to know for sure without talking to them, and even then someone can hide such a thing very well if they want to. Those who this happens often try to tell a family member or close friend about what they experienced, but they tended to get a response along the lines that there was something wrong with them, so most who have this realization just stop sharing it with others."

"And there is no way to make it happen? Experiencing Emptiness," Anders asked casually while grabbing a container of yogurt.

"Not really. All the exercises I did for 8 years, the travel to various ancient sites, spending time directly with teachers were all parts of a puzzle. But the puzzle itself has to take a final step that had nothing to do with me directly. Death has to be added to the equation somehow. That force will be needed for any deep realization, because it is only death that can drop the last ego (which Schopenhauer called Will). Only when all the egos finally fall away, can it be revealed what is beyond all egos and states of mind. As long as an ego or two are still in place, the best one can get is a small taste of Emptiness. The brink of death can push you there, but not everyone will cross. That does not mean people should go out and do dangerous things trying to be close to death, because work needs to be done to prepare for the experience. If such a grace comes, and there are too many self walls in the way,

Self can not be revealed. We prepare for something that we never know for sure if it will come our way."

"What I don't fully understand is why is this so important. Why does Anders need to see that he is not Anders. The end goal of that makes no sense to me."

I laugh. "I don't think it would. Emptiness is not the Exit door, but it is the mat you wipe your dirty feet on before going through. The dirty feet are the beliefs we have had about ourself and this reality. Emptiness is the realization that helps us begin to scrape off all the mud that has been stuck to our shoes. I have said many times, only some-thing can be trapped in a false reality, No-thing cannot be trapped by anything. That being said No-thing is not better or different than something. They are two sides of a coin. That is the whole Buddhist Nirvana is Samsara idea. No-thing is revealed when one negates something. They fit together. Just our whole lives we have had a 100% focus on the something side, which is why one needs a big dose for a while of the nothing side to balance it all out. But just as you don't want to get stuck in something, you don't want to get stuck in nothing either. That is where the work of between-ness begins, when we put our Awareness between the two and see what gets revealed. The problem is this idea that Nirvana, or Emptiness is the final goal. It is just the flip side of how we normally experience things. Both something and nothing have to take their place as equal yet useless at the same time."

*

Self Definition begins when the key error behind "going within" is revealed. This "within" is always thought of related to a dividing line between outside and inside, that being the skin of the body. So going within is taken to mean going to the inside the skin to examine one's thoughts, feelings, fears and whatnot. That is small s self definition, and is how we learn who and what our character is. We turn away the word of forms, to examine the world of thoughts and feelings.

But Self Definition is go inside the Self, to see that all of what we had previously called inside (mind, thoughts, feelings), is still outside of this Greater Self. As soon as one reaches a place where one can realize that they can witness their own thoughts, therefore "I" can not be my thoughts or how could I witness them, a shift can occur. To continue this line of examination is to reveal that all we previously deemed inside of me, is still outside of this Witnessing Awareness, because the Awareness is able to witness all these "inner" goings on from outside of it. To go inside of one's Self, eventually, is moving backwards into Emptiness.

The realization of Emptiness is not the same as the merging of the Divine Spark with the Fire, what I classify was originally meant by the term enlightenment. Emptiness is the realization that comes first, because we need to be shaken out of the solidity and importance of the world of something (forms and objects). Part of this realization is to see how much of our energy during our life has been invested in a fictional character (me). After the realization of Emptiness, if one integrates and follows where it leads, allows the energy to be re-rooted to the Spark.

Remember, the character in the dream (the Howdie thing) never has to wake up. The thing in the coma (Sleeping Beauty) is what has to be awakened. The Howdie thing has to be come to be known completely, transformed where required, then allowed to perform as the actor on stage he was designed to be, available to assist this deeper and more real Spark/Awareness. All true paths include this element of No Self/Emptiness, or at least they did before they got edited through history to instead putting the focus on ceremonies, and praying to various gods or saviours. Mr. Park, through his exercises, wanted us to bypass all of that, and get right to the heart of the process, seeing both sides of Everything (unity) and Emptiness (No-Self) clearly.

Most when they first hear these ideas about Emptiness, it seems depressing. And it is, for the egoic self we have always thought we were. That self has spent a huge investment of energy getting us to believe that its thoughts, desires and fears were the only possibilities. It has invested so much that it cannot let "us" even comprehend that there may exist something far beyond it. So it makes the idea of Emptiness seem boring, or even dangerous, to stop us taking any time to examine these ideas further. The egoic mind wants us to go back to sitting quietly, with mindfulness or a mantra, while focusing on manifesting our desires. That is its way of keeping its walls of control in tact, and be sure no one goes peeking over the fence to see what is on the other side of the Matrix.

Why is Emptiness a stepping stone for Exiting the Cave? Because only the realization of Emptiness can reveal that the body-mind and the entire world of objects is not the solid things we had always believed the were, but are projections that can be perceived and experienced. That realization comes as a great shock. All of our focus has gone into making things of reality important, and now we see that is not where the realness has always been. That is much deeper than every expected.

Is Exiting the Cave really what you want, because nothing of the you that currently believe yourself to be is going to make it. Awareness will make it, but not "you." That is where all this is going, and is why once grace starts to get close and push against all the areas that someone is grasping too, thing begin to feel uncomfortable. It is at this point the average person finds anything that will make all that tension and pressure stop. Again they think this is scary, to see that the body-mind they have identified with their entire life is just a projected actor. It has a function and a focus, and we learn to navigate with it rather than against it. We appreciate the character, root for him or her, get the best our character can attain, but after a full realization of Emptiness we no longer classify ourself as the thing we see in the mirror. We are know we are vast, and at the same time, No-thing.

Psychology can be helpful as someone works to transform and heal their mind. The challenge comes if someone does have a real experience of Emptiness, because this does not fit into the psychology framework. The experience is similar to something that they classify as depersonalization disorder. Such a disorder does exist, and it relates to a fractured egoic state from trauma. Due to trauma that the mind at the time is not able to handle, it kind of checks out. This loss is what the practice known as "soul retrieval" tries to address, to bring back the lost psychological parts from a traumatic experience. However, the experience of Emptiness, while having some similarities to the fragmenting of a mind after a trauma, is not the same thing. One after Emptiness is very clear Who they are, but the body-mind is now something being borrowed by that more Real Awareness. Since the standard psychology community has no framework, it puts the two states (fragmenting from trauma, and experience of Emptiness) as the same thing. An Additional Material article on the story of Suzanne Segal will appear on my website after this book's publication. Her story is valuable as it touches many areas presented in this chapter. She seems to have experienced Emptiness and depersonalization disorder at the same time. This as well as facing over a decade of challenges finding someone to explain what was going on for her.[51]

First you learn to "awaken in the dream" (to operate differently than one's conditioning in a way that is beneficial to your character), secondly you "awaken from the dream" (to see that the world is not the solid reality that you believed it was), thirdly you "awaken from yourself" (the Realization of Emptiness). This third realization can be both clarifying as much as confusing.

*

THE OTHER SIDE OF THE WALL

Anders has been working on edits to one of the final chapters of this book. He has been quiet, drinking his third coffee of the morning. I get the sense he wants to ask me something, and is sort of gathering up the nerve to do so.

"Howdie, can I ask you about something?"

---

51 Why her story is so interesting, is even though she wrote a very popular book on her experience, *Collision With the Infinite,* she seemed at the end of her life to have a completely new outlook on everything and wrote a new book about her new view. Sadly that book was never published and does not seem to still exist. It might have made her one of the centuries great spiritual teachers, and might have overturned many concepts of the time.

"That's the job of an editor, ask questions about what they have the job of editing."

"It is about Emptiness."

"Mmm." I figured this was the area of the question

"Is it enjoyable to experience?"

"Emptiness? The immediate aftermath of it can feel very Liberating. I mean you have just seen that all of the things you have put all of your faith on (self and reality) are not as solid or true as you once thought they were. That all the things you struggled your whole life to try to achieve, and often failed at, were just projections. How many times you said no to something, afraid that the girl saying no to a date or an employer to a job you were applying to, but then you realize there is no real "you" to get embarrassed. I mean that part of the realization is so calming. There is also seeing you are a more complete Totality, and that Totality is not something separate, it is the real you and it is here right now this second, just I spent my whole life pushing it away. And so a switch of identification begins to occur, away from all of the Matrix objects and experiences, to a more deeper realness. It can be pretty enjoyable for a while, but there are pitfalls both before and after."

"But the lead up to that experience, it just does not seem like fun the way you are describing it."

"What? Slowly chopping away every one of your beliefs slice by slice? No, that's not going to be fun." I smile. I know its not fun at all, but it is required to get to Emptiness.

"I just can't get around that every spiritual teaching I have come across that is discussing Truth, and they even use the word Emptiness in their teaching, their focus is about is finding more love, more peace, more clarity. That sounds enjoyable, not hacking off pieces of yourself with an ax."

"Well, I never said ax, hacking, nor yourself. I said chopping and beliefs, but I get your point. The lead up is not fun. Well, the first part of it kind of is, which about the only part the regular spiritual community discusses because that is about as far as they have really gone. Given again that 99% of people are on a path to feel better, to be more important, to have more sex, to fix the world, to share the afterlife with dead grandma and Jesus, then it makes sense that it is what the spiritual marketplace is selling. Granted, that part is important at the start of the path, to get the body-mind to become a better functioning and healthier robot. But that is the level these spiritual and religious traditions are operating at. It has a place, has value. But there also comes a time when if someone wants Truth, they have to stop living in their false world of comfort. A path to Truth is not about happiness, it is about seeing through the thing that believes it needs happiness. It is seeing what is beyond even the idea of happiness."

Even though we have talked about this subject many times for the last ten years, I can see that this is something that is still a catching point for Anders. He is seeking to be happy at the core. He sort of wants Truth, but not if it will get in the way of his happiness.

"Howdie, are you ever happy?"

"Sometimes I guess, I don't really think about. Enjoyable moments seem to make this reality much more tolerable; going for walks, listening to calm music, sitting by a lake. They serve a nice resting place in a world dominated by insanity and suffering. Sometimes I just sit and stare at a wall. No kidding. Since I have less and less of a belief that I need to achieve anything, sometimes I just sit there. Not really staring at a wall, just being still and silent. There is nowhere else I need to be, so I don't fight it. I can just be still. That is one of the great gifts of Emptiness, to see that all of our life we have been working hard to get somewhere, and now to see there is nowhere to get. For a while it can get calm."

"People claim they want calm."

"Not this kind of calm. They want the calm where they get all their desires fulfilled, not one where they see that if a desire is fulfilled or not makes no difference. People prefer to live a life of false, and sure they can enjoy the meditation, mindfulness, tantra and believing that because they are a vegetarian they are better than those who are not. But Truth is in the opposite direction. The path to Truth is about first letting go of false. All of it. But when you drop some false, some Truth doesn't come to take its place. You sort of see more and more of all your foundations are getting pulled out, and it can get real shaky for a while. A lot of people have had some of that feeling, but most course correct, and find a new, slightly different foundation. A few though keep going, not wanting any foundation except what they can verify as 100% True. And that can mean a long confusing lead-up period of wondering "who and what" you really are."

*

Nothing in this chapter can be fully evaluated unless this realization happens for you. Until that time, it can only remain a possibility. It is ok to try to understand this with the logical mind, even if the logical mind can never understand it. I did that too, but I had Mr. Park helping me behind the scenes with his "nothing but nothing" suggestion. In a sense, you keep this as a possibility, while you keep doing the work in your life of defining yourself and reality.

The path to Emptiness does not acquire a depth to it until one has done a great deal of work on the definition of their small s self and has gotten their "house in order." This is when the actor can begin performing its role while losing less energy from doing so. After one starts seeing their character more clearly, if one decides to keep walking, Emptiness may start interacting with you. Or rather it will begin to descend on you. I use that term descend because there is an ominous feeling associated with it. Emptiness is not ominous of course, except for the egoic identity of "me." The projected part of me knows that Emptiness has the power to remove false, and since the egoic personality is nothing but false, it knows that the closer Emptiness gets, the less trusted ego will be. This can produce a type of depression, because Emptiness starts revealing all of the ego's hopes and fears to be the same as a breeze on a cool night. Yet the process is at the same time being welcomed by the Divine Spark with a greeting of, "what took you so long?"

You have to ask yourself if the process of Exiting the Cave is something you are doing seriously, or if it is a type of entertainment or distraction? You need to make that determination to know where the path you are walking is heading. If it is distraction and entertainment, that is fine. Many are seekers, not for Truth, they seek just to seek. You know them, they run from guru to guru, book to book, technique to technique. Always something new, the next best thing, the thing that finally will answer it all. Until three weeks later when all of a sudden it is something or someone else now with all the answers. They never really want to find anything, they are just seeking to give themselves something to do. Exiting the Cave is not "something to do," it becomes the "only thing to do."

The realization of Emptiness, or the awakening of the Divine Spark, is seen by the regular mind to be quite an achievement. It tries to package anything that someone claims of importance to be an achievement. It's not. Realizing Emptiness is the simplest thing, crossing the gateless gate of Zen. Yet, crossing a gate that does not exist will require a massive effort, the result of which will be that there will be nothing of "you" left on the other side to get any benefit. The end of the search comes with the end of the seeker. And it has to be SEEN to be believed. We stop being Joe as who we are, but we continue to "borrow" Joe for worldly interactions and finding what actions will be of help to the journey of the Divine Spark. The realization of Emptiness does not change that there is a character in a world, it changes the actions and the motivations of the character.

A reminder is required here that we are not following this path to "escape suffering and pain." We are doing it to find out what is True about our self and our reality. If suffering and pain leave, then that is a bonus. The main goal is not to end suffering, as suffering likely will still take place in the Matrix as it is part of the entire basis of distortion this realm is built on. What you are doing is ending the cycle of suffering lives for the Deeper Awareness that you are. Ending of the reincarnation cycle. That happens when the main direction of our focus is no longer what happens in this realm, but what happens in that more real realm. But to get the taste of that realm is going to come with a lead up that can be very challenging. In my case, it caused me to question everything I had ever thought of who and what I was.

*

MY STORY

I will share two of my journal entries in between the one year period following my "split experience" in the Great Pyramid in 2004, and then the fall in the canyon in 2005.[52] I begin with an entry just one month after the visit to Egypt.

> April 14, 2004. *"I have been sleeping all day. I have the feeling that I may be losing the human form. I am losing interest in having anyone around me, and I have lost interest in having conversations, especially those about myself. I have no interest in telling anyone about my trip to Egypt. I don't need to tell anyone why either, just because I do not want to talk about it is good enough. The need to tell others what to do is also lessening. My two favorite phrases are becoming maybe and I don't know. People are free to do what they want and think what they want. I have little interest in what others may think of my actions. I have also lost the sense of winning and losing, what's the difference really? Everything feels so different, so strange. All the things I used to like seem to have no meaning. Who the hell am I, dammit? The old is getting ripped away. Who am I? It is a strange place to be, not wanting anything, nor wanting to do anything. A*

---

52 Both of the experiences can be found in *Falling For Truth*.

As you can see, for at least a year prior to the canyon, there was deep questioning related to "who am I?" In some ways that experience of having my awareness in two places at once in the Great Pyramid (one looking out of my body and another looking back at that body) had made me really question what I was, and it was in my thoughts almost constantly. It was also related to the understanding that up to 2004, I had worked obsessively hard for eight years, yet I was coming to terms with just how little I actually knew about anything. I kept wondering, "would I have been better off having a job and making money all that time?"I was beginning to doubt if even the path I had been walking had any real value at all.

A critical examination of our life in the material realm reveals that there has been a symbolic wall between us (body-mind) and the Witnessing Awareness that has been behind the wall. As long as one still trusts "my thoughts and beliefs," Emptiness will likely stay away. But if you want real Answers, one must keep pushing forward.

The following quote from John Kent presents how Richard Rose saw what the later steps on the path to Emptiness look like, which is not anything like people hope it will be.

"Rose has made some disturbing comments, based on his own experience, about the final phase of the path. After years of dedicated and honest search, and an ascetic lifestyle, he had expected the heavens to open up one day and strike him with a lightning bolt of exaltation, carrying him up into celestial glory. This is undoubtedly how most seekers anticipate their spiritual quest to culminate. It did not quite happen this way for Rose. Instead, what

he found was death, absolute negation of all that he had known and all that he was."[53] John Kent

The descent of Emptiness would culminate for me near the end of May 2005, yet a key preparatory element of the canyon experience was about to happen three weeks prior to the fall in the canyon. In the months leading up to that day, I had begun to see that my life was mostly an un-enjoyable experience. No activity was better or worse than another. I still went for walks, I still stopped by the Buddhist temple near my house every Wednesday night, and I still often sat in my favourite coffee shop. But mostly I was silent with my thoughts.

It was at this time that I decided to stop being a stand-up comedian. It was less about doing shows and traveling, and more that I no longer wanted to have that identity. I had had this desire to be a comedian since I was about nine years old, and had constantly been referred to as "Mr. Entertainment," as a type of mask that would make the other kids (then teenagers and then adults) like me. As long as I kept on performing, that identity would stay in place. But there was no identity waiting to replace it with. I had no other career or job lined up. All of the money I was earning would soon stop.

It was thus interesting that while I was looking for a specific show to call my last, one was offered for me on May 5, 2005, which also happened to be the highest salary I had ever been offered. I thought that this is the perfect way to go out, being paid the most money of my career. Yet I saw right away on accepting the show that it fell on the same exact day (May 5) when in 1999 I had the experience of seeing myself die in a car accident in a parallel reality. So at the time, I noticed a possible odd "synchronicity" with the performance and that day.

I do not recall much of the few weeks leading up to the show, but I do remember a tough time the night before, as indicated by my next journal entry,

---

53 John Kent chapter 16

May 4, 2005. "*First I am having a shortness of breath, as well as a need to rest a lot, a lot like a person who is really dying. An incredible apprehension is surrounding me for the last few days, as I had the feeling to want to immerse myself in something of the world. It is though nothing in the world has any joy in it. There is such a sense of having no idea what is coming, and there being no one that I can talk to about it. Obviously I am erasing a lot of personal history and identity, all in one shot. There is no question that a death of sorts will happen tomorrow. Once all of these things are gone, who am I? All of the "me's" that I tried to be, tried to achieve something as, they will all be gone. So who am I? What am I? There is a feeling of wanting to go away to Bermuda and sit on a beach for a long while. I guess I feel afraid, but I am not sure what to feel afraid of. Afraid in some way that all my past identities have not really brought me the peace or happiness I wanted. I wonder now if any identity will. I am wondering what to do now, so who am I?*"

After that show I sat at a table in the hotel where it took place, mostly exhausted. I had used up a lot of energy really wanting to give this show 100%. An ex-girlfriend wanted to see the last show I was ever going to do, so joined me on the trip. She could tell something was different, and asked me a couple of times if I was OK. I simply nodded and focused on whatever I was drinking. I felt like a death had really just occurred, albeit a small death, and nothing like the one that was about to happen in three weeks. Looking back, it was like a warm-up for the canyon. I had just dropped the identity that I had been living with since I was nine years old. The mask of the comedian was no longer there. I had really liked that identity because it made me part of an interesting conversation at a party. "What do you do?" "Oh, I'm a comedian." Well that brought a room full of people over to find out about the very unique guy. But I now desired to be something more than the mask of a comedian. Once I ended that show, hence my career in comedy, I ended the old uniqueness. I had become very average once again.

But the main reason for ending the comedian was the fact that I had just poured eight years of my life, 12 to 14 hours a day, into a spiritual search that seemed to have taken me nowhere. I had made it to Egypt in 2004, as the plan had been after seeing the *Nova* documentary in 1997. A majority of my practice was preparing for that exploration. But now the exploration was completed. So what was the point of continued practice? Why did my time in the various pyramids in Egypt not give me the "ultimate secret" that I had been searching for and thought for sure I would find there? Did the Universe hate me? Had I done something wrong? Should I have stayed with Mr. Park longer? Or had I just been fooling myself, thinking I could find something that perhaps I was not worthy enough to locate? Maybe that was the problem I wondered, that I was not good enough to find what I had been seeking. And so a part of me hoped that by dropping my main identity, source of income, and way of navigating in the world, maybe then the Universe would think I had "done enough." When I later read how Rose felt prior to his experience, I realized a similarity to where I had been after ending my comedy career,

> *"After years of dedicated and honest search, and an ascetic lifestyle* (severe self-discipline)*, Rose had expected the heavens to open up one day and strike him with a lightning bolt of exaltation, carrying him up into celestial glory. This is undoubtedly how most seekers anticipate their spiritual quest to culminate. It did not quite happen this way for Rose. Instead, what he found was death, absolute negation of all that he had known and all that he was. He claims that a mood of despair and oblivion precedes the death experience, as all of one's efforts and hopes seem to lead to nothing. There is even the sense of being on the edge of insanity; of losing one's mind. God remains silent and aloof. One*

<blockquote>
wonders if the commitment had not been conceited foolishness all along. Although many interpretations have been put forth over the centuries, perhaps this was the inner meaning of Christ's statement on the Cross as he was about to die: "My God, why have you forsaken me?"[54] - John Kent
</blockquote>

The despair being hinted at in the above quotation is not to be confused with disappointment, frustration, or the death of someone. Rose was discussing something else completely, what some have called "The Dark Night of the Soul." Most have come to believe that this means some sort of difficult life circumstances which they must fight through so that they can grow and become better humans. But the real dark night is not depression, but has its origin as seeing that the "me" thing might not what I am, and perhaps can not be trusted to be the main vehicle to take us to Truth. After seeing that, what comes next?

Along with this can come a feeling similar to that of falling off a cliff. Recall that this is the exact image of the Tarot Fool, and also of David (Tom Cruise) at end of the movie *Vanilla Sky*. This is not a call to "jump off a cliff," it is a metaphor to what the feeling of the Dark Night can be likened to. It is not the dark night of the soul, but rather just the dark night of the ego. Ego is being revealed as an impostor, and since ego is all one has known since being a very small child, the result is a loss in all of the foundations we have built to interact with standard reality. Hence the feeling of not having our foundations for a while. It's ok, you just just to get used to this odd way of interacting with the world for a while.

When the fall in the canyon happened for me, Emptiness which had be hovering around for almost a year, was revealed. But realizations are never what we expected them to be. Gifts of power and specialness did not ring down from the heavens, instead everything I had ever believed I was dissolved. I can not explain it any other way. This can also appear as an energetic explosion inside, where the deepest level of the lies and conditioning are

---

54 John Kent pg. 281

getting blown up. UG Krishnamurti called it "the calamity." If the experience occurs over a longer time, then it is similar to the metaphor of the Christian hellfire, that which will burn everything from the form that believes it is separate and important. It is pure grace, but grace is not the loving experience people wish it to be. Grace is the alchemic fire. In the following phone call Richard Rose had a student of his, Nick, who one night moved "past his mind and egoic self" to Emptiness. He called Rose wanting to know what had just happened and part of the phone call he responded,

> *"Nick (you are) scared and confused right now. It is a pretty traumatic thing when you wake up and realize that you have been living your life as a shadow in a stranger's nightmare. For a while you are suspended over an abyss, not here, not anywhere else either. You are seeing that your mind does not exist, at least as an individual unit, it's just a matrix, a port that the larger dimension anchors into. Yes, the total loneliness is what takes you away from all your contact with relativity. It comes from the realization that your essence is separated for all time from your loved ones, and your attachments to the old world. Of course you are scared. You are afraid that if you let go, you will crash into the sides of the bank and everything will fall apart. But believe me, you will find that everything keeps moving as it should, even better than if you were trying to control it."[55] - Richard Rose*

Rose reminds us that one will make their way through the experience if they do not fight against it and try to return to their old egoic world and beliefs. In the conversation above, Nick was reminded to stay chemically balanced (keep eating, exercising and sleeping), and he would continue beyond the current experience. I had a similar response from Mr. Park when something similar happened to me. He wanted me to go play golf for a few days, to

---

55 Found in *After the Absolute* by Dave Gold and Bart Marshall, chapter 14

give my mind something familiar to do while the experience just followed its own course without me trying to control it. I focused on the golf course, while the experience followed its course. I kept doing the basic things through it all. I ate, I took walks, I worked on being still (even though I couldn't sleep), and I golfed. In a week it all sort of "burned itself out," and a transformation had occurred without my ever knowing that one occurred until it was completed.

I want to return to feeling of helplessness I mentioned earlier. We hit a point where we realize that our fictional self and mind, that we completely trusted, is just not capable of getting the Ultimate Answers that we seek. We put all of our hopes on something that had little to offer. This is what was happening to Buddha under the Bodhi Tree. He was not in a deep state of will and strength to overcome all the temptations of Maya, he just saw that ALL of his body-mind resources had little value. He gave up. He surrendered. He saw that all he ever trusted in is useless in the face of Totality. He could not care about the temptations, because he saw that none of them could help him out of his moment of hopelessness. This was similar to Richard Rose lying in bed, UG Krishnamurti lying on the couch, or Karl Renz dealing with the headache. They were all in a state of total helplessness, which lead to a "death." This was the death not of the material body, but of the small s material self which they had been holding onto as the thing that would save them. For me, my helplessness was to be in a river pushing me to a waterfall that I seemed to have no logical possibility of avoiding.

But this helplessness is only the helplessness of the ego. The Dark Night ends and the dawn appears (which can take a long period of time) when one finally realizes that there is something beyond all of the egoic-mind things we have been trusting all along. The ego is what is helpless, and as long as that is where we identify, not much can happen. When the shift happens to getting knowledge and information directly from our Divine Spark, everything changes in an instant. That is the shift where Buddha was running out of options, but could now see that (in that case) his stillness could be a powerful action. He responded from Emptiness, no longer from Siddhartha. From Emptiness comes a great calm and clarity. It is not Emptiness which is calm and clear, it is where it allows our Awareness to be centered. But it takes a while to get rooted there, often the initial response to Emptiness, especially if one has not been preparing for it, is confusion.

> *"When grace comes most people try to run away from it. They don't expect it to be so merciless, so relentless and overwhelming. Grace gives you nothing, and takes away everything."*[56] - Karl Renz

No-Self/Emptiness is not scary in itself. It can be odd and confusing, but it is also clarifying and liberating. Emptiness is not a fun realization for the body-mind ego thing we have believed ourself to be, it is joyous for the Awareness beyond the ego. To cross over and move our Awareness into Emptiness, nothing of the regular self and identity can make it through. All that you think of as you has to be let go of or dropped. And if you won't drop it, Emptiness will take it for the experience to occur. This a frightening prospect to the ego, so it fights back usually through a type of depression. One just has to keep moving through it.

As the quote from Karl Renz above states, Emptiness (grace) takes away everything and returns nothing. I will say that again. Emptiness takes away everything and gives you No-thing. And it is hard to know what everything really is until you start to pay that price. Every thought, memory, hope, fear, concept, and belief has to be negated to have that realization. We like to think that the false things in our life is all the bad stuff, so if we just get rid of all the bad stuff then the closer we get to the Truth, life is going to become wonderful and joyous. The flip side is that everything you call good, all the stuff you really like and love, well we get to keep all that. A big step on the realization process is that all of that side is also false. That does not mean you have to go live in the woods or leave your family. It is not the people or objects that are getting dropped, it is the "idea" that there was a you at the core who was getting some sort of "benefit" from them. Thus it begins to be seen that objects are fine to be in one's life, and fine not to be. Emptiness will dissolve the idea that you are special,

---

56 Karl Renz, *Myth of Enlightenment*

have some sort of mission, or anything else you can believe about your self. That is the main thing that gets taken away, "I am unique and special, the world is so lucky to have me in it." It is a really hard thing to watch dissolve.

*

> *"The task of the seeker of eternity is to die while living; to know of death so that the seeker will know of all the secrets of life."*[57] - Richard Rose

If I had to simplify the meaning of what is normally classified as spiritual work, it is to prepare one's entire being to meet the force of death with Awareness and Clarity. Having a death experience alone does little to show through towards the Truth of oneself, as many NDE's seem to simply solidify their false self even more.

This death being discussed has nothing to do with the ending of the physical body, but rather the shattering of the glue that is holding all of the separate parts of the "me" together. That is why, one way or another, during an experience of Emptiness, a person will often feel like they are dying. In the canyon of course my mind was faced with the soon-to-happen death of my body by going over the falls. My survival ego dropped. I had a moment of clarity that I no longer needed to live in this reality, I could die at that instant and it would have been fine. That acceptance, a type of surrender, is what dropped the conglomerate of "me," and all of its thoughts, feelings, emotions, memories, hopes, and fears. They just dissolved, and all that remained Awareness. This witnessing clarity was recognized by itself to have been "me" all along. All of those other body-mind things had been just covers. In reality I was timeless and spaceless. But you don't have to try to "kill yourself," or any other wild notions for this to occur. The practice is to first locate, then punch holes in one's belief walls. It is those walls that have the purpose of keeping "me" on this side, and Awareness on the other. When the beliefs and dual thinking can be put down,

---

57 Richard Rose, *Energy Transmutation, Between-ness, And Transmission*, p. 65

holes appear, and Awareness can start communicating directly. The rest sort of happens on its own.

The body is not the problem, nor even the mind. A reminder that you don't need to "kill" anything, there is no need for any sort of violence against "yourself" nor "others." The identity is not meant to be killed, but surrendered. That is a very different thing. It might seem like it died or dissolved, but really it surrendered its place on the throne. In my case, with death just seconds away, "Howdie" realized he had never meant to be on the throne of control, so seeing that there was but a few seconds left of its specialness, it stepped off the throne. Awareness took the ego's place, and I realized it is what was always meant to be on the throne of my character's existence. It was beautiful, but not in the way most think. I know, everyone wants a nice experience, where you are surrounded by love, comfort and joy. That is the experience of Unity, of Everything. That is one side of the coin of Total Seeing (and I have had that as well). But to have the other side, Emptiness, to reveal itself, nothing that could be connected, or unified or loving can be in place. All beliefs have to be burned out before one can see the No-thing side of the Empty-Full coin.

This is why suicide offers no value of escape, as it is only the death of the physical body. Though it does end the current experience of suffering, it does so without the totality of the work being completed, so the soul will just continue the recycling into additional suffering bodies. Suffering will just continue in a different outer form. Thus we have to use the time available in our current material life, no matter how challenging and difficult it is, to keep up with our work of self definition and understanding. Hence, we use another day to see and drop one more bit of false, to hopefully reveal a bit more of what is True about us. Suicide will not help that process. While we are not afraid of death should it come to us, as It will come, we can not stop it, but there is no need to bring it sooner than it needs to be. We make time a friend. And we see what happens by using it a bit differently than masses use their time.

The realization of No Self can be described as the moment the bubble of belief in the character we see in the mirror every day is shattered and relegated to the state of a very well-known projection, one that we do what we can for, but no longer is our main identity. This cannot happen without the force called death. We tend to spend all of our focus only on the life part of duality, yet to see clearly, the forces of both life and death must be brought together. With the two opposites united, something that is always greater than the two can be revealed. This reconciliation of these two seemingly opposite principles, is a major step up Jacob's Ladder.

The person in the Matrix has to do a lot of work[58] to build a valid container (body-mind) to handle Emptiness. If Grace comes too soon, before we have done enough work to see through a majority of our belief walls, the experience can be quite challenging. The experiencing too early can occur from using drugs (which can open doorways one is not prepared for), from what can be called kundalini exercises (without really understanding what energy is involved in such exercises), or simply from a trauma that pushes the ego away long enough for Emptiness to reveal itself. We keep working to become a container able to handle the experience of Emptiness should it appear.

That being said, most tend to just ignore any work that needs to be done and instead engage in any distraction. John Kent clearly presented, *"All we are, essentially, is a defense mechanism against the Truth...Yet, occasionally, despite one's best efforts, reality breaks through."* And when it does, even though I have discussed confusion, there is also a pure joy to it to get a glimpse of our Divine Spark/Emptiness. As one person I know who had this experience declared, "I found the love of my life." People feel this need to search for some half they deem to be missing, but place this search towards another person out there, who we will "couple with." We spend vast amounts of time to search for this person to make us complete. Yet when it gets revealed that who we have been seeking all along has been the Divine Spark at our core, the message of seeking our other half makes more sense. That is who we want to be in a sacred marriage with, not a person in the Matrix

---

58   even though oddly later finding one did not do anything

world, or even building "self-love" for the body mind. We allow the Witnessing Awareness to be in love with what it is. When people try to say this is a world of love, and all we need is love, they are actually presenting this truth in a confused way. They make this love about the world, its objects, and the joys of their physical self. But these are all just distractions, ways of keeping us focused in the opposite direction of where Love exists, which is outside of the Matrix, through our Divine Spark.

*

TRAPS AFTER EMPTINESS

"So all the exercises you did in the years before you fell into the canyon were really just creating holes in your walls?" Anders asks.

"Yup, and holes in my head." We both laugh. "I mean there were short term benefits from all of the exercises in terms of energy, understanding and whatnot. But what those exercises were really doing was unseen at the time. They were dropping belief walls. Normally when that happens, someone just finds a new belief. For whatever reason, I chose to stay in a state of 'I don't know.' It was that openness that helped to set up the perfect moment to manifest, for me falling into a roaring river next to a waterfall. And again, what is amazing is that I never could have guessed what Emptiness would be like. I read about illusion and not being a self, but to actually have the direct experience of it, was strange and at the same time so obvious."

"A lot of modern writers say there is nothing you can do to bring about such a realization and so you should just stop. Stop doing everything."

"In a sense they are correct. Just they all have it a bit backwards. There is a time to stop, definitely. But you can not do that until you have exhausted all seeking. On one hand there is some things that you do have to find. You can't just say 'there is nothing I need to know, so go watch TV.' There is a level of knowledge that is required or one will get stuck in a type of being lost in reality. But the point is that knowledge will only take you so far, but you have to try everything out and then honestly evaluate the results. Not everything works for you, so you have to go the next thing and the next thing. Eventually you start to see that you are running out of "things" to try. You come to point where you realize you have tried it all, but still you don't have the overall answer. That is when it starts to dawn on you. The seeking can only go so far, and once you hit that point, you come to a complete stop and just stay aware within."

"And only you can figure out if you are at this stopping place or not, correct?"

"Exactly. You can not trust anyone else on the path but you. And you I don't mean Anders, but your Divine Spark. How often is that part actually speaking compared to mind is something you also have to test to find out. Castaneda called this learning to listen to the soft voice within, the voice that is not from the egoic mind he labeled the parasite, but a voice of Truth. Finding out who and what to trust is a key part of the path to Exiting. I see Emptiness as the place where the doorway starts to gets constructed. Writing is my way of integrating and understanding these ideas for myself, and perhaps might at some point be helpful for others. So in some ways I am writing this chapter to perhaps have a similar affect on someone as Eddie's blog posts were for me."

"Who is Eddie?"

"Eddie Traversa. Australian guy who had a blog around 2005 about Emptiness and No Self. Even though I had a shattering of the personal self in that river, it did not mean that I got a total understanding of everything. As I have mentioned, after the realization came a combination of clarity and confusion. Mr. Park was unable to be reached during that period of time (he was very sick and would die shortly after), but I was lucky enough to receive help from Eddie. Not only were the posts on his blog of value, but he also took a lot of time to answer my questions personally. His words helped me understand more of what had actually occurred in that canyon. He also helped to add the terms and concepts for it all.”

“What would have happened if you read those blogs in, say a few years before your experience?”

“Not much. I might have been a bit curious as to what he was referring to, but they would have meant very little to me before the canyon. But after having the very experience that he was alluding to, they were instantly understood. So in a sense, it is the same for the chapter you are editing now, it is here for whenever someone might be able to make use of it, now or later. After Eddie came across some of Richard Rose's books, and originally didn't like them very much. I found them not smoothly written and hard to understand. But later when I came across his lectures, I found him to be a terrific speaker. Rose was one of this century's true spiritual teachers, and while a great lecturer and speaker, writing was not his forte (save poetry). I prefer to read printed notes of his lectures rather than the books he wrote.”

“Same feeling here. I could not get far into reading Rose directly. But that John Kent material you showed to me, just wow.”

“About a year after putting Rose down and trying to deal with my experience from reading various Advaita and Zen works, I came across the PhD thesis of John Kent, where he rewrote and summarized all of the works of Richard Rose. It was magnificent. I still call it the greatest spiritual work, at least in the last century. Rose's material was finally presented in a way that was clear to understand, and given my experience was just over a year old, I was able in many cases to feel out the Kent material rather than read it.”[59] Kent was able to bring the core of Rose's message into an easy to understand language. I don't know how long it would have taken to make more sense out of what happened in that river canyon

---

59 The first three chapters I recommend people skip when first reading his thesis, which I think is more for the academic professors who would be judging his work. The clear writing begins with chapter 4. Dave Gold and Bart Marshall's *After the Absolute* is another text regarding Rose that can be helpful, especially as a first introduction to Rose's philosophy.

without those texts. But for a while, it was a difficult place. There are just as many traps for the ego after a realization of Emptiness as there were before. They are just structured differently, and since we have rarely dealt with these structures prior, they can catch people quickly. The lures caught me as well, and it took several years to get my foot out of the traps."

*

There are some good sources today on the subject of Emptiness and No Self, far more than existed back in 2005 when I went looking for information. My advice to you is to use discernment on anything you consider around this topic, including what you are reading in this book. That is because having a realization of Emptiness often only makes things easy for a short time. The ego will find all sorts of ways to re-frame itself into something so that it can gain importance from Nothing. I would have not thought it was possible had I not seen it occur with myself.

Some, after a realization might seek help from spiritual areas, but they often only find distorted information. They also often get told that an experience of Emptiness means that they are enlightened. This is very problematic, because the concept sold as enlightenment is some sort of perfection. If someone believes this, they will often stop all work of integration of their experience, because they believe they have achieved "perfection." That is where a book like Marina Caplan's *Halfway Up the Mountain* is so valuable. To remind us that these are just steps on a long mountain path, and not at the top of that mountain.

Some modern teachers try to present that there is nothing you can do as a self to bring about the realization of No Self, because it is all from grace or from an accident. Therefore, they say to just stop doing any work. And of course keep coming back to their 500 dollar weekend seminars. But if you look back at their own biographies, such people have had a history of a lot of doing, thinking, questioning, being alone in the mountains, or perhaps just picking up the pieces after a failed marriage or a tragic death.

They asked themselves, "Why?" There is a time for stopping, but there is a whole lot of directed action that must take place prior to that point. Richard Rose reminded us that "while realization is an accident, you have to do the work to make yourself accident prone."[60] To "stop" too soon will only stop the process. When the "stop" happens at the correct moment, it becomes magical. Thus you have to learn when the timing is correct.

That being said, even with a realization of Emptiness, there becomes challenges to deal with. Some of the problem is from the ego's reaction to what has been revealed, and some are from how the external presents the subject.

One of the ego's attempts to control the experience is vial an action that has been labeled spiritual bypassing. This is the ego attempting to hide from any pains or traumas that are still unresolved within, by created a demand that everyone around them only speak or think positively. What they call negativity is not allowed. But what they really mean is that they don't want to have to discuss anything that might link to their own inner traumas and pains. The misguided belief is that if they can control the external, they think that they are controlling their internal. It is a form of denial, and very common in spiritual circles, whether any type of realization has happened. They attempt to push the actual experience of this reality away, which really just pushes away their own inner pain. This is very common in normal spiritual circles, just after a realization of Emptiness, as more wants to come up to be seen and create a deep healing. If one is not open for this work, they will sink even deeper into the bypassing.[61]

Bypassing becomes more of a problem after seeing Emptiness, because so many of the walls that were holding back the inner pain are weakened. All the fears, wants, desires, and disappointments all just show up without warning. We are seeing what has been inside us all along, but denied because of the strong walls. This can be a very challenging time for someone who wants to try and keep all of this hidden and covered over. Emptiness

60 John Kent chapter 3
61 A good article on spiritual bypassing is https://www.verywellmind.com/what-is-spiritual-bypassing-5081640

wants to reveal everything and shine light on it so it can be healed and transformed. Ego wants these things to either remain subdued or denied. One either goes along with what the experience is calling for (and in time things get smoother), or one tries to stop or deny it, which will just make the messy stage last much longer. The solution is to surrender and accept whatever is going on within us this moment, then examine its origin, and find ways to heal and transform. Don't deny it or hide from whatever it may be. Examine and embrace it for what it is.

Another possible place to get stuck is what is called "being drunk on Emptiness." In this, a person will present that since the world is not real, it really doesn't matter what might occur: that people are getting tortured, children are being sexually abused, animals are being mistreated, or that you have traumas. They will say, "It's all just thoughts in your mind. Ha ha, drink some tea!" In this way, Emptiness is being used as a buffer from past trauma, by pretending that there is no experience of suffering in the material realm. Granted a real experience of No Self/Emptiness does begin to create a natural detachment from standard reality, however, so too comes an incredible EMPATHY for every creature in it. You can never have real detachment without equal empathy. And having empathy for others is to meet them in the state where they currently are, to converse with the person, animal, tree or whatnot as the very object that appears, as not as a superior being commenting how all the world is an illusion. The drunk state ends as one may clearly see the illusion, but meets all they come across as two beings on a very long road, and looking for friendship with them instead of superiority.

The most common trap tends to be around the idea that one is now special and important because of the experience. They have elevated themselves with a type of low grade narcissism, and there tends to be a call to go out in the world and "save" the sheep from their belief in reality. And don't forget the natural human tendency to want to share whatever we find that we deem to be helpful. When doing that from a place of balance, integrity and friendship, then one can be helpful. When one is doing it so that they can boost their own self-importance, then the likely result will be confusion and trouble. I saw this with myself (it took almost five years to clear this out) and recently I see it happening with others. It is an almost automatic egoic reflex to Emptiness, so it ramps up its false specialness even more. It is very hard to step around this stage, and only those who have really cleaned and transformed their mind well prior to the realization will have an easy time of it. The rest can get stuck here for a while. Some stay stuck for the rest of their lives.

The problem around all of these traps is that it can take anywhere from two to ten years to fully integrate an experience that was beyond the body-mind into a body-mind. Much of the first year requires more like a constant vigilance to watch every time the mind tries to make one special from having a realization, deny what they are feeling, or calls to just forget all this and focus on getting what you want in the material world. There is as much of a process of being alert to what is going on within after a realization as was in the many years of the lead up to it. The better one's inner awareness to catch these attempts by the ego to stay in control, the easier the transition phase will be. That is why I suggest a time period of quiet after such an experience, where one can not be caught in elevating themselves around others, as there are no others around. The focus can be even greater to go within and find out if and how the ego is reorganizing itself to stay in control while in this new situation of knowing.

Thus, if you have experienced Emptiness, stay open and alert with others. Don't let your ego place yourself above them. Even your next door neighbor might come out with a piece of pure wisdom that is perfect for your current place on the path.

*

BETWEEN-NESS

I need to present two things as I end this chapter. The first is that Emptiness or Nothingness is not "non-existence" nor existing in some sort of void. Nothing is both empty and full. It is not Nothingness that is non-existent, it is all that we have come to know as the material world is realized to be a shadow or a holographic projection. This is what becomes hollow, the entire material reality and all of its objects. Since this world is what we have come to focus on since birth, Emptiness will feel "empty" to the fictional self who has propped itself up as a "real and important form." Something greater than the projections does exist, but it can not be found nor understood by that which is in the material (or even astral) realm. It just lets one see through the projections, it does not negate "That Which Is," that which is beyond and prior to the false realm of projections. This is an area many get confused about so I wanted to present here, there is something Real, it is just not in the world of projections.

The second important message is from John Kent, where he presents that Rose was clear that the realization of Emptiness is not the end of the path, and that *"The 'nothing' is not the final answer, as nihilistic Existentialism or a shallow understanding of Zen would conclude."* The spiritual community tends to get trapped at Emptiness because it feels complete. I know it did for me. I have described it as a holographic understanding. My experience of Emptiness shined a giant light on one part (say 25%) of that table of understanding. That part became 100% clear to me. The problem was that, because the table is holographic, I also saw the other (75%). The mind took it as all 100% was clearly seen, when it was 25% clear, and a 75% glimpse. This mistaken understanding was with me for over a decade, because the experience will fool you into thinking you know everything intimately, when in fact you have come to know part of Totality intimately, and the rest casually.

There is a step beyond Emptiness, where more work is required. This step involves the final act of between-ness.[62] I give a relative overview of this subject in a chapter of my book *Falling For Truth*, where this idea for Rose came out of seeing how a metal object placed between two equal magnets could be suspended indefinitely. He realized that the mid point between any two things (up down, good bad, life death, happy sad) has a mid point of

---

62 The term between-ness also covers terms such as direct mind, healing and transmission, all terms I will not get into in this text but you are welcome to look into the John Kent chapter (12) suggested for more further reading.

power when one is not on either part of duality. The power lies in the gap. This gets mirrored in the *Faith Mind Sutra*, *"Tao is self evident to one with no preferences. When like and dislike are both absent, the Real is obvious and clear...If you wish to know the Truth, then hold no opinions."*[63]

What this quote (and similar ones from the *Ashtavakra Gita*) is discussing is that one needs to move to a place where one has no preferences, for each will take one out of the mid gap power point towards one of the two sides of duality. The problem is that the regular mind sees nothing but preferences. It has a preference for cereal and not eggs in the morning. It likes one book or person but hates another. The message is find a connection point that is deeper than the world of duality, to what is translated as Tao (or Absolute). From this Absolute location, one can be beyond the basic influences of the mind and the body. They can still be there, while resting in a place beyond the body that is not "labeling" one preference over another, just seeing it all clearly. This type of non-preference can only happen when one has begun to see that both sides of duality are false, and that good and bad are both just elements of the Matrix.

For a while after Emptiness one will put the Matrix (something) on one side, and Emptiness (No-thing) on the other side, and attempt to be in that middle ground where we are not swinging to either side of this coin. Near the end of the search, however, a different aspect of between-ness is used. Now instead of looking for the gap or middle ground between the two (the normal path), here we contemplate *"thought and no-thought at once; contemplating truth and nothingness, like a Zen koan, until your head stops–and then everything becomes apparent to you. Everything and nothing are on both sides of the line. If you know everything and nothing, you become in union with the Absolute."*[64] The switch is to stop "being" in the midpoint between the two as a place of clear seeing, we now use this clear seeing to bring these two sides together into contemplation at the same time. We no longer contemplate something separately without nothing also contemplating nothing. We bring the ends of the paradigm to the

---

63 Found in Bart Marshall's *Perennial Way.*
64 John Kent chapter 16, also found in Rose's book The Direct Mind Experience.

mid-point. We stop how we normally have handled between-ness and let another aspect of it sort of take command. That is when a third point, a new higher vantage point above the two is found (when they have come together and reconciled, or we could say canceled themselves out) leading to a higher and more clear Awareness. In a sense this has been the entire path to this point, only near the end does it become more clear the mechanism that has been driving it.

This is the time to STOP. I have mentioned that there is a time when all outer seeking has to end for the final answer to reveal itself. The end of seeking will eventually come with the end of the seeker, but the seeker does not end itself. It must exhaust itself, like a candle burns itself out. The stopping is not an action, but occurs out of exhausting every possible avenue for an answer. The STOP just occurs on its own. It is all about timing. If the timing is correct, this is the between-ness, where action and non-action come together at the same moment to overload the normal mental egoic capacity. Contemplation does not stop here, just ALL outer and inner searching, the contemplation of these two dual extremes takes place because there is nothing else to be done. We don't "do" it, you might say, it gets done to us because we have exhausted the thing trying to do it all "my way."

This is where the practice of acting for the sake of acting earlier on path was a preparation for this stage. This practice from Carlos Castaneda, which I discussed in *Falling For Truth,* was to perform actions that there were no reason for doing. One such example is to remove all the books from a bookshelf, but don't clean the bookshelf, just put all the books on the floor, then put them all back on the bookshelf in exactly the same arrangement. Doing such actions for no logical reason makes the egoic mind livid because all normal actions are based on achieving an end result that will please the ego. By learning to do small actions such as this for no reward, over time will begin to create a gap where larger actions of "doing without a reward" can occur. The bulk of the later spiritual search would fall into this type of seeking. From this more and more is found the best action, is non-action. After a lifetime of doing, we will finally learn the power of stillness and of knowing when it is time to perform an action which the stanza 12 of the *Faith Mind Sutra* describes of those who have not come to this understanding, "*The faster they hurry, the slower they go.*"[65] One could present its corollary for those who have had a taste of Emptiness, "*the slower one hurries, the faster they go.*"

Rose also makes a unique comment about where this path to between-ness ends, that being where you keep watching everything in what we call mind, both with the mind and what is beyond the mind, until an explosion occurs. That is the second element of this final stage of between-ness, a bringing together of regular mind and Greater Mind, into witnessing together. And after that occurs, Rose claims that "then awareness is not in FRONT of the mind anymore."

That is interesting. If you ask just about anyone where their thoughts occur, they will point to their head, and more directly, to the front part of the head. What Rose is suggesting is that after between-ness has taken its final act, then we will no longer feel that we will be witnessing reality via our head, but from another location. I do not feel that Rose is presenting what Suzanne Segal described in her bus stop experience[66] (where she became the witnesser of everything from a point outside of her physical body, which is a sort of depersonalized experience). My sense is that Rose is suggesting that since pure Awareness is never localized to a body-mind, on realization it might operate its center from a variety of locations. What that means is perception of the Matrix from this point on is no longer tied to the normal rules we were all conditioned to follow since birth.

This is what happened for me in the months following my canyon experience. The standard mind was no longer the center of my awareness, and thought mostly did not occur. When they did, a thought was seen as something completely separate from that which was witnessing it. The witness and the thought were two separate things, and most of the thoughts that did arise were seen as petty and useless. This stayed in place for four to six months, after which began a fading process where Awareness would shift

---

65 Bart Marshall, *The Perennial Way, Faith Mind Sutra*

66 Whose story will be presented in detail in Additional Material that will appear on my website

between being within "normal mind" as it used to be my entire life prior, and sometimes in the place beyond mind (a location that I can not really put into words). This continues to happen right up to today.

The point of this chapter was to try and provide the flip side to the work, that all we have taken to be true and real, likely isn't. It is all layers of deception, one Russian Nesting Doll through the next. The work to Define oneself, and move through the stage of Emptiness is also not a fun process, but leads to a Liberation. Only it is not "you" who will experience the Liberation.

> *"Anyone who has seen the truth would not want to change anything but their own erroneous view of things."*[67] - Richard Rose

This has likely been a difficult chapter for you to read, because this was a very difficult chapter for me to write. I can only hope that some of what I am trying to make a point of can be garnered. One of those points is that Emptiness is a key step on the ladder to Exiting the Matrix. Emptiness reveals that all that we believed we were is but a projection, and that something greater is behind it all, which is shown to be the only thing real the entire time. That begins to cause a shift to rooting in this Awareness, and thus giving less attention to the external Matrix, including the body-mind. That does not mean the material realm or our form is ignored. We do what is needed to do, but no more than that, and all excess is let go of.

You can not Exit the Matrix by having your focus be on it and its creation. You have to step out of it. We want the access the Power that exists in the Pleroma. Truth is not a thing, an object, or an idea. It is what it is on the other side of the gate, a gate only the Divine Spark can walk through, a gate that is gateless. She does this after thanking the character in the dream that she borrowed for their work and experiences together, then wiping her feet on the doormat of Emptiness, removes the mud of the material and astral

---

67 David Gold *After the Absolute*

worlds, and glides past the threshold. The Divine Spark does not need to be "carried" across the threshold, she is quite capable of passing to the Celestial Fire and Pleroma herself.

> *"The Great Way has no gate; Thousands of roads enter it. When one passes through this gateless gate, you walk the universe alone."*[68] - Mumon

68 Mumon Ekai, *The Gateless Gate*, early 13th century

Chapter 5

NEW AGE DECEPTION

"There is no 'New Age.'
There is no 'Old Age.'
There is only madness,
and waking up from madness."[69]
- Richard Rose

The New Age Movement has been at the heart of most spiritual seeking since the 1960s. It existed long before that, just in other names and forms, but when the first round of revolutionary youth wanted to bring down governments and instill fairness and sanity to the world (this was before any hippies existed), all of a sudden a new phenomena swung onto North America called The New Age Movement. Few at the time (or even now) can see that the implementation of this movement was not organic, it was manufactured. And given that just about everyone today has been involved it its teaching and ideas in some way, it is a program that has to be examined and unraveled. When someone gave up on religion (the story of their youth) a new one was required. The New Age fit the bill of a new story for one to believe in.

*

A young filmmaker named Vikram Gandhi got curious to learn why people become so enamored by gurus. He started to do a documentary, but quickly found that most were frauds, looking simply for money or sex. He wondered why do we need spiritual

---

69 Found in John Kent *Path to Reality* pg 85, chapter 4

leaders at all? So he decided to impersonate one (calling himself Kumare) and set up shop in Arizona, growing a beard, taking on an Indian accent and began promoting a message of "self-empowerment." His 2011 film *Kumare* is a unique insight into the guru-follower dynamic. Simply put, his ruse quickly got so out of control that he wound up getting a group of somewhat devoted followers rather quickly, and he himself started to wonder if he "actually was" a real guru.

When he finally revealed himself to the followers as a fake, they felt he really had been a guru to them, and what he had shared had been helpful for them. Perhaps at the core, the majority are just looking for a decent parental figure, one who actually has a few useful life suggestions and ideas. It really was a most interesting movie to look into this dynamic.

The Kumare experiment is similar to a special that UK hypnotist Derren Brown made in 2015 called "Messiah." Here he traveled to Sedona and tricked many of the city's spiritual teachers into believing his hypnosis and sleight of hand tricks made him a true psychic. It ended with him performing a contacting the dead seance using the technique of cold reading, and shocking the people there to the depth of what he could know about people's deceased relatives. His point was that the so-called psychics were likely frauds like himself. But there is a shade of gray to this. It is not so easy to pass such a label on everyone.

Are all teachers, gurus, satsang givers, and psychics fake? Well no, but the question really becomes, how much of what they are doing or saying is genuine and true, how much is honestly intended help but caught up in misperception, and how much is outright fakery? The percentage of truth will be much lower than anyone hopes. This gets even more so when the guru's main job is to sell love and happiness. All they need to do is to put themselves into a bit of a stupor when they sit in their "wonder chair," set up hypnotic environment, and voila! The people fall in very easily.

I noticed this when I went to these type events in the past, or more accurately, dragged to them by friends of mine. It did not take long to notice the hypnotic speech patterns, the repetitive statements about being happy, and that suffering was just a thought in the mind. Then afterwards I would say at least 50% of the attendees were leaving the session with what I call the "glassy-eye" look. The same look you notice from people who are high on drugs, only the drug here is the "carrot on a stick hope" of being happy, increasing your wallet and getting all the sex you can possibly handle. I am amazed many of the glassy-eyed people were even able to drive home.

And when this drug high happens over several days of "retreat" or daily meetings in an ashram...the glassy-eyed look can last for a long while. That is what the New Age is all about, a drug for the masses so that they will not see the real situation of this reality. A cover up of the real truth of reality.

That is because one of the biggest lies put forth on the modern world has been an idea around enlightenment. Mariana Caplan put it brilliantly in her book Halfway Up the Mountain, "*The most common, widely held fantasy about enlightenment is that it is freedom from suffering, the transcendence of pain and struggle, the land of milk and honey, a state of perpetual love, bliss and peace. Enlightenment represents the collectively-shared dream of an idealized and perfect world of pure beauty and joy. It is not only a New Age fantasy, it is the secret wish of all people. It is our shared dream of salvation. But it is only a fantasy.*"[70] Richard Rose had a very different presentation of what enlightenment is, one that seems vague on one hand, yet is clear that it is not about some sort of happiness or bliss, but a type of between-ness and described it as, "*The tension between being and not being,*" and "*The experience of nothingness and everythingness simultaneously.*"[71]

Of course happiness sells. The "New Age" supposedly gets its name from the presentation that this reality will very soon enter the processional Age of Aquarius, moving from Pisces where we currently reside. This shift is presented as a new Golden Age where everyone will become happy, living in a wonderful high

---

70 Mariana Caplan, *Halfway Up the Mountain,* chapter 2
71 Found in John Kent *Path to Reality* pg 268, chapter 15

vibrational frequency. Few know that the phrase New Age is linked to the ideas of Madame Blavatsky and the Theosophical Society from the 1870s. But we will come back to that. However not much tends to be written that this New Age of Aquarius might not be the Golden Age everyone is wishing for, but perhaps an age of complete technological slavery and control. Besides, this whole talk about the cycle of ages is also up for questioning, or why it has any value to us at all.

*

Religion makes its promise that you get out of suffering by believing in their savior and the reward is eternal happiness after you die. The New Age repackaged that to say, forget about after you die, you can have your happiness and heaven right now, all the time. The New Age is promising perfection, utopia, endless bliss, endless orgasms, all wrapped in a veneer of saving the planet, the dolphins, and the unknowing masses. The New Age is a drug. I was "hooked" on it for a while myself 30 years ago. Luckily, I got off it rather quickly, but it still took years to sort through various foundational beliefs that get into us from being around the ideas.

When one looks closer at how the New Age has been packaged, what they see is that one deception (religion) is being covered over by another deception (New Age spirituality). As long as people fall on one side of this duality, no one is looking for the third point that transcends both of them. Similar to politics, the system just wants you to choose one of the two offered sides, they don't care which one, because both of their choices lead to the end result the system wants. New Age spiritual movements are not really in opposition to religions. Actually they are all working hand in hand with them, just two faces of the same package.

People should have seen through the lies of the New Age, guru, and spiritual teacher game during the period between 2020 through 2023. During these four years, the most open lie put on the human population in the last one hundred years was on display twenty-four hours a day. And the majority of the gurus said nothing. They in fact encouraged compliance with the lie. If you claim to be in the business of Ultimate Truth, but you can not see

123

a massive lie happening constantly in relative reality, how could they possibly be trusted to present Ultimate Truth? They can't. Because they showed their whole existence is really about money, followers and power. Not Truth. The few that did talk about what was going on during the previous four years are the only spiritual teachers left who I still listen to, and have developed great respect for. I dropped the rest, the same as any other false we come across.

But what is this Movement? There is much more to the New Age phenomena than spirit guides, chakra balancings, crystal singing bowls and tantric sex. It is about the belief that a full world-wide Utopia can, and will be, established. This movement originated in the 1800s out of Theosophy, which had as one of its goals the creation of a new world religion, monitored by a one world government. These concepts were running in the background for several decades. It just needed the conditions to make it mainstream.

By the 1960s when this term New Age began to be applied, there was no real face to the movement. Several authors and speakers were later linked to sort of being its "founding fathers" but at the time were more individuals sharing similar ideas. In the 1960s, the early stages of the movement promoted drug and sex highs, which seemed to link closely to the ideas found in Huxley's novel of the future *Brave New World.* All the gurus and Satsang masters may not even know it, but that is the end goal of the movement, a system similar to that novel. The civil uprisings of the 1960s, when revolt seemed a real likelihood in the United States, is when this movement magically got rolled out. It was one of the key responses to the rebellion that was forming.

Recall that the 1960s started to have too many young people seeing through the lies of the government, the banking system, of everything. JFK's death and the start of the Vietnam War just helped solidify the seeing. These original rebels were not hippies (as they were not yet invented), these were young university students, well educated, those most able to clearly see the corruption surrounding them. Their goal was to take down the entire government system. And the government was worried because they could speak clearly, they could organize, and they were serious.

The initial anti-war movement was led by this group of intelligent young people. The government realized the best way to slow them down was not to retaliate against them directly, as that would have brought even more to the side of opposition, so their idea was to create an infiltration into the opposition. This was the hippie-New Age movement of the 1960s. If you look back into the real founders of the hippie movement of the 1960s, the ones who pumped the money into making it happen, you come across key connections to various government agencies. The goal was to intermingle this new generated movement with the current anti-war movement, and in essence, confuse the two. Pretty soon all everybody was talking about was the drugged out hippies and not the real anti-war protesters. The original group could have taken down the government, while the hippies were lucky to take apart a bean bag chair. And it didn't take long for any real threat to be completely turned into something that the government could control.[72]

Recall that the first hippie movements did not happen in San Francisco as generally presented, but rather in Los Angeles (where one finds Hollywood). They were all pretty much small cults around one charismatic leader, along with a bunch of young sexually promiscuous women. That was the draw for a lot of the first round of hippies, join a group where you could have sex with a bunch of young women all day. This all coincided with the Laurel Canyon Music scene, firstly to promote sex and drugs, then to promote peace, love, and meditation. Many of the key musicians of the period had fathers who were high ranking members in the US military.[73]

When things were still at a flash point of the young people against the government, this is when the gurus from India began to

---

72 An excellent book on this period is *Weird Secrets Inside the Canyon* by David McGowan

73 See the book *Weird Secrets Inside the Canyon* by David McGowan for more information on the connection of musicians with the military

show up in the US to teach meditation along with the focus on "happy" thinking. The attempt was to make standing up for freedom or rights a form of negativity, and instead teach a focus only on being positive. Not that the gurus could be said to be "in on it," as most likely they believed what they preached (well most of them anyway), but that does not mean it was all just a control plan at its foundation.

One of the biggest lies the New Age movement propagated was the idea that one should never have a negative thought. That all we have to do is force our mind to be happy all the time, and then all of our suffering will just vanish. And even if that could be true (which it is not), the world still continues to suffer. But no one really seems to care about that. People can claim to give their prayer for world peace every Sunday night, but they refuse to acknowledge that world tends to keep getting worse, they do not even question if what they are doing is not only a waste of time, but maybe even THE CATALYST for making it all worse. Ignore what is really happening to the world, and pretend to be happy.

The New Age Movement can also be categorized as the "love and light" religion, and is a passive movement. An aware person is honest to the situation around them, and will stand up for what needs to be resisted. The passive male will sit with his eyes closed and do nothing, especially if some woman will give him a blow job later for doing nothing. That is the world we now inhabit. The feminine was under attack for centuries, then beginning with the 1960, the masculine came under attack. We have almost lost the depth of power of both the masculine and feminine now.

Granted there is a time for a passive approach, but that is very far along the path. Of course ask almost any seeker where they are, and they will tell you they are almost at the top of the mountain, a couple of more weeks to total enlightenment. That is why Richard Rose's metaphor of the path that he labeled Jacob's Ladder, a part of which is to honestly know which rung they are on, is so important to one's knowing what practices they should currently be involved in. One of the big switches in the New Age, compared to the shamanic-monastic traditions they claim to have originated from, is that the New Age has made the starting point the end of the path. Almost no one even knows such a switch occurred. Asleep is now awake and everyone can drink their smoothies, wear their white robes, clean their chakras and the end is just around the corner. Deceptions abound everywhere.

Most would say America lost the Vietnam War, but as it turned out, that was not really the war that was being fought. The US government was fighting a war of control to stay in power, and they won that war handedly. And the New Age Movement helped to quell the real protesters who could have toppled a country. By 1980, pretty much all of the US had been pushed into the New Age Movement and any talk of taking down the system, either Wall Street or the government, was long forgotten. Then rampant cocaine abuse and disco music made everyone party to 3AM. Life was "good."

Granted the New Age, like any religion or cult, is not fully false. It can't be. Anything 100% false will always be seen through rather quickly. Thus the way forward was to mix in some key truths and then distort them (the preferred method). Truth from fiction then becomes hard to spot.

A large majority of those drawn in to New Age teachings are suffering from deep traumas in their past. They are seeking for a way to overcome all of this past trauma in an attempt to feel better. Even if something feels a tiny bit better, they will keep doing it (this is why the alcohol and tobacco industries makes so much money). Others feel alone, maybe even having to have made the decision to leave their family unit after years of abuse, and then just want to find a group they can feel a part of. Others simply don't feel they fit into the regular world and want to find others who think like they do. The gurus play on that...bring in the flock feeling alone and make them feel welcomed and loved. It does not take long for them to empty out their bank account and move in, because for them this pain is much less than the pain of working hard at a job just to have an apartment, while feeling alone and estranged from reality. I am not knocking anyone who has done this, on the surface the choice makes sense. But a few do not have feeling better as their main goal, but in actually finding out what the origin of this insane reality that could even be a world of such trauma and suffering, so that requires a very different approach than the what is found on the spiritual best seller lists.

A sad truth about how the New Age movement could gain such popularity is that it preys on people who are in some way emotionally suffering. They are in pain, and the basic promise "to be happy all the time" is hard for anyone with deep inner wounds to just pass by. But is any of this going to really do what it promises, or just give a short term band aid to cover over the bleeding? Many people will leave the 200 dollar weekend meditation retreat feeling wonderful, but then in a week the drug has worn off, and the inner pain is back. So the student hauls out another 200 dollars and goes to the next retreat. This goes on endlessly until someone decides to do real inner work and allow their suffering to be honestly seen and transformed. The work is always within.

The New Age also promotes many "healing techniques" some of which can actually be valuable and helpful. However, too many declare themselves "healers" without the years of training and work it requires. I know several who came out of "healing sessions" more damaged than when they went in. A certificate from 3-week healing course in Bali, or a one month online workshop is not enough to be a healer. I have come to find out that true healers, of which there are a few in this world, have had a lifetime of learning. There is as much to know and transform about oneself as there is to learning specific techniques. The great healers will come out of first having healed their own pain and trauma, transformed their own darkness. There are some good healers out there, and again if there was one word I would suggest when going to find one, is look for integrity. Everything you think that word represents is what you are looking to find. Integrity is a word that is very hard to find in the modern world, yet I can verify, some that embody this word still do exist.

In the course of my odd 15-year illness, I saw a lot of healers, and many of them New Age types because, well "you get desperate." So I personally know the dynamic that keeps this system going. Yet NONE and I mean NONE of the New Age healers provided any real help. The help that took me up a step was always from a healer who was revealing what I had to do to transform myself. They were turning me into my own healer. Each stop on my healing journey included a key piece of honest knowing about myself and my "life story." The "healing" came from me, from something deeper, after I could see through another of my belief walls that was keeping the in-balance in place. They just acted like a pointer and guide, less someone "fixing" a problem.

Another promise of the New Age is providing people some sort of a saviour. Once one rejects the Jesus story, where else can they go? The New Age comes with wonderful replacements like Beings of Light, the Galactic Federation, karmic gods, helpful aliens, or spirit guides. The astral realm is full of helpers is their presentation, but few want to see that the astral realm is mostly filled with demonic archons masquerading as helpful entities. People are taught to take whatever they meet in the astral at face value, so it is no surprise that they tend to get "faced."

The same goes for much psychic work and channeling, as the Derren Brown mentioned special revealed. One might ask; "Who is there to channel in the Matrix?" Well archons of course. There are no higher loving beings just sitting around waiting to talk through some "channeling guru." These archons pretend to be whoever the channeller wants them to be. If they want to talk to Jesus, Buddha or a dead relative, then that is the mask the archons put on themselves. There is only one saviour that you ever need, and that is your Self. All the rest is in one way or another just an outward distraction. When real help comes, it does not come from an outside source connected to the Matrix, it comes from from within. Doctors, acupuncturists, herbalists and the like are helpful for getting the body in a more stable state energetically. But then we have to take the energy they have helped us accumulate with some "base healing" to go within and see what is at the core of the issue, and find the link to What we are to let us know what we really must do to complete our healing. As I mentioned the best healers I came across taught me how to take my stored energy and go within to seek my own transformative power.

The prayer scam is one that is found in just about all current religion or spirituality. In the immediate aftermath of one of the recent hurricanes on the US East Coast, a person wanted to help. So they set out to get supplies that they could drive to the affected areas. He wound up getting a lot of donations and just before he left posted a message on his website "thanking God for hearing my prayers to bring relief to these suffering people. The Lord is good." Can you see the fallacy that this person, and a majority of the world, lives under? The underlying belief is that there is a loving God. But this God does not seem to do a very good job looking after anyone, as this realm remains a torture chamber of suffering. This omnipotent God could have stopped the hurricane, thus caused no damage, death or suffering at all. Yet God did allow this. So now one is thankful that help appeared, and thanks the very same god who created the suffering to begin with. He should be thanking the regular humans who came to donate to help alleviate suffering in a psychopath reality.

Of course, none of this praying ever helps. The bombings continue, people go on getting slaughtered, kids keep suffering, rapes continue, and animals get abused. People have just given away their energy, and becoming prey to the very being that could have fixed this place from the start (or any time since). Can you see the scam that the Fallen Creator has set up? Pray to the same psychopath who is getting the benefit from all of the suffering that they structured into this reality. It is an amazing system, and even more amazing that the majority have not seen through it all.

Next to synchronicity (which I discuss in detail next), perhaps no part of the New Age movement is as popular as the "manifest all your wishes" programming. Here is where the old "law of attraction" ideas were re-packaged. All one has to do is focus on material rewards, and then imagine you already have it. Want to have big muscles, a big dick, big tits, big wallet, all you have to do is imagine you have it. Which is total insanity. To see their needs to be an intention, and then making actual steps within reality is how anything gets done. The imagination just provides the direction. But it has kept millions focusing on manifesting all their desires, instead of looking deeply into what a desire is, where it originates, and ask how much focus they should put on any of them.

SYNCHRONICITY

Synchronicity is one of the most misunderstood of the New Age concepts, and might be the one that has taken the most root in the average consciousness. This is a term originally coined by Carl Jung, and proposes certain meaningful occurrences emanate from "forces much greater than chance." I would agree with part of the idea, but like everything here, it gets muddled. This claim becomes that almost ALL co-incidences are "meaningful," and are set up by a loving deity for the purpose of your evolution, thus you should automatically follow and accept every co-incidence that appears. No one is asking the base question which is, what exactly determines if a co-incidence is meaningful or not?

Everyone has had some odd synchronistic happenings in their life. Most every famous novel has a unique or lucky meeting as the way to get the story started. Yet if one looks closely at these synchronistic moments in our lives, there are co-incidences that have led to positive outcomes, and there have been other ones that have led to trouble and difficulty. What is interesting is how the ones that have led to pain and suffering tend to not be labeled by the term "synchronicity" or "meaningful co-incidence," but rather "bad luck." For a while I got caught up in this type of belief structure as well.

I will share a personal example of this. Just before I went to play hockey overseas in the mid 1990's, I wound up on a small network TV sketch comedy show in Ottawa. That was an odd co-incidence in itself, because I never knew this show existed, so I was not trying in any way to be a part of it. It just showed up after doing an impromptu impersonation gig for a friend at a charity function. But as soon as the appearances on the TV show occurred, and the possibility of it moving to bigger things, a boatload of other co-incidences started happening around my hockey career (which had pretty much ended). At the time, I should have seen that some type of set up was going on. Everything seemed to start moving towards something I had been interested in since my teens (being in television comedies), and all of a sudden a whole set of co-incidences appear which wanted to move me towards what I had been "told to want" (professional athlete). I followed the hockey route, which led to very little opportunity, and passed on staying with the TV show, which could have opened various doors in performing and writing.

My theory on this is that most of the co-incidences in our life are not from our Self, or from a loving God (since there isn't one), but from the archons, acting similar to the "men in hats" that were manipulating the lives of Matt Damon and Emily Blunt in the movie *The Adjustment Bureau*. These archon hat-men only cared that humans followed specific pre-approved life scripts. Everything in people's lives were being manipulated and controlled to keep them on the record grooves that the archons wanted. The final choice made in the movie was for the characters David and Elise to decide to be together to which the "hat men" agreed to. First of all, why do we need to have some alien hat-men say our choice is acceptable? The catch to their "choice" was later revealed that their coupling was in an "earlier life script" that was changed at some point. Thus the couple were not going to a life of their own choosing, just another song on a record chosen by the archons. In fact, I am not sure that one choice that happened by those characters in that movie was a REAL CHOICE. Every bit of their lives was some type of manipulation coming from the archons.

Even when the archon Harry was saying he would help David to connect with his lover, he was setting up a giant trick. He told David that the bureau's weakness was water, so they should meet on or next to water. As I will discuss in chapter 7, the Matrix is symbolized by water, so water would be the archons "strength." So Harry was tricking David. By being close to water, he was in fact being able to be constantly monitored. Harry being a helper is the same misdirection as Michael pretending to help the humans in *The Good Place*. Why should David have believed anything he was told? Thus the entire "breaking out" part of the story was a giant trick to make David and Elise believe that they had somehow by the force of their own will overcome the entire system, and escaped to a world of their choosing. The depth of manipulation played on the two of them, is an example of how much we are subjected to in this world.

In my case I see that the hockey co-incidences were to throw me off something that could have been a much more interesting direction, and perhaps one not on any "original script" which is perhaps why I was so driven towards it. So it is clear to me that we do run into various co-incidences in our lives, but not all of them are wonderful like we are told. There are very nefarious forces at work behind the scenes with all of this.

But sometimes there are co-incidences that are not coming from outside of us (from the Matrix and its archons) but from our Divine Spark. Granted it is rare, for she needs to project out a lot of energy to do this, so chooses very carefully when to create these. Thus once in a while there is truly a helpful co-incidence in our midst. Those are one's, when you can verify their origin, that should be followed without question. The problem is that these manifest very rarely and they tend to be subtle in their presentation.

The idea of synchronicity exploded in the 1990's, mostly thanks to the popular book *The Celestine Prophecy.* Just after that book's appearance, came a number of movies about synchronicity. One was *Serendipity* (2001) which presented how a woman lets coincidences choose her actions...which of course leads the two main characters to "live happily ever after." *Magnolia* (1999) had all of its characters connected in a very complex way. *On the Line* (2001) again has a series of coincidences that eventually leads everyone in the movie to live "happily ever after." *Sliding Doors* (1998) was about a woman following two lines of events. *Run Lola Run* (1998) had a time loop with multiple timelines. Interesting that this is also the exact period of time when movies like *Dark City, The Truman Show and The Matrix* were released. It was almost like the two sides of seeing reality were being pushed into the face of the masses at that very time, which would automatically create confusion.

But the start of the recent "synchronicity movement" seems to be the book *The Celestine Prophecy,* written by James Redfield in the late 1980s. He packaged many New Age and Eastern philosophies in the book, yet never once used words such as karma or reincarnation so it could also appeal to religious followers. I don't want to make this discussion about Redfield, he was a therapist for abused adolescents for several years, which is a challenging but important field to be involved in.[74] I want to focus on this message of the book, which had quite an impact on a lot of people at the time, including me.

While there were many New Age elements discussed in the novel, synchronicity was front and center. The claim was that these co-incidences were now happening more frequently because we are getting close to a global raising of consciousness. The co-incidence idea was being linked to what could be called the idea of ascension, or an evolution of consciousness where we can pray our way to happiness and no more wars. All of these co-incidences were designed to help us raise our vibration so that we would soon join the more perfected realm. I have already discussed how well these praying and wishing for a better reality have worked out. As I write this, at the end of September 2024, this reality appears ready to explode, not join together for a Kumbaya sing-along. But the core of the synchronicity message is that God loves you, and therefore co-incidences must be God leading you to a better experience. This thinking though might have made it even easier for the archons to manipulate people. At least this was probably true in my personal experience.

And yes, sometimes there is a deeper force that is Real and is interacting with us. This not something outside of ourself, but our own Divine Spark, but rarely does she speak with us directly. That means most of the communication one is receiving in any

---

74 Info on Redfield and Celestine Prophecy from
    https://en.wikipedia.org/wiki/James_Redfield and
    https://www.celestinevision.com/james-redfield-formal-biography/ , and
    https://en.wikipedia.org/wiki/Human_Potential_Movement

moment may coming from something outside of ourself. Our job is to not just blindly follow any synchronicity, but notice and ask questions of it. What is being presented, why now, who might gain from me following or not following this possibility? We learn to see the signs of archon interference so that we can turn away from those set up traps. Yet we also learn to notice the times when the Spark within has set-up a doorway for us to follow. An example of this for me would be the *Nova* Egypt program that came on when I was 28. This moment had a different tone to it than a normal co-incidence, was subtle in its manifestation, and was internally explosive when noticed. The direction the Divine Spark wants us to follow are often not to happy places, but towards seeing what is True. The false wants to lead us towards more comfort, importance and getting us focused on material goodies. I share this to keep in mind when the next co-incidence appears in your life. Dissect it, and ask where is the synchronicity originating, and where it might really be trying to lead you?

*

LOVE AND LIGHT

The love and light myth is a big part of the New Age Movement. Everyone says they want liberation and enlightenment, because they believe this means constant happiness and eternal comforts. One tends to lose interest in this subject if they realize that the enlightenment they claim to seek would require complete dissolving of everything they believe. They prefer to have the caterpillar to go with them while becoming a butterfly. It does not matter that all the systems out there in the retreats and books don't work, and have never worked, because people keep lapping it up. People are paying big bucks to be reassured that they can wake up while staying asleep.

Most do not want to even consider that the force of love (in the materiel world) may just be a code embedded within a type of computer program, as a chemical urge to find a mate, have kids and then raise them to create a new batch of slaves. Schopenhauer called Romantic Love the most important part of his concept of

Will (the force that controls most everything a human does) even to claim that the "genitals are the source of the Will."[75] Not that there is anything wrong or evil about the experiences of love or even sex. They are enjoyable experiences for the body-mind. But that is all they are, not signs or pointers to a higher spiritual way of life. They are codes hardwired into the human robot in order to be sure new babies get born, and they get looked after so they get old enough to have their own babies. When one finally understands that there can become a questioning. What then is beyond the program of material world love?

There is a Love of course, but that is outside of the Matrix. What we call love here (which is generally a really strong like or desire) for either a spouse, child, dog or hobby, all links to the program designed to get us to function in specified ways. And there is nothing wrong with this feeling. The problem is to turn it into something special, something beyond a computer program, and apply overloaded importance to it. One then chases it, demands it, and demands that others act in specific ways to keep triggering this inner chemical reaction. When one sees through that, it becomes a feeling that can either be there or not, can come and go, and thus one takes a key first step to release from a big chain in the prison material Matrix.

Any emotion is a tool to be seen and used, but not grasped onto. One goes inwards to explore these emotional holes within, not to fill them with something else, but to see and unravel their origin. That is the opposite of what spirituality and religion have done, changed the focus from seeing that one exists in a false projection designed to act as a trap, to one where the outward search is to get a much of this chemical reaction (emotional love) in the body as possible. This is why love is the main blast one will receive in the standard NDE experience, because it was what one was really seeking for most of their life. Is there thus any surprise that this strategy of blasting the newly dead soul with an overwhelming supply of the love feeling has a 99.9% success rate for the archons in the after-death realm? We have to take the 0.1% open space that is in our favour, to a place of clear thinking,

---

75 Arthur Schopenhauer *World as Will and Representation* vol 2 p. 514, 533

questioning and stillness where we can navigate what is best for What we Are, not the archons. That is the reason for the writing of this book.

*

Some might suggest that this chapter has been very harsh, and I guess in some ways it has. It was written because just about everyone who has been doing any type of seeking in the last fifty years will have come across the ideas of the New Age. And due to the intensity of the marketing, the prettiness of the packaging, and the promises of hope have tended to sway literally hundreds of millions of people into these concepts. And the teachers are as confused as the students.

That does not mean basic elements are bad such as: using crystals, checking astrological charts, pushing acupressure points, having herbal teas, sitting peacefully, or changing to a healthier diet. They all have value for the character in the Matrix. The problem is when what can be called natural ways to assist the body-mind attain a form of balance, gets turned into a type of long-term hope for the world or that one's spiritual evolution is tied to the material betterment of the character. Like most religions and systems, the New Age has a goal of comfort and happiness in the Cave, not honest examination of the Cave, with the eventual direction of returning Home.

Chapter 6

ORIGINS and ENDINGS

"Some are afraid lest they rise naked. Because of this they wish to rise in the flesh, and they do not know that it is those who wear the flesh who are naked."[76] - Gospel of Phillip

This chapter is an overview of the subject of creation of the Matrix and of the group of beings we call humans. Where do we come from? You can go to various religions, spiritual groups, even cults, and they all have an answer for this question. Why is knowing about the creation of an illusionary simulacra important? Let's just say that if the prison bars are not examined, one will not notice which of the bars is actually not solid and can be removed.

I am going to examine two areas. One is the Gnostic creation myth, generally found in the Apocryphon (Secret Book) of John, and the Gospel of Judas. Interestingly, I have just found the original Coptic versions of these texts and have begun to read them directly (with the help of a Coptic dictionary) but it is slow work. I will not be finished with this personal translation before this book is completed, so in time I may have more to add.[77]

Likely the best overview on this subject is the work of Angeliki Anagnostou in the first half of her book *Can you Stand*

---

76 *Gospel of Phillip* 11, http://www.gnosis.org/naghamm/gop.html

77 This Coptic version as well as information about dictionary can be found at https://marcion.sourceforge.net/nag-hammadi-library/apocryphon-of-john-nh2-en.html

the Truth. The second consideration for this subject is a vision that I had in 2009, that on the surface seems quite at odds with various ancient creation myths, yet perhaps not so. This vision is where I will begin the examination.

*

VISION

The vision I had in 2009 can be read in Additional Material 7. I am not claiming this vision is the truth, only that it offers a different perspective as opposed to what is normally presented. This vision happened in the midst of a series of ceremonies that I was doing with a medicine man friend, and after one of those ceremonies I went to lie down. When I did the detailed vision appeared before my inner sight. It presented a couple of unique ideas. The first is that it was not the Creator that made humans per se, it was nature itself that made humans, and did so for a purpose. It was to help release a trap that the Creator (Lucifer) had put nature in. That puts my vision in somewhat opposition to the base Gnostic texts, who present that the human form (not the Spark) was made directly by the Creator and archons.

That humans might have a different origin than usually presented made quite a bit of sense because humans just do not fit in here on Earth. We have no fur for warmth, so need tools, fire and shelter. We are quite fragile, have a wide range of illness, have problems that make no sense for dealing with the environment (such as colour blindness) and are the only creature it seems that has a parasitic ego. Religion attempts to present that humans are superior to nature, but if nature itself was our creator, this idea of superiority gets turned on its head. The stories of humans being made out of mud or clay also links into my vision, though instead of a god doing this it might have been much less super-natural, but no less magical. Read the vision and come up with your own conclusions.

Already in my vision from 2009 was the idea of being caught in a type of trap, and that there were requirements to Exit it, and that humans had the job of helping with that for all beings in the Matrix. One other element of this vision that I find interesting is that I claimed, "Nature knows where the doorway is and what to do when we get there." So that now to me is interesting for it indicates that knowledge of the process of Exiting the Matrix does exist here, and that nature is the one who knows the mechanism.

So perhaps the complete understanding of the Exit process comes from interactions with nature? I hear the question, how does one interact with nature?

*

NATIVE TRADITIONS

This turns back to where my time with the Native Medicine people comes in. Up to this point in this book it may have seemed that I have ignored what might be called Traditional Knowledge, discussing only Asian and Gnostic philosophy. I want to remedy that shortage now, for the Native teachings of how to be in harmony with nature is one of base foundational work.

Today standard Native traditions were relabeled during the New Age Movement under the term shamanism, usually applied to white people acting in a Native way. Each tribe or culture has its own words for men and women of knowledge, those who provided assistance for the community in many areas. One type of these were those who acted as Those that become the intermediaries between the human and spirit worlds, which is what this shaman word today is meant to signify. Modern Medicine People tend to see those who label themselves as shamans to be usurpers of their traditions, and often label them as plastic, such as those selling ceremonies which Traditional people never charge for, or who are attempting to pass themselves off as holy people (only not having gone through the long training and initiation that each specific tribe requires).

That being said, one does not have to have been born of a Native tribe to learn how to personally interact with nature. That is one of the cores of being human. Learning how to communicate with a tree or how to find out what plants in the area are edible is not "shamanic." How to heal, bring rain and the like is. But these cultures interacted with the natural world in a far more deeper way than most think. I was able to learn this from direct time spent with these knowledge holders. For general overviews I would suggest works such as *Fools Crow* by Thomas Mails (which discusses Fools Crows' methodology of healing) or *Shamanism* by Mircea Eliade (which presents various accounts of tribal peoples from over a century ago). Of course the best advice would be to leave the plastic shamans behind and go find a real deal man and woman who still lives on a reserve and follows the old ways. They taught me more than any book possibly could.

In Native tradition there is an understanding of how this realm has been structured from years of continuous study. They see a natural order that has been set up, and if one works with that order, you might say that nature will work along with you. This type of inter-relationship sustained societies for a long while. Yet our current human society of the last 150 or so years, has mostly been built on going against this natural order. Everything is now the opposite of how it should logically be. And Natives know this change did not happen by accident, it was planned and orchestrated. With this loss of natural understanding, came the loss of what could only be called "sane ways of living" in this reality.

At their origin there were many insights in Traditional cultures regarding Exiting the Cave. Mircea Eliade's excellent 1951 book *Shamanism* details many areas including ideas such as initiation ceremonies where one goes through a type of ritual death and dismemberment (the experience of having every part of one's body taken apart in the experience, "cleansed," and then reassembled to become a new person), or the creation of an inner light or a mystical inner heat and fire (similar to a Baptism of Fire).[78] Yet, all traditions get distorted over time. Things move more towards how to impact the material realm, often via prayer to unknown entities and forces. I discussed this in *Exit the Cave Book 1*, asking is one praying or becoming prey? I mention this to keep my readers from getting too deep into any tradition, no

---

78 Mircea Eliade, *Shamanism* initiations pgs 59-61, fire pgs 412, 437, 474, 476

matter how wonderful it may seem on the surface. They all seemed to start out as clear seeing, but in time they get shifted and altered into something else. It is a reason that I suggest that people work with many traditions, as each only has a small part of the origin still within it. Thus you have to get pieces of the truth from various places, and put them together yourself in order to complete the larger jig saw puzzle that all of these traditions were once directly mirroring.

But certainly there is no better place to go to learn of how to interact with, talk with, and be a co-helper with nature than the various Traditional Peoples all over the world.

*

To finish this opening set of information I want to have a short discussion around the ideas of souls. I fully assert that not just humans have souls, all living creatures have a soul. A soul is not the same as a Divine Spark, a soul is an energy source that causes what would be inanimate (dead) to be living. The Divine Spark can be a part of any of these souls, connected with any creature, not just humans. The soul can be seen as a piece of Matrix energy, combined with a life force. If that life force is a Divine Spark, there is the possibility of philosophical depth. If the life force is a "Matrix-mirror," we get what I called the Automatic Human in chapter 2.

Many claim that animals cannot leave the Matrix. I disagree fully. I concur that anything that is in the Matrix can leave it, be they people, animals, rocks, trees, or even staplers. Those who are connected with a Divine Spark have, lets say, a more possible direct route, but any creature can turn its awareness within and connect to the Pleroma. Doing so they are 75% of the way out. Animals have an advantage in that they do not have a parasitic ego structure as humans do, so they do not have to spend years overcoming this implant of self-importance. On the negative, they tend not to have a natural philosophic outlook. However, I can certainly say that I have come across some animals in my life (a few pets and a few in the wild) that are as philosophic and as wise as any Zen master. Within a simulated reality, all forms are equal. Humans are not special and on a pedestal, just structured differently than the rest.

If my vision from 2009 is correct, that it was not Lucifer directly who made us but the forces of natural world as a way to help all escape the Matrix, then it would make sense that we should stay connected with nature in this material realm. Thus whenever I eat now, I not only thank the food I eat (which died for my character's continued living) I let each bit of food know that I, in thanks, want it to link with me, so that when I leave the Matrix it is welcome to come along and join me (as they have joined me in some manner from the eating) in a combined Exit. I do the same with animals that I have come to know, trees that I cut for firewood, even the pens and paper I use for writing. If they have a core that has originated from outside of the Matrix, and they wish to return Home, they are welcome then to share the trip with me, in gratitude for what they shared with me.

*

GNOSTIC ORIGINS

When it comes to the study of Gnostic origin myths, most would suggest that the prime alternative researcher to study would be the writings of John Lamb Lash. He was my first foray into the subject almost twenty years ago, as he was one of the first to examine the Gnostic texts from a non-Christian perspective (most researchers want to think of the group as early Christians). It took another fifteen years to come across the writings of Angeliki Anagnostou and *Can You Stand the Truth*. Not only is she an excellent researcher and writer, but by being a natural Greek language speaker, she was able to consult many of the original texts and re-translate them for herself, providing some very unique and important understandings. What I share here is inspired greatly by her book, yet this origin of the Matrix section will be a brief overview.

A second connection for this chapter is the Cathars. In writing this chapter, I went to read some recent published articles about them, and was left disappointed. No one really understands this group from Southern France, who were killed off by the Church of Rome in the 1200s. They tend to be presented as either Native Indians, Buddhists or versions of 1960s New Agers. That is likely because there is no frame of reference today for what they may have been. When a researcher understands that this group has as their number one goal to end the reincarnation cycle, the only modern system they can think to compare them too is Buddhists. So they write as if they are two and the same.

And, who knows, maybe that is true. There is a possibility that early Christianity and Buddhism could have well been the same thing, as the 2007 movie *The Man From Earth* suggested. But if the Cathars were not Buddhists, then what were they? Granted they did seem to have a connection to the Earth and living in a very simple way. However, there was far more. Firstly they had to come to the point where they realized that this entire realm is an evil trap, and as such they would reject all of it (save for the bare minimum required to keep the body alive in order to continue all of the practices required so they would not be coming back here).

When it comes to all of this, one has to ask, why should we trust the Nag Hammadi codex? Are they really better than any other set of creation mythology? My only reason to say that yes they might be is because we got them in their original form. They were not passed on from one group to the next, over the course of 1500 or 2000 years as other religions and mythology were. These documents were hidden at the time they were written, and stayed untouched (seemingly) until they were found in 1945. Only such things as Ancient Egyptian Pyramid Texts (inscribed on the wall of Old Kingdom pyramids) and a few others can be called "original sources." They may not be perfect, but they are about the best we currently have.

The *Nag Hammadi Gnostic Codexes,* were named after the Egyptian town close to the caves where a Bedouin peasant found them in 1945. I find it interesting that perhaps the most important written document to help one Exit the Cave was found hidden in a cave. These are leather bound books of a "pre-Christian" group known by the Greek inspired word Gnostics. Gnosis means wisdom, or divine wisdom, and this group may have been the descendants of the last of the Egyptian Mystery Schools. If you sound this word out in English it can become "Know Isis" which also might explain more of where the origins of these texts lay. Prior to the find there was little information on this group, the Christian Church having burned and destroyed as much as possible. These codices, are the direction needed to find the Christ (Cosmic Revealer) within, and rid of the force that opposed it, which they labeled archons.

I am only going to give a brief overview. I recommend you read the original texts[79] for yourself, and read Angeliki's book for more detail on them.[80] What her book helped me to understand is that the majority of ancient texts are not presenting details about one creation, but two. That there was an Original Creation (before this Matrix) and then there is the creation of the Matrix/Cave. Granted most of the information in ancient texts are about our Cave creation.

Of this original "pre-Matrix" creation, there was what is described in the Nag Hammadi texts, particularly the Apocraphon of John, as a Father. This is an Absolute Being that was not created. The logical mind works in duality, thus it operates with beginnings and endings, births and deaths. To have the presentation of a being without creation is impossible for the regular mind to understand. The Gnostic texts give us no further indication of this issue, as if it is obvious. This Father Being has an equal female half, called Barbelo, who together as One reside in a realm of light known as the Pleroma. From this original creation a sort of emanation occurred, where what could be thought of as filaments of light came from this now male-female Being. The filaments became known as Aeons (each which were a combined

---

79 Entire Nag Hammadi library can be read at
    http://www.gnosis.org/naghamm/nhlalpha.html
80 One criticism I have of her work is that she never defines exactly how she came to
    her knowledge. The book is laid out as a fictional mystical story, where she meets a
    dream-like Hermes figure who "instructs" her, but there is no indication of her own
    traditions, teachers, or life story.

female-male pair). This type of creation is mirrored in the Ancient Egyptian creation myths of the Ennead and the Ogdoad, with their pairs of matched male-female deities.

Anagnostou interprets the Gnostic texts to claim that each new Aeon created its own universe (by each half combining with their opposite gendered consort). She claimed each used a tree to make the creation. What she means by a tree (in the Pleroma) is not fully explained. She claims that there was one tree that was dead, and thus was left aside and not to be used for creations. This would be the tree that would be used by the Fallen One to create a new false universe, ours. That is an interesting interpretation of the Genesis Garden of Eden-Tree of Knowledge symbolism, but because she is not really explaining what a tree means. It sort of gets left hanging as a non explained symbol.

Various Gnostic and Cathar myths indicate how this current Matrix reality came about; generally with the suggestion of a wish from the Aeon Sophia to create on her own without her male consort. Some suggest the original Christ is this consort. Why she wanted to create this way is not explained. Why does "wisdom" want to create on its own, given that it is wisdom, it should have known the possibility of a dangerous action? Because the reasons for her wishing to create are not revealed, one has to take that metaphor to mean something beyond what it seems. Another question not answered is why it must be a feminine deity to make the original mistake. Of course, this is the origin of later blaming Eve (feminine) for a fall for humans.

The texts indicate that she gave birth to a hideous creature, rejected it, and tried to hide it. This creature became known as the Fallen Creator (Yaldabaoth). He decided to follow in his mother's footsteps and also create his own world without a consort. The "Apocryphon of John" indicates that this Fallen One turned himself into a lion-faced serpent and "moved away from his birthplace (Pleroma)." What is interesting is that the Apocryphon of John states *"He created realms for himself, with a brilliant flame that continues to exist even now."* This flame is likely the white light that is seen in NDE, thus this light is more than just a recycling set up, but also the very force that lion-serpent created the

Matrix with. The sun we see in the sky is likely a type of symbolic presentation of the original light (whatever that is) to be used for creation. This would thus make sense why this creator would be associated with the name Lucifer (fallen light being). It is important to realize that this brilliant flame of the texts is not the Celestial Fire that would be brought into the Matrix later to give it life. From here, the creator began to manufacture helpers, called archons (rulers), to assist with the continued creation process and then with the control of this realm. These are the demonic beings of the higher realms, and an entire section of the Apocryphon names them specifically.[81]

After making the archons, the Fallen One needed to create a functioning reality. After doing so he declared, "I am a jealous god and demand you have no other gods before me." Of course, this statement indicates is that there are other gods, for whom could he be jealous of if he were truly at the top of the totem pole?

There are various versions of how Sophia attempted to stop the creation happening, and how the first human Divine Spark (Adam) was tricked into entering the realm. There seems to have been a creation in the Pleroma of something new that the Apocryphon of John simply describes as, "The Man exists." There is no mention of what this Man is, where it came from, why it was made, just now all of a sudden it is there. Yaldabaoth on hearing this called out to his archons,

> *"Come, let us create a man according to the image of God and according to our likeness, that his image may become a light for us. And they (archons) created by means of their respective powers in correspondence with the characteristics which were given. And each authority supplied a characteristic in the form of the image which he had*

---

81 Genesis in the Bible is a bit confusing as there are a couple of references about the Original Creation, yet most of it is about the creation of the Matrix. In Gnostic terms, God-Jehovah is Yaldabaoth, and the various helpers (angles) are the archons. Apocryphon of John from http://www.gnosis.org/naghamm/apocjn-davies.html

> *seen in its natural (form). He created a being according to the likeness of the first, perfect Man. And they said, Let us call him Adam, that his name may become a power of light for us.*"[82]

This section of text is very important to understanding what the Gnostics had to say about the creation of humans. Firstly is that the humans in the Matrix are a copy of what was in the Pleroma. The phrase also adds "according to our likeness." This "our" would be referring to the archons, but why need to have an image of one thing and a likeness of another? Do humans have the image of "the Father" and the resemblance of the "archons." It is very confusing. Another element that the Apocryphon of John presents is that the creation of the Man was done so that the image may become "a power of light for us (archons)." The most important word here is power, an indication that humans were created to power the AI system for the archons.

The Apocryphon claims that 365 archons made the first Man, or we could say implanted time (365 days) and space upon the creation. However, the creation was lifeless and did not move. The Father was asked for help, which he did by letting Lucifer borrow Eve (not a female deity but the life force). Why the Divine Father helped Lucifer to bring life to this flawed creation is not explained. One suggestion is that it was done so that a trick could be played, but why Lucifer needs to be tricked is also not answered. Why did the Celestial Father not just shut down the Matrix immediately upon seeing that it was a flawed creation?

What the Apocryphon of John does claim is that the Father gave advice to the Fallen Creator to blow into the face of the newly created Man. When he followed this advice, he wound up blowing the spirit of Sophia that he had within into the psychic soul body of the new man. The man gained life, while Lucifer lost his greatest power (Sophia).

Lucifer was not pleased by this occurrence, and thus began to get the archons to trick the perception of humans into focusing

---

82 http://www.gnosis.org/naghamm/apocjn.html

on what material gifts could be attained, rather than using the inner power for Liberation. Placed into terms of my vision, nature is doing what it can to try to guide us, while the archons are doing what they can to trick us. The second great trick was to get the humans to create the bars of their own prison. That was done by getting the man in the astral realm, to project out a material reality. On top of that, to then project themselves into the same realm, and then to forget that it all was just a projection. Exactly where and when the Divine Spark makes it appearance is hard to say, for it is not specifically mentioned in the texts. The texts refer more to an idea that within a person is a divine seed, a spark of knowing, and a light of intelligence. Granted the Greek word for breath was Pneuma, but this was not so much a breath of air, but this breath was spiritual, and as such relates to the breath that Lucifer was tricked into putting into the human. Thus, in this case this Spark or Pneuma is related to Sophia.

The two types of creation might have been skillfully presented in one of the plates that appear in alchemist Robert Fludd's book *Utriusque Cosmi...Historia (History of the Two Worlds)*. One of those plates,[83] by famous engraver Matthaeus Merian, presents the universe. At the center sphere is our material realm, which includes the words "elementum Aqua and Terra (elements of Earth and Water)." This central area includes the signs of the zodiac, as well as images of various plants, animals and minerals. Sitting on a ball globe is a monkey-like creature holding a compass open towards a second globe. One of the monkey creature's arms however is chained to a larger female figure which is standing outside of the inner circle.

Her body, which could be classified as being in the sky realm, while her head (surrounded by stars) pokes into a fiery circular "angelic" realm above that. The image of the woman represents the Divine Spark, though most researchers would claim that she is Sophia. She too is chained above to a hand coming out of a cloud that breaks into the angelic (demonic archon) realm. Within the cloud is the name of God, Yahweh, written in Hebrew.

---

83 Plate from the Science History Institute Museum in Philadelphia and can be looked at in more detail at https://digital.sciencehistory.org/works/fvm4tyd

Most would think this is the good god, but why would the Good God be chained to the Divine Spark? The chain-er is of course Lucifer/Demiurge.

Another interesting piece of information in this image is that the Divine Spark is shown with a sun on one breast, and a moon on the other. Her sun shines a light beam down on the material realm. Yet within the "star" realm there are three suns and a moon, each who also are shining light down on the material. Thus, the Divine Spark is shown as giving off light or power that is not the same as that being given from the sky from the Sun and Moon. To create power, a battery needs a positive and negative magnetic pole. Is that what the Sun and Moon are in our realm are, a symbolic battery that powers the realm, and designed to hide the deeper Sun (power) that exists with the Divine Spark?

I don't want to go more into this subject of creation, you can look more deeply into it if you wish. I do want to conclude with one interesting claim that Angeliki made in a 2019 interview that in her eyes the Fallen Creator (Lucifer) was originally not evil. While we could call him misguided or self-important, it was only as he begun to create his AI simulation from what she referred to as the dead tree did something go wrong. The deeper he went into this creation, which she used a metaphor of a black hole to describe, he reached the lower layer which had a type of sickness that the did not know about. From being in this area he became sick as well. This sickness changed Lucifer, where at first he was glad that the Divine Spark had entered and was powering his universe, and allowed this Fire to come and go as it pleased, but once becoming sick with a type of delusion, he become angry towards the Divine Sparks. With that, he shut the Exit door and kept the Sparks in his simulation as hostages. However, certain Gnostic scriptures indicate that Sophia thought the creation by the Demiurge was an abomination from the start. I am not sure where she gets the idea of an infection from, nor do not see this indication in any of the ancient sources I have examined to date, but it is something that could have some possibility for those who want to examine this in more detail.

As I have suggested, it is my opinion that there were not many Sparks that entered the Matrix, only one Celestial Fire. When the Fire entered, Lucifer as his way to keep the fire inside his creation (thus keep it powered) split the Fire. He "divided" not the waters but the Fire. Once again the water and the Fire are switched around in the myths to symbolically hide what was really going on.

> *"This spiritual degradation, in contrast to materialistic progress, is apparent in every subsequent generation, when it passes the baton to the next one. There is then, this intense feeling that the new generation is 'inferior' to the previous one. people believe that this feeling is the result of the 'generation gap.' But it isn't...This is why most of the real saints relinquish any kind of activity in the world of Lucifer....When someone finally chooses to follow a spiritual path (a pure and ethical life); he has some chances of success, only if he moves against all this downward vortex of materialism that humanity is following."*[84] - Angeliki Anagnostou

This is similar to what Mr. Park would to tell us about what he called the two serpents within us. I mentioned this in *Falling For Truth,* that one of the exercises we did was to lay down on a bed while he hit our back in various places with a rice spoon. We had no idea what he was doing until one day he told us he was hitting the head of the downward moving serpent. He claimed we had two serpents in our energy body; one was designed to move us upward to higher states, while the other is to drag us down into the mess of the material. I thought this was a metaphor until one day after one of his semi-painful smacks, I felt something wiggle away inside my body. Oh crap, I thought, he is correct again!

Both are the twin sides of duality, thus both (what we call good and bad) are of the material. One must silence both, yet most

---

84 Angeliki Anagnostou *Can you Stand* p107-109

try to silence only the negative one and thus feed the positive one. Granted it can make sense to tackle the material one first, as most are more deeply rooted in material world traps than spiritual world traps, but both of them (and their connecting weaknesses and astral counterparts) have to be silenced. We cannot kill the snakes; we can only make them quiet. We put them to sleep, only then can the "Sleeping Beauty" within be woken.

Yet if one can awaken Sleeping Beauty, and get the inner serpents to become still, one does not find bliss and happiness as the gurus promise. Instead, one is catapulted beyond duality into Emptiness. One sits in a type of contentment, as one sees that all we thought of as "ours" (emotions, feelings and thoughts) were not really ours but part of an overriding system designed to push our energy body into places where it could be eaten. We thought we were getting energy from our feelings (particularly the happy ones) and that was partially true. However, a big percentage of that energy was going to other beings. One has to learn how to get energy from the Pleroma, through the reawakened Spark. It is here where the power of the realization of No Self, the use of controlled folly, and the turning away from the material to dwell within the spirit all play part of this deep stage of practice.

We want to awaken the Divine Spark and put the twin serpents within to sleep. This has been one of the great misdirection of Eastern philosophy, the idea of using our attention and practices to awaken the kundalini and get it to rise, which will in turn give us all sorts of powers and psychic abilities. This is another of the many traps of this realm, designed to give us "manifestation goodies." What we want to do is put the serpents to sleep. We want them to become still. It is what Mr. Park was doing with his hitting of the head of these inner serpents with the rice spoon. He was not killing it (for they cannot be killed) but giving it a good sting so that it would stop moving for a while, where the idea was that we could re-harness our inner energy toward a place of inner silence (the nothing but nothing), and we use that awareness to no longer feed the serpents with any more energy. They would then stay in their "stung" state and remain in relative stillness. We are not doing this to find some sort of heaven/nirvana (which is still a part of the Matrix, just the nice half) but to be in the exact middle of duality. We do not want to energize either side of the serpents (positive or negative) we want to wind up in a permanent state of what Rose called between-ness, always residing in the gap between all opposites. That is where true power can be found, and where we exist in a mostly detached way from the Matrix.

One finally comes to understand the early Gnostic ideology when one realizes that the Christ figure did not come to create a liberation for people from sin, but to Liberate Sparks from the entire Matrix. Buddha and Christ wanted to free people from reincarnation, and thus had no interest if people were happy, wealthy, fulfilled or anything else within the dream. Almost all spiritual teachings are somehow presented as how to get better results in the physical material world, and how to get more wishes fulfilled. Christ's quote in the "Apocryphon of John," "*And I entered into the midst of their prison, which is the prison of the body. And I said, He who hears let him get up from the deep sleep.*"

As long as there is still a love of matter, a belief in its importance, and the need to focus on one's own successes over failure, then this is where all of the attention is going to be drawn. One cannot spiritually evolve in the material; one can only learn how to awaken that which has no origin in or of the Matrix. Spiritual work occurs in the Self, which is why the main process is termed Spiraling Inward.

*

ENDINGS

When one realizes that their reality is a type of simulation, it means two things. The first is that it thus has a beginning, and secondly, an ending. Every video game has a point where the game can no longer continue and one way or another will end, and the player can choose to restart the game again or not. Our reality is no different.

This began to get clear for me when I was writing my book *Exposing the Expositions* on the 1800s World Fairs. Once the basic narrative was shot through, that they obviously did not build 700 acre sites just to blow them up with dynamite six months later, something else was going on. The most likely scenario for me was that the world went through a type of reset, where someone or something in control did not like how things were, pushed a button to pretty much "wipe it clean," and then start a new version of it. For me these fairs were the coming out point from that reset. I am however very questioning on the "goodness" of the previous worlds. Part of my work of writing the Power of Then was to show that Old Kingdom Egypt was somehow trying to be a helpful civilization for humans and wisdom. I no longer feel that is the case. In writing on the Fairs I had suggested that it was possible that the world of these buildings was meant to bring harmony and balancing energy to people, and that is why they needed to be reset. I question this now. It is just as likely that this realm has since its inception always been one of control, loosh harvesting, manipulation and suffering. It may have been structured differently during different time periods, but the core intent behind it all has been the same. Was living in those 1800s cities really any better than living in a modern city, beyond that they may have been aesthetically nicer looking? Perhaps not. It is a question that is worthy of deeper study.

I fully believe that we are watching the start of a new reality, a new world. From that standpoint the New Age has it correct, the problem is that they see this newly coming world to be a wonderful one of higher vibration. However as I mentioned above, this realm has likely been a trap from moment one, has been designed on distortion and suffering. There should be no reason to think that any newly designed world will be any better than what has been. Certain individuals and small groups figured this out and devised ways for them to Exit the insanity, but they were never at the top of the systems totem pole, always working behind the scenes from much lower, sharing with the few they could really assist.

This to me is perhaps the most important element about the current state of the Cave. My sense is that the simulacra we have known, will literally be shut off. Westworld is ending and a new park is being built. This is where things are headed, and the new reality is going to far more trapping than what has been seen in this one. Granted both are illusionary realms within a false Matrix, just the deeper one gets into the quicksand, the more work is required to "wiggle" one's way out.

While the second half of Angeliki's book is also about the way the current material reality will end, she used *The New Testament* text "Revelation" as her foundation. Revelation is not the only ancient text that seems to discuss the "end of the world." Another interesting one is the Norse myth of Ragnarok. Norse mythology is very detailed and complex for anyone who has not had some background in the gods and tales. For that reason I will not go into the specifics of their end of the world tale here, but I suggest if you are interested to read the excellent overview found at the footnote.[85] But the most interesting part of Ragnarok is how nothingness is infused directly into the tale. The suggestion is that after the gods have had their great final battle, the world will sink into the sea leaving only the vast Nothingness. In old Norse this was known by the name Ginnungagap. It is interesting to see that in this world (usually translated as Abyss) ends with the word gap, which in Norse means the same as in English.

I have discussed the need to be in the gap between any two of duality, and this place of between-ness is where the power exists. You have to be in a gap of between-ness with the concepts of creation and ending as well. There is only an appearance of a creation, and the appearance of ending, but when you hit that still point between them, that is where the power is found to propel you past both of them one step higher on the ladder.

A key part of Angeliki's thesis is the belief that when this Matrix was created there was a time limit put on it. However the Demiurge and the archons also know this, hence their idea of creating a new simulation to keep the Matrix structure operating after the supposed end point. John Panella has also suggested this same idea (new simulation will be happening) but he adds another option. He presents that those who do not Exit the Cave, nor go into the next more trapping reality, will wind up in a time loop of

---

85   https://norse-mythology.org/tales/ragnarok/

the current world we have been living. I looked into his idea, and present some interesting historical dates around his hypothesis in the Additional Material.

Angeliki and I have similar ideas that a new 5-D trap reality is being put together as a way to suck in the mass of souls who will not take the Exit that currently exists. The ascension story is another trick being prepared for decades, one played on "New Agey" types of the population. As I mentioned in my earlier book, "D" to me refers to depth, as in deeper into the quicksand of the Matrix. 5D would thus be a far denser place than 3D. We do not want to go deeper into the quicksand, we want to get lighter, we want to move towards 1D (oneness).

She presents a very specific breakdown of how our current reality will end, and she may well be correct, but with all prophecy one can never know for sure until it happens. Her claim is that the sky will become flared up, various sounds will be heard (including trumpets), and strange natural phenomena will appear. After this, various demonic beings are released from the areas they are currently behind the scenes to come into this realm and wreak havoc. The current controllers know this is coming and are doing their best to prepare a cover story that they feel will be the most likely to fool the masses (nuclear war, asteroid, alien invasion) to have an explanation for what they are witnessing. Yet again it could just be a moment like when we turn off a television, as simple as just blackness. We have no idea what such an ending looks like, so should keep all possible experiences open for examination.

How bad this new simulation might be was presented by Phillip Corso and Dan Burish, who suggested that the creatures encountered at Roswell in 1947 were not aliens from another planet, but humans from the future. These humans had found ways to travel back in time to try to stop what they called a spiritual calamity that occurred in their past (our near future). If this thesis is correct, what they call the calamity could well be the creation of a new simulation, and all the humans that went into it became trans-humanistic robots. It is why I suggest that all of what is being done right now in our current reality is not about putting chains in place for this world, but to lay out the principles for the new reality soon to come.[86]

The only answer is to reject all of it, to be finished with any and all levels of the Matrix simulation, but what most seem not not understand about that idea, is that the main rejection that has to occur is as much to the person we believe ourself to be as to the Matrix reality that makes up this world. Angeliki relates an Exiting similar to the Rapture idea of the Gospels, where certain "chosen ones" will be snatched up by Jesus and disappear from the world. The problem with the Rapture idea is that it is presented as a lucky tap on the shoulder that comes when Jesus thinks you are perfect enough, or simply had enough faith. Thus, there is still very much a "me" that this rapture is going to save. The idea of being snatched up is another likely misdirection to keep the separate "false self" projecting its form and waiting for the saviour moment, just moving to a new reality to keep this going.

One can Liberate their Divine Spark from the Matrix. It occurs from a combination of complete Self Realization, along with a detailed examination of the simulation and how it is constructed and kept running. Both of those completed chores I feel will create the Exit portal instantaneously, but I do not see this as a "being chosen," nor the need for an external saviour to do something for us. As long as you are still a some-thing that needs to be saved, then you are also something that can be tricked or trapped. Nothing can not be trapped or need to be saved. It just needs to be brought out of its coma.

*

The closer our simulacra gets to the end, the likelihood of it spinning out of control is high. I am not sure that the Fallen Creator has a total handle on this reality anymore, and is in a sense having to constantly do damage control on what is happening in this place. That is all going to lead to more confusion as the end approaches. I think most everyone can relate that just about everything in our world no longer seems to make any sense.

---

86 Information found in Anagnostou *Can You Stand the Truth* pgs 591-670

Once again, all of what is discussed in this chapter needs a disclaimer. There was no origin, and there will be no ending. There is however the appearance of a world, an origin and ending. Only that which is false can begin and end. Truth is beyond such opposites. One's focus is not to wake up IN the simulation; one wants to wake up FROM the simulation. This can never be said enough times.

The trans-humanistic 5-D agenda is one trap. It becomes easy to attack this new agenda and label it as evil with the intent on trapping human souls, which it is. But from an Exit the Cave perspective, everything in our current reality is also a projected trap. Thus at the core there are two tricks that are being played at the same time now. One is the trick of our current 3D or 4D reality, while the other is the new reality, which will likely be presented as an alternative when our current world seems to be too dangerous. The trick comes (often from what tends to be called truth movements) is the focus on how good this current Earth reality is, compared to the trans-humanistic one. While rejecting the next simulation is useful, without also seeing through the lie of this one, solidifies a grasping to this current reality. The Matrix has you no matter which side of these two choices you fall upon. That is how duality is set up, no matter what choice you make, it is within the framework of what the Matrix has given you to choose.

I should remind that these ideas are similar to the ending concepts of what is known as the Hopi Prophecy. This prophecy discuses a shift from what they call a fourth world/creation (ours) to a fifth, and appear in part on a rock known as Prophecy Rock near Oraibi, Arizona. Interestingly, in spiritual presentations their new ascension realm is presented as 5D. Thus we likely are not in a 3D realm like we are told, but instead 4D. You do not jump from 3 to 5, but 4 to 5. 3D would have been the previous simulation, while we are in 4D which would symbolically match the fourth world of the Hopi. Each of these previous worlds in their cosmology ended with a cataclysm, then a new world created, a new turtle placed on the back of the old turtle. To their way of thinking, the previous worlds did not end, they continue to exist. I found it interested when I did this research on the Hopi while I was writing my first book *The Power of Then,* that there were elders who suggested that certain rocks could be lifted up and the third world could still be seen taking place in a hole under that rock.

As the prophecy relates to today, several signs are claimed to have been realized. Only the final one is left, which is after the population gets too "wicked" and human life becoming too Koyaanisquatsi (Hopi for life out of control), there will be a falling of heaven, and a Blue Star will appear in the sky, manifested by a Kachina spirit. After that the prophecy claims that all "ceremonies" will cease. What exactly would be the Blue Star seen in the sky. Plasma outburst? Supernova? Something faked. After this the one the Hopi call Bahana (True White Brother) will appear from the east to find "uncorrupted" people and take them to the fifth world. Some have claimed these prophecies are made up in the 1950s because they were not found in books prior to that. Other sources suggest that these ideas were kept secret until a tribal meeting in 1948 where it was suggested they take their message to the United Nations.[87]

This prophecy might as much indicate information on the change to a new realm, as much as a trick to those who believe the prophecy. Because the move to the new fifth world is presented as a good thing, where the "spiritual ones" will be entering this world, while the "material" will be left in this one. Again why would anyone want to go into any world in a Matrix created by an insane deity? Why would another world have any other purpose than loosh harvesting? Most of the Hopi prophecy, from the standpoint of "how to live in harmony with nature," is very useful. But is the end result of it to lead to continued entrapment in a new realm? I leave that for you to decide.

Assuming that this current (3D or 4D) reality is soon ending, my opinion is a combination of my own Vision, the works of Anagnostou, Panella and what Robert Monroe called an aperture in his book *Ultimate Journey*[88]. There seems at the end point there will be three choices, and it does not matter if the soul

---

87   First presented in book form by Frank Waters in his Book of the Hopi (1963). Other suggested resources are Thomas Mails book The Hopi Survival Kit (1997) the article and referenced videos of a lecture by elder Thomas Banyacya, Sr. at https://sacredland.org/hopi-prophecy/, criticism found at https://en.wikipedia.org/wiki/Blue_Star_Kachina, and information about the 1948 meeting at https://www.blackmesatrust.org/?p=658

is dead or alive at this point. Those are: go to the next simulation, or start a whole new time loop cycle in this reality, or Exiting the Cave past the symbolic Exit door. Of course even the idea of Exit door is another false projected idea, but for a while it can be a useful tool for our focus as we go through this work. But even the idea that there is a door will at some point in the journey have to be left behind. The gate becomes gateless when one has realized that there is No-one to walk through it. Still the Divine Spark Exits, by revealing to itself fully that there No-thing of it which is capable of being confined.

---

88 A full examination of what Monroe reported of his travel to the exit door in that
   book will be discussed in one of the Additional Material sections for this book.

Chapter 7

THE FOLLY OF ONENESS

"There is no we in one."

As they say in horse racing, we are now in the home stretch. Maybe it is also time for everyone to take a stretch, a small break, as there has been quite a lot of material up to this point. And even now as we get close to the end of this book, there will not be any "here is what you should do" speeches. I can not tell anyone else what they should do, as only you can figure that out. This is a book of my opinions, experiences, and the ways that I have come to see this reality. Nobody can have a system that will work for everyone, because each person's path will be a unique journey through their own life story. One only takes what they can from another's experience, and only uses a portion of that for which to build their own unique path.

*

Anders and Liv are finishing their two-night visit to my home, on a one week vacation they are taking in the area. This gave Anders and I a chance to have a complete discussion over my reworked final chapters. He had seen an earlier version and was rather surprised with the depth of changes that were done.

We are sitting around the table having breakfast, well actually Anders, Liv and my wife are. I eat early in the morning, so I am just sitting there with them and listening to their conversation. It is nice to have guests visit for a few days. And it is just as nice when the guests leave. I like to have a quiet calm environment, and I would assume that is similar for just about anyone who moves deeper along this path. Again, I could be wrong about what others may want, but it has certainly been high on my list.

I live simply. I like to enjoy the natural world, find time to read a bit, sit and observe what goes on, and then contemplate what my senses have taken in. In my comedy days during the 1990s, my life was an endless amount of unique occurrences, like a television show. I could have created a *Curb Your Enthusiasm* clone based on my daily life experiences. Now, my current life could never make it to television, as most would likely find it quite boring.

Anders begins the conversation around the end of the book, "These chapters sure went through an overhaul. But given what I previously read, I think this was a very good idea. I know this work has been challenging for you."

"I realized that I had to make some changes, Anders. What I was originally attempting to do was write what would have been an entire book into one chapter. For that reason alone, it was creating problems. I realized that it needed to be three chapters, one to present some key foundational areas, and a second to act as a type of prologue to the next book, and one for a proper ending."

"Next book?" Liv asks.

"Yeah, I realized that was the answer. Don't try to squeeze in a whole bunch of stuff into what would be one disjointed and rushed chapter, would be a disservice to this material, and would be disservice to all of the information that preceded it. The material should be carefully examined, personally lived, and then well written."

"I thought you were done with the writing after this."

"I thought I might be as well, but likely not. Because I have a process to present. Maybe I should explain. Originally the final chapter was to be an evaluation on the merits of spending long periods of time in silence and retreats from the material world.

Yet, I had not done such renunciation in around twenty years, thus I do not feel I have tested the practices enough lately to give a detailed opinion of them right now. All I can provide are some overviews and suggestions."

*

Liv wants to take the conversation to a question she has been wanting to ask. "Howdie, I would think that Exiting the Cave has to be real simple. I mean it can't be complex, it has to be something everyone can do. Is your book describing this simplicity."

"Is it complex? Probably not. Is it something everyone can do? Theoretically, yes. My estimated likelihood of anyone completing it? Almost nil. This is based on the standard ancient idea that 0.1% of 0.1% will fully awaken in their lifetime. By that, I take it they meant the requirement to have reached the state of Total Knowing where they can then Exit the Matrix. That math means 8,000 today would make it. Even if you bump it up to 80,000, that is still a very small number overall. It is a process that requires the utmost of commitment needed to burn through the core of every lie and deception. The lie of love will likely be one of the hardest for the average person to get through. It is easy to see the stuff we hate as a type of trap of the Matrix, but so much harder to also see that can also be what we most love."

*

ONENESS

My answer moved Liv to ask another question. "About oneness. I mean we are all one right? It's all just one, so how can there be any problems with a Demiurge, traps, or even distortions if we are all one? We all merge back with the Divine at some point, and me and the plate and the table and God are all one. I can't see how there can be any problem."

"It is a good question, Liv, and only lately, have I finally understood the fallacy behind the whole concept. I now see the idea of oneness, as perhaps the biggest error made by the spiritual community. How often is some "enlightened" person presenting that the world is wonderful because "everything is one," or "we are all one?" By those statements alone, they mean that all objects: fish, bears, staplers, rocks, chairs, me, and you (and the experiences that they have) originate from the same source, which they see as God, or whatever term they want to substitute for it. And while partially true, it is also partially false, but almost no one can see the false part of the concept."

"Oneness is false or God is False?"

"Yes." I stop and smile. I guess I felt I needed to tell her a bit more. "I will explain. There is a Celestial Fire that originated in the Absolute of the Pleroma, which is outside of the Matrix. The Matrix was manifested by the Fallen Creator in error. When this happened, the Matrix and the Pleroma became separated from each other, and thus no longer were 'the same.' After the creation of the Matrix and its inability to be 'alive,' the Celestial Fire was brought in (or tricked to enter) the new false Matrix to make it alive. And here lies the problem: There are now two different "one's." The Celestial Fire is a one and the entire Matrix is another one. The Fire was divided and split into many Divine Sparks. From the standpoint of the Sparks, there is only one Celestial Fire from which they all originated from, and which has its origin outside of this entire reality. The Sparks have absolutely NOTHING to do with anything in the Matrix, while EVERYTHING within the Matrix (all of its objects, including the body-mind of any person) is part of the one of the Matrix. These two ones are not the same. An error gets made believing the objects, thoughts and experiences are the same as the Divine Fire. Simplified, the Matrix is a false 'one,' and the Divine Fire is a True 'one.'"

"Two different ones? Has anyone ever thought of that before?" Anders asks.

"I haven't seen a direct reference the way I have just said it here, but that does not mean that these ideas have never been intuited by others. But Lucifer has done a good job over the last few centuries editing out any information that tried to reveal what I just presented. The Spark/Fire is the only True element. Everything else is a projection, either directly from the Matrix itself or part of a trick to get the Sparks to project inside of it. But all of the projections originate with the Matrix. You could use an analogy that from the standpoint of the Matrix, prior to any manifestation, all that existed was an AI computer code. This code is the 'one' origin source of everything that appears within it. A multitude of projections are possible, but only if they fit within the original code that was provided. All the objects are one from the standpoint of the Matrix, but NO objects are One from the standpoint of the Celestial Fire. Whether any object has a Divine Spark at their core or not, makes no difference from the standpoint of its Matrix form.

So when a spiritual teacher proclaims 'we are all one,' or 'everything is one,' what they are really saying (without realizing it) is they are linking everything material, and its original Creator, with that which is spiritual. That is the error. As soon as you link anything to the material realm, you are discussing the Matrix and its Fallen Creator. Yes, all objects and experiences are one, based on having the same Matrix source code from the mind of Lucifer/Demiurge. But none of them link to Pleroma, which has nothing to do with the Matrix. It is something completely different. And that understanding is what has become distorted and even lost to the modern world."

*

I give them both a long explanation during our discussion, but I will simplify it for my readers here. The Fire from the Pleroma has nothing to do with objects or experiences. It is what is hostage in the Matrix system, and thus is not like all the others. A person, a tree, or a bird does not Exit. The Awareness behind them, if it was originally part of the Celestial Fire, can Exit. Howdie does not leave the Matrix, for he is always a projection from and of it. Pure Awareness can borrow the Howdie-thing as a vehicle for its own deeper work to Exit the Cave. The more awake it is, the more it can be the driver of the Howdie-car. It sounds bad on the surface, what will happen to "little old me?" Awareness, which is what you really are, has been wanting to have "your" full attention since your conception. The Matrix has just done a good job to deceive you into trusting the mind, thoughts, feelings and sense perceptions. Once the shift to Awareness gets made, the Howdie thing becomes happy to let its Truth be the guiding mechanism and not the thoughts and feelings which had been its previous guiding tools.

For those who may be confused, consider the Out Of Body Experience. When you have an OBE, as I have had a few times, there is a witnessing from Awareness but there is no longer a material body that one is witnessing from. You can see your normal physical body, yet are outside of it looking back on it, as if seeing yourself through a mirror. Yet something I call "me," an indviduality, is still present, just it no longer has to be centered inside of a body. It is much more vast than that, just it has been mostly walled out so that only a tiny piece of their real Awareness is allowed into the body-mind, meaning the Matrix part of us is mostly running the show. That is why none of awakening the Divine Spark is in any way negative, yes some of the focus on the body-mind goes away, but that was never the truthful part of oneself. Awareness is, and the more walls that get taken down, and the more Pure Awareness can be the main perception point, the more clear the body-mind becomes. It is the best way I can explain this.

When we drive our car and arrive at our house, we get out of the car and leave it in the driveway or garage. It has done its job, to help us navigate our trip back to our home. Then we go inside and do our "house related" activities, and we completely forget about the car, until some time in the future, when we feel the need to use it again. In the case of Exiting the Cave, the vehicle body (and more importantly the identity) is going to be left behind. We thank it for the job it did, and appreciate the suffering, sacrifices, challenges, and navigation of obstacles it had to do. But the body-identity is part of the everything of the one Matrix, as opposed to ONE (Fire).

Liv had been sitting in somewhat a stunned silence while I was presenting this information. At first there was a fighting type of energy, an outer sign which I detected that there was an inner battle happening within her. But this fighting energy seemed to slow down as the conversation continued, and she became more still. After she calmed, she took about thirty seconds to respond. She looked far off to her left, processing, gathering thought...and then it all spilled out, "Oneness. The spiritual oneness claim. It's all garbage isn't it? This whole 'we are one,' and 'merging with the Great Divine.' Total garbage!"

"Yes, there is no 'we' in one. Besides, there is nothing to merge with. Even when I say that the Divine Spark reunites with the Celestial Fire, that is not really true either, as it is just a metaphor for the regular mind to use while going through the process. Do you now see how the phrase 'we are all one' is perhaps the biggest misdirection in the spiritual game, yet true at its core?"

"Fully. I can't believe I never thought of this before."

"I guess all these big revelations require certain steps to happen. That is why someone can't force their new realizations on someone else. A person has to be in the correct place and time for something new to be able to even be processed. All objects are indeed one, because they all originate from the Matrix. But not the Ultimate Witnesser of those objects, they are not the same."

"Is this were the origin of detachment comes from? This understanding that Awareness is not an object?"

"Of course. It should finally begin to make sense as to what that word really means. Do you also now see why groups like the Cathars were so clear about the need to reject all in the material realm? Because they understand that only the Spark/Awareness is Real, and everything else is part of the false (Matrix, code, projection). That includes even the body-mind vehicle they were borrowing. The only focus was to awaken Sleeping Beauty and symbolically rejoin the Fire, and have that fire baptism. And that will not happen if the main focus is still on the material realm or the self, because the world will take the majority of our available energy. Again, the material Matrix is not to be ignored, run away from or denied, but the level of energy and attention that we put towards it drops considerably after such realizations."

"Liv will still be in the world?"

"Let me put it all this way. Studying the Matrix to uncover it as a set of coded information that can be navigated has some value. But you don't study it with the belief that it will lead to a spiritual transformation. The study of the Matrix reveals the structure of the prison; while the study of the Self reveals the Exit.

*

I could tell we were moving to some very core places with Liv and Anders with this conversation. Sometimes I get to a point where I have to make a decision. Have the people I am speaking with had enough of an information explosion for one day, or is there room for one more? My sense today is that there could be room for one more, so I give it another serving. "Liv, do you know the difference between water and fire symbolically?"

"No. Well sort of. I guess water is said to be about emotions and that is why the Native Tribal Societies might have the bear as a symbol of...Ugh... oh." She stops. "Is this going to be another two oneness type thing? Are fire and water talking about a different oneness?"

"Yes, you have it. A realization happens when one sees through the illusion of the Cave. An Awakening happens when one sees through the illusion of the self. And when the Divine Spark becomes energized, in a sense gets switched on again, that is enlightenment. It is the final state where the Spark is connected to the original Celestial Fire. This is the Baptism of Fire by the Christ figure presented in the Cathar theology. But this baptism is not about the person becoming perfect, special, holy, wonderful, or full of love. It means that one has had their Divine Spark not just out of its coma, but also reconnected, thus it burns as a mirror of the Celestial totality. When this occurs, you could say there is no interest, and no magnetic pull to the false white light of the Lucifer Matrix. But all this is not the way this word enlightenment is commonly presented. The Cathars were correct in claiming that they had to become a body of light, but this gets mixed up and turned sideways in the modern way of seeing things. You see this today with people claiming to be a Cathar, wearing their white robe and playing a pretend game of being perfect, special, perfected, or pure. This is the standard way 'Enlightenment' gets packaged."

I continue, "These modern enlightenment concepts are connected to the idea of water, especially the drop in the ocean metaphor. It is often used in spiritual terminology to discuss how all is one. The drop of water (or a wave) appears for a short time as something separate, but then returns to the fullness of the ocean. Where does the wave begin and where does it end, or what is not ocean is what these famous spiritual texts present? When one sees that the water metaphor is meant to represent the oneness related to the Lucifer Matrix, these metaphors begin to be seen as a type of distortion, as water here is representing the Matrix. Could this relate to the story of Jesus walking on water? That he was symbolically walking on the Matrix, and not sinking within it, rising above the entire false realm? Gives that story a whole new presentation does it not?

"Oh wow," exclaims Anders. Now he too is processing in a big way. "The walking on water story always seemed like a just a look how holy the guy is story, but this idea that water is representing the Matrix gives it an entirely different meaning. We are not looking to not sink into water, we are looking to get to a Christ-like state where we no longer sink into the Matrix. Not by being holy, but by being an Awareness that is not of the Matrix so is not bound by it. Just wow!" Meanwhile Liv seems almost giddy with excitement. I know they had long ago let go of their early Christian upbringing, having moved into various New Age thinking in their 20s. My sense is that they may revisit some of these New Testament and Gnostic texts again as they have just sensed far deeper metaphors present than they had ever thought were there.

"The Matrix is all a projection from of an AI code, one that is a copy or reflection of something more real. Water is a major reflective element in the material reality. It is how Narcissus falls in love with himself, from seeing his reflection in water. What is viewed on the top of still water is the mirror projection, seemingly looking like the real original, but is just a copy. Everything in our reality is also a mirror projection like this. We have learned to believe the projection, to trust it as real and true, and not go looking for the source. Thus to the Cathars, a water baptism was the sinking of one into the oneness of the Matrix and Lucifer, at least symbolically. To not be walking on water, means one must be "light", a being of Fire which as long as it stays above the water, can burn endlessly if it has enough fuel."

"And in the Bible?"

"Even Genesis, which is mostly talking about the creation of the Matrix, has water as its primal element. This first element being water is found in most cultures, such as the creation myths of Ancient Egypt. When water is being separated from water, or from the sky, it is putting the computer code into action. With a Baptism of Fire, one was not sinking into the Matrix, but walking in the Pleroma. Does it make more sense now why this distorted topic of oneness is so important?"

"Why has no one ever talked about this."

"Maybe they did, just no one listened to them, so they stopped talking. Or if their stuff was written down, it later got edited out. Trust me I am not some sort of world genius as the first one to figure this out. I mean the symbol takes on so many levels. Water and fire just do not go together, if water gets on fire it puts it out. A little bit makes steam. But steam is still just heated water, a cloud. Fire is different completely.The Divine Spark is the full side of Emptiness and resides in a symbolic Heart, while No-Self is the empty side of Emptiness and resides in Awareness. The Matrix is just the Matrix, it does what it does. And we shape our own experiences and our own private world within it, based on the rules it provides. And those rules can be overcome, but generally, when someone gets to the point where they can start changing all of the rules, Emptiness has become so blown out of their egoic self that they no longer have an interest to change anything."

"*The Matrix* is a movie full of water symbolism. The code of the Matrix is symbolized by falling rain for example. "

"Good for bringing that movie up. If you look everywhere you will see water in those movies."

Liv has been mostly quiet and just listening to the conversation, but this now perks her, up. "So. Neo in the *Matrix* movies. He is called 'the One.' My guess is that you see that reference completely different now?"

"The question becomes which One is he? The Spark or an object from the Matrix? If he is identifying as an object in the Matrix, thus being false, then would he not be trapping himself in the very projection he claims to be Exiting? Hence the problem with the red pill-blue pill that nobody noticed. On the surface you can see the choice was between a water baptism and a fire baptism. But Neo got tricked. He choose the red pill, so fire, but did you notice that he took the pill with a glass of water. So the water overrode the fire. Hence all the red pill symbolism we have seen explode after that movie, especially in the so-called "truth movement" is not really the great revolutionary awakening information they think. They too have swallowed the red pill with water, so are looking for how to have their fire baptism in the midst of the Matrix. How to use a bit of seeing to make their prison cell nicer and more comfortable. And I understand the urge to do that, I really do. But it has been attempted for thousands of years, through various simulations, and nothing has ever changed. The idea of fixing this reality is just another trick within a trick."

I continue, "That is why Mr. Park told me early on that a choice had to be made on the path. That choice is to either walk the material road or to walk the spiritual road. He was clear that at a certain point in time, you can no longer walk both. I of course thought I knew what he meant by the spiritual road, a sort of adding spiritual things to one's daily life. It took almost twenty years for me to begin to understand the depth of his statement, or maybe I am just a bit slow on such things. You can't reach the spiritual realm by performing material world actions. The material world at a certain point has to be dropped so all that "exists" is the spiritual. Maybe it took my reading of texts such as the *Faith Mind Sutra* or the *Gospel of Judas* to open access to the clarity within to start to finally understand his message."

*

GOSPEL OF JUDAS

The Gospel of Judas is an interesting Gnostic text not found in *The Nag Hammadi* documents, but from the *Codex Tchacos* discovered in the 1970s near Minya, Egypt. This text is mostly known for where Christ comes to talk to his group of disciples, and laughs at them. Only Judas manages to see what Christ is laughing about, and as such is able to receive a much deeper instruction.

The text begins with the disciples praying over bread and Jesus laughs at them. They ask him, "*Master, why are you laughing at [our] prayer? What have we done? [This] is what's right. He answered and said to them, "I'm not laughing at you. You're not doing this because you want to, but because through this your God [will be] praised.*"[89] Jesus laughs at the disciples because he sees that they are doing what all religious people are doing, praying to the creator of the false Matrix for personal and thus also false favours. They can not see the very subject I pointed to above, the existence of two differing onenesses. They can not understand that Christ is not from the Matrix. He is either a type of holographic-type insert from the Pleroma (The Cathar belief), or is a being with a fully realized Divine Spark, thus operating wholly from the Pleroma and not the vehicle-body observed in front of them. Either way, the figure known as Christ had only one purpose for being "seen" by others, and that was to reveal the deception of the Matrix to those who would listen and those who could take action upon what they had heard.

Christ then tells his disciples that "*no generation of the people among you will know me.*" Again, meaning that he is not a

---

89 Quotes from https://www.gospels.net/judas which uses the translation of Mark M. Mattison.

flesh and blood design of the Matrix. The key part of this reveal is for those listening to not to put him (Christ) on a pedestal, but rather to get each person to see that which they Are (Divine Spark) is also not a part of the Matrix. That at their core, they and Christ are equal. What he Is at the True core of Oneness, is also what they Are. Instead of taking this pointer to the depths of understanding (which would unravel all of their sense of self), the text claims that the disciples began to *"get angry and furious and started to curse him in their hearts."*

When Jesus asked if they were strong enough (spiritually) to face him, and only Judas did, -though he did not look Jesus in the eye. He understood that Jesus was not from the Matrix by saying, *"I know who you are, and where you've come from. You've come from the immortal realm of Barbelo (female half of Pleroma), and I'm not worthy to utter the name of the one who's sent you."* Because Judas knew the difference between the Matrix and the Pleroma, Jesus took him from the group for private teaching. Much of the rest of the text includes the ideas that the God whom the disciples were praying to was really the Fallen Creator, as all material objects, experiences, fears, and hopes are not from the Pleroma.

The last piece of this text to highlight is when after the disciples have realized they are living in error and ask for help. Jesus responds with, *"Stop struggling against me. Each one of you has his own star...Truly I say to you, the pillar of fire will fall quickly and that generation won't be moved by the stars."* I am sure most readers by now will realize that the inner star he is referring to is one's Divine Spark, from which they (and He) originated from.

It becomes very paradoxical discussing all of this. That there is no reality and nothing going on (hence detachment and silence and stillness are an obvious response), while at the same time the experience of the reality continues, one designed to create the maximum confusion, lies and manipulation possible (which requires clear seeing, action, direction and focus). And both sides are equally valid and important, at varying times, in varying degrees, depending on what the dream is throwing at someone.

ALLOGENES[90]

One of the most valuable pieces of information for our understanding also comes from the *Codex Tchacos,* called the Temptation of Allogenes (Stranger). It does not appear in the Nag Hammadi works, however there is a text simply called Allogenes (The Stranger). They are different presentations, but the material is linked. The Allogenes in the Nag Hammadi presents information about the Pleroma. The Temptation document is difficult to locate either in book form or online (see the above footnote). It is another very clear presentation of what I have been describing about this confusion of oneness.

The text begins with Allogenes (the Stranger) praying to what normal translations suggest is God, the normal loving creator thought of by the masses. But this text is clear that the prayer is to the "Father of the Ages...to reveal the mysteries, so that we may know ourselves; specifically, where [we've] come from, where we're going, and what we need to do to live." I could say that this is pretty much what we are asking ourselves. The text claims this is happening on top of mountain known as Tabor. This Tabor is generally thought to be a mountain in Lower Galilee, but as I have mentioned in my series on the mysteries of Southern France, the Cathars fully believed that Mount Tabor was Mt. Segur.

Satan (representing the False Creator) and described in the text as "the one who binds the world" appears and first tries to discourage one's seeking by claiming that even though one is walking up this mountain, they will not find anything. But Satan claims that if they come to him and the world they can have "silver, gold and clothes" (material world goods and experiences). Allogenes rejects Satan, "Depart from me, Satan, because I don't seek you but my Father, who is above all the great realms; because I've been called 'Stranger,' since I'm from another race. I'm not from your race." Here the text is describing what I have been

---

90 Info on this subject can be found at https://www.gospels.net/stranger, https://en.wikipedia.org/wiki/Allogenes

presenting in this text. He is rejecting Satan (Lucifer) seeking The Father (origin in the Pleroma) thus indicating there are TWO elements- Matrix and Totality. He says he has the name Allogenes (Stranger) because he is a stranger in the material world, meaning not from this realm and claims clearly that he is not of "Lucifer's race" or we could say "Lucifer's Matrix code." He is the Stranger here as his origin is from another reality.

Satan continues his attempts of temptation, until finally the Stranger responds, "Depart from [me], Satan! Go away, because I don't [belong to] you." The deceptions failed because the Stranger was able to stay strong in his Ultimate Intent, that to reach the True Father in the Pleroma and thus nothing in the Matrix could be worthy of his energy or focus, and The Fallen Creator has no more that he could do, "And when he had been defeated, he went away to his place in great shame."

Once he has stood in his power and rejected the Lucifer Matrix, a transfiguration occurs. The Stranger calls out to Father to have mercy on him, and to save him from all evil. He asks to be seen in what he calls "this deserted place" and asks for "indescribable [light] shine on me." This deserted place is likely referring to a mind freed of focus on the material (or astral for that matter) Matrix. The indescribable light being asked for would be the Celestial Fire, the light in the word enlightenment. The Stranger might be said to be asking for the Baptism of Fire.

A shining cloud comes to surround and shine on the Stranger. It speaks to him, suggesting his prayer was heard and that it had come to tell him the gospel before he leaves (the Matrix).

The text then comes to a similar idea that was found in the *Gospel of Mary Magdalene* mentioned in chapter 3. Here the light discusses six powers (desire, darkness, ignorance, death, kingdom of the flesh, and foolish 'wisdom' of flesh), while the Gospel of the Magdalene had seven, (darkness, desire, ignorance, jealousy, carnal inebriation, intoxicating wisdom, and devious wisdom. These powers will attempt to bind the Stranger as he leaves, and demand to know where he is going. With each of these powers the instruction is to present to it, "*What bound me has been killed, and I've been released. I'll go up to my Father, the One above all the great realms. And it will release you.*" Interestingly the text describes these beings that will be asking these questions are angels, of which I would like to see the original text to see what this word translated to us as angels are. No matter, we know it is describing archons.

It seems much more of this text existed originally, but all that is left is but a few sparse fragments from this point onward, a few lines with the suggestion not to have fear.

This text is important for our work for a couple of reasons. The first again this idea that there is a oneness from the Pleroma (what we are) and the one of the Matrix (everything in manifestation) which we are not. He rejects all temptations (and likely fears and deceptions) from Satan, and after fully rejecting everything that could be thrown at him, one could say that the Stranger has regained his complete power of the Divine Spark, so the Matrix no longer could bind him. The second is that it is discussing this sort of Q and A that one must go by, which are the tricks of the chakra system. One has to let go all of the binds to matter, all of the binds to fears and temptations by sinking back into what we Are, this Light or Fire being discussed. And as I have suggested we avoid any of this in the journey Home, by having so dissolved the Matrix from our being, that the Q and A does not need to happen, as we have in a sense answered all of these questions based on our actions that we took while still in a body in the lead up to the journey home.

I would suggest the importance of the entire set of the *Codex Tchacos* because while there are only four texts within, they are all about Exiting the Matrix. The Gospel of Judas and the Temptation of Allogenes have been presented. The other two texts that appear in the codex are the First Apocalypse of James (the text that reveals the attempts of the archons to seize souls and demand a toll from them (loosh energy) and what one needs to know to be past them. I discussed some of this text in the first *Exit the Cave*. The final text is known by the title 'From Peter to Philip the

Apostle,[91] but is mostly a text of Jesus in discussion with his disciples.

*

A NEW WAY OF ACTING

> *"Things matter to you. You asked me about my Controlled Folly and I told you that everything I do in regard to myself and my fellow men is folly, because nothing matters. Certain things in your life matter to you because they're important; your acts are certainly important to you, but for me, not a single thing is important any longer, neither my acts nor the acts of any of my fellow men. I go on living, though, because I have my Will. Because I have tempered my Will throughout my life until it's neat and wholesome and now it doesn't matter to me that nothing matters. My Will controls the folly of my life."[92]* - Carlos Castaneda

One of the standard questions that I often get from my Locals community surrounds "how do I interact with the world once I see it is not as I had previously believed?" The question tends to be something along the lines of how they can become more honest and authentic with everyone they interact with, so they can discuss the truth as they see it constantly. Some add that they want to help "wake up" their family members and friends who seem not to listen to them when they share "what's truly going on" in the world.

All of this is another element of the New Age overlay which is still presiding in one's system. That New Age idea being that we have to find our "true self," and then become a new person (often with a new name) to share our new "higher" understanding with

---

91 http://www.gnosis.org/naghamm/letpet.html
92 Carlos Castaneda *A Separate Reality* chapter 6

everyone so that we can live in a more authentic way. The problem they felt is that the person they were were living beliefs and a life story that was what society or their parents wanted for them. The believed remedy is to remove this actor, and now they can become a more real person. Few seem to understand that the actor IS the real person, and what they are really doing is substituting one actor for another one, that they believe is somehow more valid. They keep believing there is a "real person" somewhere, and if they just begin to forcefully project this new person it to everyone, that the world will now have to accept their position. But none of this involves anything that this book is suggesting.

What I have to come to see is that the character I constantly play, Howdie, has a robot-like functioning mechanism (which we might call instincts, cellular imprinting, personality traits, and certain preferences from what it likes to eat, what hobbies it likes to do, what it enjoys to discuss). I am not trying to stop the robot part of the body and try to take total control of all of these various processes, many of which came immediately at conception or birth. The body was created in a certain way to do certain things in the world. And you can overturn much of this coding, but fighting the base nature of the body itself is not the best use of our energy. Most of it is fine as it is. All that is required is to notice the gap moments, the spaces where the robot is in low function mode and then slip in from deeper Awareness what needs to happen.

One does not need to change much outwardly (what we do, what we say, what our name is, what we talk about), we change what is going on internally. Or we could say, we let the majority of the body do its thing as required, while we sharpen Awareness to be more clear about the inner thoughts and feelings (so they do not spin into something that could lead to a problem). But this inner world of what we believe or understand does not need to be "projected" out to the world as a way of showing how great and truthful you now are. You only need to be aware of your inner state, and be comfortable with what you observe there.

As for waking people up, I tend to ask, "Oh, you probably tried to tell your family and friends all about what that was going on." They would nod along, and then I would add, "And when you told them your honest seeing, the reaction you got was for them to push you away as fast as possible." They tend to nod again. People get a real shock when they found out that most of the world out there is not that interested in hearing about whatever truth they have uncovered. The more you begin to understand about deep subjects, and if you start talking about these things to the average person, you are going to get hit with tremendous resistance. A sleeping person does not like to be woken up. Sleepers like their sleep, and their dreams.

Generally when one finds something they think is of value, the natural human tendency is to want to share that with others. But if you start to be honest, especially with people who know you well, they will not want to listen because you are not behaving and talking like the person they have already boxed you into being. Who you are supposed to be is fixed in their mind. They have built an entire structure of who you are, and they expect you to fulfill their view. Change worries most people, because if their mind can not instantly classify everything that is outside of itself, it becomes very frightened. If we start acting differently, people don't know what to do. So we fool them, we act exactly as they expect. That is where and idea called Controlled Folly comes in, which I will get to shortly.

Yes one should still seek people to have honest and deep conversations with, but the further we go in our path, there will likely be fewer people that we can make such friends with. Most of the time we will be in a type of floating along mode with the masses, just discussing what is expected at the moment: the weather, Jim's new deck, the football game, the price of gas, and whatnot. So we test the waters, we wait for a good moment to slip in a small mention of something deep and see if they take this up and ask us more questions about it. If not, we just carry on and forget those discussion points

You can turn this hook and fishing thing into a type of game, throwing out the little possibilities and having fun with the reaction. Even if someone gets a bit offended or concerned about what you have mentioned, you can always just respond that you were joking and simply go on to some safe topic. They will soon forget that you ever brought it up. You have to be honest with yourself of course, never lie to yourself within, but when it comes to dealing with the outside human reality, one has to sort of keep the actor and the role going on mostly to keep one's energy intact. We don't need to get into battles with people for no reason.

On the other hand, we don't lie either. We won't believe one thing and pretend we believe the opposite. We just learn how to present the understandings we have in such a way that we feel true within, yet not bashing against anything without. We don't need to convince anyone of anything, but we don't have to agree with others either. It is fine to just say I disagree with that, and move on to some other subject. Choosing sanity in any moment is always a good option. That does not mean you have to fight insanity, just choose not to associate with it, and choose to stay clear to ourself within. This is the message for just about anyone who has figured a few things out about reality, and gone through a few inner transformations.

However, once one has had a realization of Emptiness, things get a bit different. Now it is not so much that you see yourself sometimes in actor mode, but more that you realize that what you really are is something much deeper and fuller than the human you always thought you were. A big part of this "seeing" is that the entire Matrix is a giant insane suffering-generating deception that can never be fixed nor improved. *"The longer I live, the more I dislike this place,"* is how Richard Rose described being in this reality.[93] Reality is a giant trap and not the wonderful place we had always been told. This understanding stops the need to try to fix the world, and even to manifest our desires. We now see that all our life we were always working towards certain successes, and to constantly avoid of failures. But upon the realization of Emptiness, we grasp the concept that both winning and losing are equal in the life of a video game character. We also see that the majority of the "success" we searched for was not attainable, since it had nothing to do with anyone's merits, nor even

____

93 Richard Rose 1980 lecture, John Kent *Path* chapter 4.

their hard work. Most success has come because a person was from a specific family or belonged to a specific secret society. That understanding also allows one to drop all of the personal shame held around one's failures (especially around career or finances) as we begin to see the system was always set up for the majority of people to fail. There should be no shame at all in losing a game that was rigged from the start.

Once one sees that the world, and especially human society, is one giant insane mess, the realized one tends to come to two options to move forward. One of those options is to just leave society completely, going to live in an out of the way forest hut or on a mountain. The other option is to re-enter the societal world, meaning to re-enter the dream with the actor. This is the more challenging of the two options, but I consider it the more powerful choice. Escaping or withdrawing completely from the human mess has its merits. Small retreats of total silence are required to be able to hear the deeper voice of inner Truth, and get a break from the non-harmonious effects of modern society. Native Medicine Men still go on one or two vision quests a year, where they spend several days fasting, praying and being open to messages from beyond their body-mind. But the key here is that in all of these cases they did not stay in retreat permanently. The Medicine People would return from these "moments of aloneness," and come back to their communities to share what they had found, and be of service to others with it. Richard Rose suggested at least one long retreat alone (up to 30 days) once per year to get the mind focused and clear, and then return to see what you will do with things learned on the retreat.

Anyone can be a good meditator in a quiet dark room. The better test is how good can you meditate for three hours seated in Times Square in New York during rush hour. Being in the world is more of a test than the silence of a monastery or on a mountain top. The point here is that there is a time for sanctuary from the human world, and a time for immersion in it. One part of dealing with day to day reality is to see just how much of your realization have you integrated. How much is True Awareness running your show? How much do you really have your "house in order?" Only by testing in the day to day reality can the answers to these questions be found.

Once one has decided not to go live life in a cave but continue to interact with the world, a new way of acting must emerge. You don't get rid of the person you know as you, you learn to move it in ways where it "rubs against" reality less and less. You still keep up your empathy for other creatures, and demand the liberated way of being for the character you play and you don't bow down to that which takes you from your sovereignty. And of course, you take many breaks entirely away from the human world. You don't live in a pretend glassy super happy state of bliss while ignoring the suffering and injustice of the inane surrounding world. Nature might not be any more "real" than the human world, but it does allow for more breaks from all of the egoic craziness the human world entails.

But there is a way to proceed with interacting with the human world. How to act like we are behaving as if the world is important to us, while within we know differently.

I discuss my concerns around Carlos Castaneda in the Additional Material, but this subject is one that I think he (or whoever wrote those books) was very clear on. What he called Controlled Folly first appeared in the second book in the series, *A Separate Reality.* It could be seen as a revised practice similar to what might be described as "Acting as a Non-Doer" in Asian philosophy. It was also mentioned it in two later books, *Eagle's Gift* and *Power of Silence,* though the meanings of the term were changed, and the change was never explained.

Don Juan makes his first comment about this term in chapter five when he discusses that he wished a peyote ceremony had taken place with his grandson rather than his friend and says, "*We must know first that our acts are useless and yet we must proceed as if we didn't know it. That's a sorcerer's Controlled Folly.*"[94] The entire practice is presented in this one sentence.

Folly is a word that means something similar to foolishness. The point is that ALL actions one is partaking in this reality are folly, because everyone believes that what they are doing is important, either for themselves or the world as a whole. Actions still occur though always knowing that the outcome of any action is no longer important. How much different is success or failure to a video game character? When one sees the world as it is, but continues on acting "normal" within it, one is still partaking in folly, but one is doing it as a strategy, thus the folly is said to be controlled. The control is not to act in some sort of elevated way (like gurus and spiritual teachers often preach). We perform the same as everyone else, and thus we can move around in a type of camouflaged way. No one will have any idea what we really know, so no targets get placed on our back. We can then do the inner work we need to do in private, with a more clear energy from not "fighting" against all of the belief systems surrounding us.

Controlled Folly can be put into place upon seeing that the world (achievements or winning) are not the important concepts that we had previously believed. When all that goes on here is given an overlay of being equal, a new way of behaving is called for. But just because you see things in a new way, the other 8 billion do not. As mentioned above, the average person gets into trouble by trying to tell the rest of the world why they are wrong, but few (if any) ever come to see things in your "new way." So, in order to continue to interact with the masses, you have to appear to think and believe about the world the same as them. One learns to continue to act as their character has been built, yet they do not personalize any longer what happens from the action's act. A proponent of Advaita or Zen would suggest actions arise, but they are no longer the "do-er" of those actions. The action and them are separate. Controlled Folly is taking this idea one step further.

One is no longer looking to gain glory, riches or specialness from any of their actions. They might occur, but that is not the

---

94 Carlos Castaneda *A Separate Reality* chapter 5.

reason behind an action, only to see what is the most "efficient" way for the character to act in any moment. If a neighbor needs help with painting their fence, you can help to paint the fence, even though at your core you know that from the standpoint of Ultimate Reality there is no fence and no neighbor. We act the way everyone expects us to act, so we can navigate reality in the smoothest fashion around other people. It is an amazing way to keep interacting with the insane Matrix until the Exit door materializes. We keep being kind and helpful, but now we are not doing it so some god will give us "good boy or girl" check marks for us to get into heaven, we do it just because it is the best way to respond to an insane world.

I can say that the three Medicine Men that I spent time with appeared as incredibly ordinary in almost all of their interactions with me. They seemed no different than the woman at the post office, or the guy who would sell me shoes. It was only when being with them in a ceremonial place, such as in a sweat lodge, that they became very different. Their power showed up, things happened, and knowledge appeared. I realized that the power around them was always there, it's just that they just very carefully chose when and how to reveal the power so as to not have too many "prying eyes" on them.

Don Juan clearly points out that the key word to describe this practice comes from seeing the world as unimportant, which is not the same as worthless. He presents that all actions are equal (since they occur in a fictional holographic projection, my words) so one loses their self-importance in things like comparing and judging actions with others. All actions are equal in such a reality. Yet by choosing a pathway of reducing suffering for self and others, we simply respond to live in a more empathetic way (so in some opposition to the make up of the Matrix)...but even that idea might be an example of folly.

Richard Rose spoke about this subject privately with people he perceived who were at the point of understanding and implementing it, described the way he went about everything he did in the world as *acting as an actor.* Don Juan similarly stated,

"My acts are sincere, but they are only the acts of an actor." We have always been a type of actor, but now one is aware of this fact, so they now know "why" we are acting.

One does not implement Controlled Folly to "be an actor," or to "help out the cosmic director." One implements Controlled Folly to give the outwardly impression that they believe in realness of reality the same as everyone else, all the while residing in the Emptiness that is behind it all. This may seem like denial, or even a trick we are playing with ourselves, but it is none of these. We are both accepting the false world and at the same time not accepting it. Within the stage play called life on Earth, various chores need to get done, so we assure that they do. The end result is that the wood gets chopped and the water gets carried, but never any longer to we think that "we" chopped it, or "we" carried it, or even that it was important to do, just simply the tasks were called for to be done. If someone says that the barn has to be repaired today, even we know from a depth of seeing that nothing needs to be done right now or even done at all, yet if we choose to assist with the request to help, we fully agree that it is important and needs to be done now. We give the fullness of our help to complete that project, all the while knowing that it didn't matter in the grand scheme of the Divine Spark or the Pleroma if the barn was repaired or not. Today, tomorrow, or ever. Reality gets its actions, we get our interaction with the world, but we no longer give the Matrix various places to drop its hooks into us.

This topic, like everything else in this book, is very difficult to explain in words, and why I highly recommend reading chapter six of Castaneda's book. The back and forth conversation is perhaps the best presentation on acting in the world without being the "do-er" of the action. What should be said is this idea is not something to be used in order to justify negative behavior. That is not what this practice is for. It is about being able to smoothly fit in, with a world that you no longer fit into.

Granted should one come across another who has also had the realization of Emptiness, there would no need to use Controlled Folly with such a person, as you are now reside in a similar place of seeing. When no one else is present you can interact with such a person as a true equal and with complete honesty. Thus finding another with the realization of Emptiness becomes a great gift for both, as the two can share honestly and help understand one's personal pathway.

LISTENING

A core element of spiritual practice is usually placed on the sense of sight. Even Castaneda labeled the ability to know the depth about anything by the term Seeing. Granted, a few spiritual traditions do push feeling to the top of the list. Yet generally at the bottom of the "important senses" practice of all key traditions is listening. Which is odd, because Mr. Park, and a writer named Julian Johnson, both suggested that our way to the Totality was through the ears, not the eyes.

One of the many reasons that Mr. Park wanted us to follow a path of stillness was so that we could silence the regular mind long enough to hear what he called "the sound of the universe." He claimed that with enough stillness, one would hear this cosmic sound, which he claimed was similar to the hum of a computer. At the time, I was not seeing reality as a type of computer simulation, so I didn't take his suggestions too far. Now of course with a change in how I understand reality, his metaphor becomes more poignant. A few times, when very still, I have come across a very unique buzzing sound, nothing like tinnitus (ear ringing). It was a sound that seemed everywhere and nowhere. I am sure is what Mr. Park was pointing out.

The book *Path of Masters* was written by Julian Johnson in the 1930s about his time with what he declared was a spiritual master. While I do not agree with many messages of his work, there are a few areas in the book which are quite well presented, one being how everything in this reality (including all religions and spiritual traditions) are now covered with layers of distortion. Johnson's key message was that one needs what he calls "a living master" to end the reincarnation cycle (Exit the Matrix). Certainly, being able to spend time with someone who is at the Exit door (but has yet to walk out) can provide not just the steps that they took to reach the door, but also a type of transmission where the view at the door can be given to the acolyte. One consideration here is that anyone's true master is always their true self (Divine Spark), and even wisdom that comes from an external teacher has its origin within. In my view, a living master gives someone a much quicker pathway to turning on that Spark. Though I also believe that if the connection to what is True within is clear, then our Spark and its wisdom can be clearly "heard."

The reason Johnson claimed that the living master was important was to help direct the student to what he called the Audible Life Stream, and compared the sound to an electro-magnetic frequency. James claimed that this sound would be like a draw for us that we could follow, similar to the thread of Ariadne in the Labyrinth. However, this message has its belief that it is originating from a loving god. Mr. Park is also discussing this sound, but I do not recall he ever told us to "go" towards it. He just told us that it was important to hear the universe. What if this sound is not coming from outside of the Matrix, but is the sound of the workings of the core computer at the heart of running the entire Matrix? Perhaps that is the core practice to try and learn to hear it. Just as there is a white light trap that occurs in the after-life, perhaps there is a type of humming sound that is also a type of hypnotic draw for those not aware of it. I mention this because this is something I am currently working on.

*

PRACTICE

Those who have read my books or listened to various interviews I have done know that I went through a seven or eight year period where I was doing some type of practice almost eight hours a day. They wonder if I still do so. And my answer is not anything anymore that I would classify as that steady. When I feel the urge to do Qi Gong or a recapitulation, I do so, but nothing is structured and daily as it used to be. I do a practice when the call comes in the moment to do it.

One element that I do practice each day is what I would call my evening close down and protection before going to sleep. It involves a connection with our Divine Spark. Why is the topic of connection with the Divine Spark so powerful?

I began the first evening of the last intensive I had with asking those present to have an examination of the Matrix while in a meditative-type state. I had them see the confines of it, and the force which is "binding" them. Because of the group presence, none of them felt any fear during this examination, even when they got some views of the dark entities that "control" the Matrix.

Then I had them see and connect with their Divine Spark, which many then described an overwhelming power that they felt as soon as this happened. A power and clarity that had always been there, but which they felt they had previously been distracted from connecting with. With that power, while they could still see these forces and beings of the Matrix, but they now KNEW that there was nothing any of these beings could "do" to them. All they could do was attempt to scare them, but as long as they stayed rooted in this "Truth" of who they really were, the beings were just a scare tactic designed to draw their attention back to the Matrix. When they returned their awareness back to the house where the sessions were going on, I can say that many of them were almost beaming. I don't use the word "beaming" lightly, as it was a reflection of the Fire/Spark they had made the connection with. The beam was their own Self. And it was very noticeable.

One of the things I've learned about the Fire/Spark is that it can help us sleep better. While twenty years ago I would do some various protections before going to sleep, over time I became somewhat lazy with this pre-sleep practice. Around 2021, I began to notice a large intrusion of archons starting to get into my night time dreams. They had been there for 25 years of course, but these intrusions tended to happen perhaps only once a month. They were not so much creating a type of nightmare type scenario (though at times those were there as well), but often were just disguising themselves as someone I knew from the past, usually an old friend or ex-girlfriend that I had not seen in a long time. Since my "guard was down" as I was glad to see and old friend, it was like I was forgetting to see just what was behind any of the faces appearing in the dream. When I woke up many mornings, I felt off-kilter, and with odd thoughts in my head. I remembered the dream that I just had, and having a meeting with my old acquaintances, and quickly realized that the meeting was terribly strange. I also quickly realized that I had not been interacting' with the "image" of an old friend, I was interacting with an archon using my friend as a mask for its attempted manipulations.

Some days it took hours to realize this happened, and each time I had to in a sense "clean out" the dream from the night before. Shortly thereafter, my energy would stabilize. When this began to happen more and more often, I realized that I needed to catch this manipulation before it began, to put a type of protective layer up before I went to sleep. But I ran into a problem. When I did this twenty years ago, I would surround myself a type of coloured light which connected to some sort of what I thought was a spirit being or protector. I realized in 2022 that these "beings" were of course archons in disguise. What that meant is that for almost ten years of this practice, I had been asking for protection from the very beings I was asking to be protected from. A neat game being played.

So I made a drastic shift. I decided instead before going to sleep that I would try to make a connection to my Divine Spark. I feel her awake and aware. And I then asked for a golden energy to radiate from That Which I AM (her) to come and act as a type of protective shield in all areas that my fictional character exists in (material, etheric, astral, etc.). I also add in one or two other small elements (which are my own personal addition), and which each of you can add your own additions), and then go to sleep. I tend to wake up fine on mornings when I did this, having had a clear and deep sleep. And on the other hand when I forgot to do these pre-sleep preparations, I did not sleep as well and sometimes had cleansing work to do in the morning.

Why I believe this practice is so valuable is because the protective energy force for the sleep is being generated by the Divine Spark, and not being asked by something outside of the True. Truth is always more powerful than false, so by making that the core of what such protection is means that it has a power beyond what we can think. You can take this one practice and turn it into something even bigger of course, this was just something about sleep to get people started, as I know many out there are presenting how much trouble they have sleeping. This is something that has helped me so I thought I would share it.

*

I want to finish this very important chapter with another reminder how difficult it is to first see, and then navigate this very strange reality. No wonder so many eventually give up their seeking, not from lack of ability, but from being overwhelmed by the sheer volume of the layers of deception. That is why if one does not have a clear Intention to reach Truth, Liberation, Totality, or whatever capitalized word you would like to use...it is easy to wind up in quicksand.

Yet, no matter where in the quicksand you are, you can get out and keep moving. It becomes finding this more real Awareness, for that is what you can trust. That Awareness can be described as Emptiness, and it can also be termed a type of Stillness. But a Stillness that is active, not passive or empty. Empty is full of possibility, and it is this conundrum that must be worked through. The way to do that is via Silent Empathetic Detachment.

As much as there is the challenging work of spiraling inward, so too is there a requirement for stillness. Times of just being and perceiving. Not attempting to get anywhere, do anything, achieve anything. I will end with a favourite quote from one of Japan's most famous Zen poets,

"Too lazy to be ambitious,

I let the world take care of itself.

Ten days' worth of rice in my bag;

a bundle of twigs by the fireplace.

Why chatter about delusion and enlightenment?

Listening to the night rain on my roof,

I sit comfortably, with both legs stretched out."[95]

\- Ryokan

---

95 https://www.poemhunter.com/poem/too-lazy-to-be-ambitious/

Chapter 8

SILENT EMPATHETIC

DETACHMENT

"My barn having burned to the ground,
I can now see the moon."[96]
- Mizuta Masahide

I will walk a completely new path for a while, and I will document that journey in a new work, perhaps as a type of memoir. The key areas of process will be silence and detachment. But not the way people tend to think about those two words. During the course of the last 25 years, I have had periods where I have done this type of work, from sitting still for several hours beside a river, in pitch-dark rooms for the entire night, or hours of gazing. This stage is a bit different than that, or you could say that those types of practices were the warm ups.

Part of my work going forward will be an examination of texts. Some will be those which classify as Christian Hesychian (the Greek goddess of stillness and quiet), as well as Asian tests such as the *Ashtavakra Gita* and the *Faith Mind Sutra*. I will put the suggestions within them into practice and test their value directly.

---

96 https://en.wikipedia.org/wiki/Mizuta_Masahide

I am calling this testing period Silent Empathetic Detachment. I will discuss these three words in this chapter as to what I mean by them, as opposed to what the standard spiritual community means by them, and how they can be of value on our Ultimate Pathway Home.

*

NOISE

> *"Noise is the most impertinent of all forms of interruption. It is not only an interruption, but also a disruption of thought."*[97] - Arthur Schopenhauer

If one thing has defined modern society in the last fifty or so years, it may not be the rise of computers, or zombie-people walking into streetlamp poles as they stare at their phones. At the core level, the modern world might be classified as one of excessive noise. Noise is different from sounds. We can be in nature and the sounds we hear (a running stream, the chirp of birds, the wind blowing through the trees) do not create a sense of disharmony or negatively affect our nervous system. These sounds calm us down almost instantly. Any city is the opposite of this, a cesspool of noise: car horns, jackhammers, helicopters. Then walk into any cafe or restaurant and all you hear is high-pitched animated conversation, overtop of music that is forcing everyone to speak even louder. Most people today do not even just walk when in a city; they have to have earphones on so that some blaring music can be pumped into their heads. Then just as one needs a break for the constant sounds of the modern world, they go home and turn on their TV or computer to view a movie or program to get another dose of guns, car crashes, crying and yelling.

The increase of noise is not by accident. One of my original mentors was John Anthony West, author of *Serpent in the*

---

97 Arthur Schopenhauer essay "On Noise"

Sky. In that book on the symbolist understanding of Ancient Egypt, he presented, *"the daily life of city dwellers today is technically a form of mild but persistent torture, in which victimizers and victims are equally affected. And all call it 'progress."*[98] Things have gone far downhill in the noise department since he wrote that in 1979. Places of harmonious sounds are almost gone now in the human city world.

The Pursuit of Silence in a World Full of Noise is a 2011 book by George Prochnik. It presents his search of going around the world looking for people who still value to be in a noise-free environment. Excessive noise is not good for the human nervous system, which can quickly become overly stressed from excessive sound. Just one trip down a busy street can get your entire nervous system out of whack for hours. Done day after day, this overloaded stress on the body can lead to all sort of health issues. There is a reason that in the ancient world, one of the first elements of the healing process was the addition of harmonious sounds to the patient, to stop the stressful sound vibration the ill body was presently producing. Noise, and especially noise that the mind recoils from due to its disturbance to inner equilibrium, puts the entire human form in a type of flight or fight state. People are walking with anxiety from the noise that surrounds them daily. No wonder so few can see reality as it really is, they are bombarded with noise day after day, and their inner world is just in coping mechanism from it all.

So when the average person says they are looking to achieve some silence, what they really mean is they want to find a location where they can spend time without a lot of excessive noise. And that is a valuable first step. We need to actually have the "space" to be able to hear what is going on within our body. We need a space where the dose of electro-magetic frequencies are less so that our nervous system can be somewhat still. There is a reason that in the Greek world Hermes was the over-seer of the nervous system. For one has a challenging pathway to wisdom (Hermes) if the nervous system can not be still and calm. Those are first steps on the pathway of Knowing.

---

98 John Anthony West, *Serpent in the Sky* pg 26

Noise is also related to the idea of being busy (no time for inner stillness). Ask someone how he or she is and the usual answer is either "fine" (which means I have no opinion) or they might respond that they are "busy." They are not presenting this message as a plea for help as in "I am so busy, I have to figure out how to get my house in order." No, they are wearing that message like some sort of badge of honor, "Look at me, I have so many things to do, so I must be important." This is such a strange way of presenting oneself as doing well. How often would you hear the opposite of this, when you ask someone how they are receiving a response of, "I'm quiet, not doing much. Just sitting around with my dog or cat, or being alone in the woods a lot." To find real stillness and simplicity seems almost forgotten by most of the modern world. There is a reason the message of the old monks, both East and West, was that only in silence can one hear God. Of course we are not going to fall for the "hearing" of anything from the Matrix, but you get the point.

But this chapter is about Silence, which is different than the absence of sounds or "being in a quiet location."

*

SILENCE/HESYCHIA

"Having no destination, I am never lost."[99]
Ikkyu

Silence is the base of the entire process. And it might also be one of the most distorted of teachings of the entire spiritual community. In the beginning stages of the search, finding some inner silence is not for the sake of silence itself (as presented in meditation classes) but to give the witnessing awareness some space so it can examine thought. We slow the mind down so that "we" can see thoughts, feelings and emotions clearly for the first time, and have the capacity to ask where does this come from, or why do

---

99 Zen poems of Ikkyu

I have this emotion? Be clear enough to look out into the world to be able to see it without inner dialogue, thus perceive it as it is. By teachers telling students that their goal is to have a still, calm mind, they are actually blocking this early stage of the process that is meant to take place. Silence for the sake of silence is much later in the process. The early part is to gain some space from noise (inner and outer) in order to look at things for the first time.

Making the search for silence itself the core of practice is a trick. The spiritual gurus have taken something near the end of the process (sitting in silence when one is withdrawing energy from the material realm to place it all on what might be called the spiritual) and turned that state into the pathway to reach it. The claim is that an enlightened person sits in silence all the time, so if you want to reach that, you need to imitate what he or she is doing. This of course is the complete opposite of how such a man or woman reached that place. No matter how many times Rich Little impersonated Jimmy Stewart or Richard Nixon, he never once became Jimmy Stewart or Richard Nixon. He was always Rich Little impersonating a celebrity. It is the same with those who attempt to sit in silence to become like the Buddha. It does not work that way. You do not imitate a rung of Jacob's Ladder, you do the work on the current rung you are on to reach the next level yourself. People do not want to deal with the work of true spiraling inward that is required to really move up the spiritual ladder, so they prefer to pretend their way to the top of the mountain. Given that being happy is the number one goal of the majority of seekers, it is no surprise that false promises are big sellers. And getting some space away from noise (either outer or inner) tends to make one feel better, so it seems like the "thing to do."

Stillness however is different from silence. This is happens when Awareness can shift from the physical form to the deep being that we are. Because the Divine Spark can be personified by being still, but this has also been distorted by putting it in a coma. Sleeping Beauty asleep is a type of still, but it is externally forced upon it, while in its natural state she is Stillness. There is a difference. It is this place that Asian texts such as *the Ashtavakra*

Gita is pointing towards. That Stillness is not an activity, it is the center of one's true Being.

That is why having one's house in order (especially the mind) is so important. For should we reach this point of Stillness within, we don't want anything "floating around" that can still operate as something to grasp onto that can pull us from this center. You can also say that when one reaches this Silence, it will reveal the state of our "house."

I want to share a bit of an overview on what is known as the path of Hesychia, the Greek word for stillness. Well, actually, it is the name of the Greek goddess for stillness and peace, but today the goddess part tends to be ignored. Hesychia has perhaps become the key element of Eastern Orthodox Christianity and presents its roots to those known as the Desert Fathers and Mothers of 1500 to 2000 years ago.

The historical claim is that many early monks, with famous names such as St. Anthony and John Climacus, left various Egyptian towns were they were born (the reason given due to persecution of Christianity), to live solitary hermit-lives in the Egyptian or Palestinian desert. This Roman persecution of Christians is only claimed to have lasted a few decades, yet people continued to leave the towns for the desert. This increased as monasteries formed around the original renunciants. If this movement away from towns happened to get away from persecution, why did this practice continue even though the persecution ended? Perhaps they chose to leave only because the ever expanding cities of the day were creating too much noise for their required inner examinations. There may be another reason for their going into the desert as I will discuss in the Anthony Additional Material.

It is normally presented that these hermits were seeking God or oneness. A key question at the heart of this material is to ask to which oneness or god was their work of silence directed towards? As we have seen, no matter the methods, the direction tends to all trace back to Lucifer and the Matrix. Of course, the person does not believe that is where they are sending their prayers or energy. Nevertheless, one's belief does not matter. What matters is the depth of understanding of how this realm is structured, and the specifics of where one's intent is really directed. The Desert Hesychists, at least in how the texts are presented, seem to have very much believed that a loving creator made the material realm, and in many cases it seems that the "god of all objects" was where their intention was flowing towards.

One of the most popular of the early Fathers is John Climacus, who is the originator of the text *The Ladder of Divine Ascent* (this ladder being Jacob's). He was a 6th–7th-century Christian monk from a monastery on Mount Sinai who now has a feast day on March 30. His text has three sections (steps), which include 30 virtues (rungs) which explain subjects such as exile, solitude, silence, detachment, and obtaining virtue.[100] At the beginning of this book he presents; *"Our God and King is good, ultra-good and all-good (it is best to begin with God in writing to the servants of God). Of the rational beings created by Him and honoured with the dignity of free-will, some are His friends, others are His true servants, some are worthless, some are completely estranged from God, and others, though feeble creatures are equally His opponents."*[101]

This same good god idea was still in place in the 1330s when Gregory of Palamas presented his famous responses to elders in the church who were critical of Hesychianism. In Palamas' very interesting responses, he at one point very clearly wanted to indicate that the Hesychians were not dualists (Manicheans or Cathars) when he responded to a question about nous (ability for deep awareness) being in a body and stated, *"Brother, have you not heard that the Apostle says, your body is the temple of the Holy Spirit which is in us'...Then why should anyone who is endowed with nous think it is improper to bring their nous into a body whose very nature it is to be the dwelling*

---

100 https://en.wikipedia.org/wiki/John_Climacus

101 St. John Climacus, Translated by Archimandrite Lazarus Moore *The Ladder of Divine Ascent* (Harper & Brothers, 1959) section 1.1

place of God?...the truth is, brother, that these words apply more properly to those heretics who claim that the body is an evil thing made by the Wicked One. As for us, we believe that it is bad for the body to be caught up in carnal thoughts. But it is not in itself wrong for the nous to be in the body, since the body is not evil."[102]

Now of course we do not have their direct words presented to us, for the current texts are claimed part of an original oral tradition that were later written down. The Middle Ages was a time when much of history and religion was going through tremendous revisions. My sense is that all of the writings of those we call the Desert Fathers were quite likely edited at some point, and perhaps any "heretical" ideas (such as an evil creator) purged from the writing. The point is that we don't really know for sure why these men and women went to the desert, or what they really did there. We only have what the book compilers in the Middle Ages have told us about them, which might be true or not.

This brings us to another question. Why does one need to renounce the material world, if a wonderful loving God made it? This is where their ideas do not make sense. If their ultimate goal was to join in unison with the Creator of matter, then there should be no need to live the life of a hermit. One should immerse oneself into the world of objects and experiences completely. My sense is that the origin of this movement to the desert was something very Gnostic or Cathar at its core, that in time (like all systems) were infiltrated and distorted. I do not doubt that many went into the desert under the belief of renouncing the world, to join with the Creator of that world, but logically that makes no sense of action. I suggest that be kept in mind when looking into any of the ideas within various texts, unless we know the underlying motivation for one's practice, it is hard to be able to determine the value of that practice for Exiting the Cave. We are not looking to improve our prison cell, we are looking to break out and never return.

No matter which side of the argument one might be on regarding the reasons for the hermetic life in the desert, there is

---

102 Gregory of Palamas in *Holy Hesychia* translated by Robin Amis in response 2.1 pg
   30

useful information in these texts and it should not be instantly rejected due to some possible foundational errors that may or may not have been at the original core.

One area I found very interesting in looking into Hesychian philosophy is that their work was far beyond just silence and detachment as is often presented. They had a three-step process in a variety of areas. This is similar to the three-step process of Mr. Park, Richard Rose's Jacob's Ladder, and the system of the Medieval alchemists. These three stages for Hesychists are presented as Katharsis (purification), Theoria (illumination), and Theosis (becoming God-like).[103]

The Purification stage has its focus on the rejection of all non-pure or tempting thoughts (known as thieves), whom John of the Ladder described as looking to "steal one's cluster of grapes." A great amount of time at this stage was directed towards having clear attention. A big part of their early work was the reciting of what is known as the Jesus Prayer, a short sentence (Lord Jesus Christ, son of God, have mercy on me, the sinner) that is repeated over and over as a mantra. My main concern with this prayer is the belief created that one IS a sinner, and thus there would be no examination of the origin of the Matrix to see if Lucifer and his archons may be the real origin of any so-called sins.

The second stage, Illumination had at is root great mental discipline, and of guarding the mind (from the thieves previously removed but still looking for entry). The teachers were clear not to try this part of the work too early, or it could become something that causes more delusion rather than clearing them out. The final stage of Theosis can be thought of as taking the now clear mind that is guarded and rise it to the Divine. This raising and connecting is often presented as reaching "light." It is this final stage when the work of Stillness calls for its most focused action.

John Climacus claimed that stillness, "I*s the rejection of all noisiness as something that will trouble the depths of the soul. The final point is when one has no longer a fear of noisy disturbance,*

____

103 Information on the three stages can be found at
    https://en.wikipedia.org/wiki/Hesychasm Wikipedia

when one is immune to it.[104] The task is to learn how to keep awareness of what is happening within at a top level, no matter if we are alone, in a line at the grocery store, or in the midst of a challenging dinner party. The time completely alone is to sharpen this skill, so it can be as strong when in the world of people.

*

Richard Rose suggested that the path gets more intense the further one goes,

> *"This is what happens when you start backing away from what is unreal. When you start out it is a wide path. There is all sorts of garbage you can get rid of. As you go on, the path gets narrower, and the things you have to let go of get very precious to you. Finally there is no escape, you go through the funnel and that's all there is to it."*[105] - Richard Rose

I fully understand the reasons for people wanting to extricate themselves completely from human society. Once one sees that all systems in society are built and run by beings whose main purpose it is to confuse, distort and create suffering, then why would someone want to have any part of it? Thus the question from many who have seen through these layers, why stick around society at all? I have felt the same many times myself in the past. A complete hermetic life is one thing, but even a monastery is not a solitary pursuit. There are other monks, communal chores, daily songs and the like. So there really is fully leaving society, as in living completely alone day after day. All other options still involve some interaction with the human world.

My sense is that the focus should be less on the need to fully leave society (unless things get so difficult such as wartime), but to find a way of life where one is not fully immersed in society constantly, and at the same time has ways of personal alone periods from it. When I lived alone, I used to take one week periods

---

104 John Climacus Stanza 27
105 Dave Gold, Bart Marshall *After the Absolute*

where I never spoke to anyone, saw anyone, did my walks during the night hours when few people were up, just to spend seven days without interactions. However is that really the way to live an entire life day after day? Those in my life who shared their wisdom with me did not seem to think so.

Mr. Park and Richard Rose both spoke about the value in spending periods of time alone in solitude (up to one month for those who can put aside that amount of time) in order to go within. Longer than that and one might be considered to be running away. Recall that Native Medicine Men still go on regular vision quests (which they call fasts) where they sit still in a natural power spot for usually 3-4 days at a time. These opportunities of solitude give one the space to be able to hear what is happening within, while at later stages of the process, it is so that one can sit with Being.

The periods alone are also to sharpen this ability to be in the silent center, so as to treat this experience to act as a Controlled Folly when re-entering the world, which will allow (even in the midst of an action) to operate from a stillness. I can say that I have seen this many times in my life, the ability to be in action, noise and activity yet remain still within. "Charge up that battery" while on retreat, in order to make it work more efficiently around people.

A woman I used to know back in Canada worked a normal 9-5, five days a week job. However, on Saturday and Sunday, she stayed in her apartment in complete silence. She did not answer the phone, go anywhere, and most of the time just sat in stillness. If I wanted to talk with her about something on the weekend, I would have to wait until Monday to get in touch with her. For her, the only way she could be in a calm stable state when interacting with city life during the week, was to retreat away from it every weekend.

But to the crunch. What is really meant by this seeking of solitude and letting go of noise, is not about just being in places without sounds. First off there will most never be a place without sounds, even the forest has sounds (even though they are harmonious). Some might suggest that the word silence is meant to indicate that the mind of the practitioner, thus to sit with a blank mind. But this is much deeper.

It is a work to sink back fully into what we are. Which is Emptiness. It is the still place where Everything exists in possibility, yet not manifested into the material realm. It is not "outside" of the Matrix, but we could say at the point of being in the Awareness as the Divine Spark. Thus the more of this Stillness becomes our moment by moment experience, the external world becomes less "intrusive" to this inner world. Being in Stillness has nothing to do with anything happening in the material world, but relates to a sinking back into what we Are. From that place the material realm is seen for what it is, a projected theater of far less significance than the Stillness. It is something beyond words. Thoughts have no place there. But one does not reach Stillness from having no thoughts, this is the error of how it is presented. One reaches the point of true Stillness, and the thoughts are forced to stop on their own, as happened in the canyon for me.

*

ANTHONY

Perhaps the most well-known of those who chose to live in the desert was Anthony. He became immortalized, firstly as being the first to have a book written about him in the 4th century, and secondly for the story of his temptations becoming one of the most depicted images in Renaissance artwork (painted by such famous artists as Giovanni and Michelangelo). Generally the paintings have Anthony in a cave, with an alter that includes books and a skull, being tormented by various demons or Earthly temptations while he is resisting all of them. Resisting temptation is related to detachment and release of desire.

His story has similarities to the temptations presented to the both Buddha and Jesus. According to the chronicler of the Anthony story, Athanasius, the Devil fought Anthony by afflicting him first with boredom and laziness, then phantoms of women, and finally with demons and wild beasts which beat him to almost the moment of death. He resisted and rejected all through the power of prayer. Eventually the temptations and attacks stopped. Anthony had resisted long enough that the Devil had nothing remaining and left.

There are a few unique paintings of the Anthony story that seem to depict him at the end of his process (he no longer seems to be tempted). The point of these paintings is that if we reject the Matrix lies and demons long enough, they they lose their steam of control and deception. Yet the way the images show, if you look closely at the symbolism, is that Anthony is doing far more than just his rejection of objects or experiences in the Matrix. What is really going on is that Anthony is detaching from Anthony, as much as the demons or temptations that are being manifested.

Anthony is presented in *the Philokalia* as having one of the best quotations around the power of commitment I have come across, *"Intelligent people must ceaselessly remember that by enduring slight and passing sufferings in this life, we gain the greatest joy and eternal bliss after death. Therefore, if a man falls when struggling against the passions and wishing to be crowned by God, he should not lose heart and remain fallen, despairing of himself, but should rise and begin again the struggle to win his crown. Until his last breath he should rise whenever he has fallen; for bodily toil is a weapon used by the virtues, and brings salvation to the soul."*[106] That is power, and that power to never turn away from his Ultimate Intention is one of the main reasons for his overcoming of the various temptations and fears thrown at him.

I have a small section on Anthony, around some curiosities about where he was claimed to be in the Egyptian Desert (and if Ancient Egyptian sites were involved in his choices), as well as a mention of a connection to the Rennes Le Chateau mystery will be a part of the Additional Material.

---

106 *Philokalia* Anthony 76 "On the Character of Men and on the Virtuous Life," pg 238

DETACHMENT

> *"Real detachment means the death of preferences of all kinds, even those that seem to other men as the very proofs of virtue and good taste."*[107] - Evelyn Underhill

The story of Anthony naturally leads to a word much thrown around in modern spiritual literature, detachment. This is another of the misunderstood words. Detachment tends to be symbolized as ridding yourself of your desire for a BMW or finding Mr. Right. However, those actions are just altering preferences of the actor on the stage. Non-attachment as it is thought of today is not the way to Liberation, but a by-product of it. If non-attachment were the key to waking up, then every homeless person would be enlightened by now.

Letting go of things, be they clothes one does not wear, or childhood parental beliefs, is not really what is meant by detachment in the ultimate sense. The core attachment is not of a person to an object or experience, the attachment is of the person to the person having the attachment. The final detachment that has to happen is to release the attachment one has to the false self. John Kent presented Rose's view of detachment wonderfully,

> *"One should learn to watch all that is before one's mental view with complete detachment and resist the urge to interfere with the life-experience one is witnessing, and even to note that the desire to intervene derives also from this person that is seen and is not of oneself (meaning the inner or anterior self). This passive backing away from oneself occurs while respecting the paradox that one must*

---

107 Evelyn Underhill, *Mysticism: A Study in Nature and the Development of Spiritual Consciousness*

Modern spirituality has taken two erroneous positions. The first is that physical objects are a problem and that one must give them all away and live with just the clothes on one's back to feel any sort of freedom. Of course there is some truth in that. The more objects we have, the more pies we have fingers in, the more mental-activity and grasping there likely will be. While we don't actually have to get rid of every object, we have to see that all things we have are "possessions." As such we have to be ready to let them go at a moment's notice and not to feel sadness for their disappearance, yet at the same time not feel them as somehow a burden. As I first presented in *Falling For Truth,* if I am digging a hole, it is nice to have a shovel rather than use my hands. I appreciate that the shovel is there. When the hole digging is over I have no need to continue to "have" the shovel. Until the next time it is needed, it is fine to be used by someone else. Tribal cultures tended to view various tools as less of personal possessions, but things available for the entire tribe when needed. They would not need 50 shovels for 50 families for example, when 5 shared ones might be sufficient for all.

Granted, the great spiritual teachers of history were not hording objects and money, building magnificent temples, or gaining self-importance. They needed little from material reality, only their basic sustainment. They know what is "required" and what is excess. That might be one of the key sentences of understanding: to know what is required and what is excess. If we feel we need a car, we get a simple and reliable one, not twelve sports cars. If we choose to live in one location, then there will be some sort of structure, but it will not be a mansion, temple, or anything extravagant. Fools Crow lived simply, Richard Rose lived

---

108 John Kent *Path* chapter 14

with only the kitchen of his house having any heat on during the winter. Lakota medicine man Clayton would always give away any money that I gave him, but would accept a bag of groceries for his empty fridge. Anything more than required was not needed and thus if it appeared, was given away. This is the opposite of the standard world where the message is to get as much as you can, and hoard up wealth and objects for that is the only way to be happy and powerful. The standard world is about pushing people to find ways to be better and above everyone else, the great teachers about how to find ways to live in a simple equal way with reality.

Usually those who go into extremes of detachment living, at one time had great desires for "goodies" of the world, be it food, money, sex, or power. Thus when they get a hold of this realization, they see they are on the far end of the grandfather clock pendulum, so the mind tries to balance this by swinging as far to the other side as possible, extreme asceticism. This is how the dual mind works, feel it is too for one way, it pushes to too far the other way. That tends to be what happens with either worldly excess or renunciation of the world. As has been suggested many times, the work is between-ness, to constantly keep dual forces at bay. If one sees they are living in excess, becoming an ascetic will not work, as eventually the pendulum will again swing to the other side. What one must look for is the balance point between, where there is no asceticism or desire for excess. The pendulum would then become still. Perhaps that metaphor can better explain why the ideas of Stillness and Detachment actually go together.

This inability to find the still point of the dual pendulum, is what is at the foundation of creating all sorts of rules for oneself (or others). At the still point between extremes, one knows what they need, and what is excess. No thought needs to be given to it, what is needed is obvious. If a human is in this realm, there are requirements for some things. Even the Cathars who saw every object in reality as coming from an evil deity, still ate food, had a blanket and had a fire burning to keep warm at night. Like everything else in this realm, there is nothing wrong with food or sex, or trees, or swimming, or singing, or birds. They are just projected objects and experiences in the realm. They are false from the standpoint of the Pleroma, but the various rules of how or why one should interact with this reality makes things very confusing. Why should one reject "nice" food to eat only simple food? What is the determination of what food is "simple" enough to eat? Why eat some food, but completely renounce sex? Why then not be like food and reject "nice" sex and have only "simple" sex? You can see the contradictions within all the rules that are rarely presented into a logical framework.

*

TEXTS OF STILLNESS

The *Faith Mind Sutra*, also known as the Hsin Hsin Ming is ascribed as being written by Zen Patriarch Seng Ts'an around 600AD.[109] The first Asian text I read thirty years ago was the *Tao Te Ching*, because it was the most well-known. I found it a rather average text, but because it was so highly regarded I felt the problem had to be my level of understanding. But when I came across the two texts mentioned above, I realized that these were true classics. The Faith Mind is just 27 stanzas long, but packs a lot of punch for so few words. It presents things in a very clear way, such as how it discusses detachment,

> *"If you wish to know Truth, hold no opinions. To judge and choose is the disease of the mind. When Truth goes un-observed, the mind roils with self-centered striving. No good can come of this."*

> *"Do not become entangled in outer life, nor indulge in feelings of detachment. Serenely abide in What Is, and all such dualities disappear...."*[110] - Faith Mind Sutra

---

109 The translation of these texts I have chosen appears in Bart Marshall's *The Perennial Way*. I have done this partially by having Bart as a spiritual friend on the path, but more because his personal realization of Emptiness allows him to translate the text in a way that those without such a realization cannot do.

110 *Faith Mind* stanzas 2 and 4 in Bart Marshall's *Perennial* pg147

In the case of the Faith Mind quote above, it is suggesting that as long as the mind is operating in a dual way within reality; either enjoying the beautiful side or afraid of the ugly side, the Matrix "has you." The trick is to not put any importance or value on anything the character does or experiences in the Matrix. The quote is neither suggesting to be focused on what is happening in life, nor to attempt to be detached from it. Doing either will in a sense be putting importance on anything going on in reality, and as mentioned in the last chapter, only when seeing the "non importance" of what happens in reality can one act as the moment requires.

The Ashtavakra Gita is one of the most magnificent spiritual texts written. It is the presentation of a conversation between master Ashtavakra, and his disciple King Jankara. The text begins with Jankara asking, "How is liberation attained?" Ashtavakra answers him as to the method, after which Jankara declares himself enlightened. However, Ashtavakra sees holes in this supposed claim, which Jankara continually attempts to prove his "completion." Ashtavakra and Jankara go back and forth, until after 100 full lines of dialogue (in section 18) Jankara's spiritual ego finally shatters and he reaches the state he had falsely claimed to be in at the beginning of the Gita.

> *"Give up desire, which is the enemy. Give up prosperity, which is born of mischief and good works. Be indifferent. Look upon friends, lands, wealth, houses, wives, gifts – and all apparent good fortune – as a passing show, as a dream lasting three to five days.*
>
> *Where there is desire, there is the world. Be firm in non-attachment. Be free of desire. Be happy. Bondage and desire are the same. Destroy desire and be free. Only by detaching from the world does one joyfully realize Self.*

You are One, Awareness itself. The universe is not aware, nor is anything in it. In reality, it does not exist. Even ignorance is unreal. What is left to know? Attached as you have been to kingdoms, sons, wives, bodies, pleasures, life after life, still they are now lost forever.

Prosperity, pleasure, pious deeds...Enough! In the dreary forest of the world, the mind finds no rest. For how many lifetimes have you done hard and painful labour with body, mind and speech? It is time to stop."[111] - Ashtavakra Gita

One of the key elements of the exchange is to present that desire is an enemy to awakening. The spiritual community puts its focus on fear as the bad guy, not desire. That is because the modern spiritual marketplace is set up to provide ways for people to get their deepest desires fulfilled. They sell enlightenment or a new car as the same things in the marketplace. It is all about getting more things for you, so that that you can reach your "potential," "improve," "fix some problem," and become powerful, important, or just elevated from others.

Actually, it is not really desire itself that is a problem. When we are thirsty, having a desire for water is a good thing. The problem is that this desire mechanism has been altered by the ego as a way to attempt to obtain objects or experiences that will make us feel better, or said another way, provide dopamine releases in the brain. That is what most desires are, a chase for a feeling, then linking that feeling to an outer object or experience. Thus we do not want to eliminate the desire mechanism entirely, it serves a purpose. What this passage is getting towards is any desire that is not coming from a quite logical place of what is currently needed by the body-mind. What else beyond that is required? What excess is required? That is the question to keep in mind, what is required currently, right now?

---

111 *Ashtavakra Gita* 10, from Bart Marshall *Perennial Way* pg 117

In the above stanza, Ashtavakra claims that all of the world is a dream, a passing show. Thus, his point is why focus and chase after desires, when the very things you desire are illusion? That is another reason the modern world has pushed video games on young people, they want the idea in the subconscious that the "attainment" of illusionary things is valuable. The text also claims, "Where there is desire, there is the world." The world of objects is dependent on our projection to keep it running and drawing our attention to it. If we drop our desires, then the objects of the physical world lose their luster and we start to ignore them. In addition, when one begins to ignore the physical world, they are being like Buddha under the Bodhi tree, St. Anthony in the Desert, or Christ on the mountain. It seems like we are turning our back on temptation, but since the focus towards those objects is what reality is built on, in a way, those desires are also building the entire Matrix.

Reducing the grab towards any desire will not cause standard reality to disappear, but there will be a subtle movement of energy from its normal direction (outward towards objects) to inward, strengthening of the pathway to the Divine Spark. Energy flows where attention goes is the saying, and that is one of the many things this small sample of the Ashtavakra Gita is pointing at.

Lastly, the text asks how many lifetimes has one followed the acquisition of desires in the world? Obviously none of those lives have led to the ending of the reincarnation cycle, or one would not be here having this life experience. Therefore, the text is asking why not try a different approach from the one being lived by everyone all through history. The call to stop following the normal pattern of living for the dealing with the Matrix. This is not calling to ignore reality; it is calling to put one's energy focus on that which is greater.

PROVIDENCE HYMN

I felt that one key examination in this final chapter should be to discuss the final section of *the Apocryphon of John.* The final part of this document, known as "The Providence Hymn" tends to be ignored by most commentators. Prior to this, the text mostly refers to the story of the Pleroma, the Fallen Creator, the creation of the Matrix, and the entrapment of the Celestial Man (Fire). The ending Hymn is different and I recommend you read the complete version of it yourself.[112] What I will do is present the most important parts for the discussion.

This "Providence Hymn" is describing the pathway Home. It is describing the call to awaken and return to one's original light (Fire). If you can get to the point where you "Become" every word of this hymn, no other books or texts would be needed.

This hymn itself is giving an overview of the coming into the material realm of Providence (a female deity from the Pleroma) for the purpose of awakening and freeing the Divine Sparks that the earlier part of the Apocryphon presented as having become trapped. Interestingly, it is not a Christ male figure there that is depicted as entering, but that which is feminine, perhaps seen as a form of Sophia. On the other hand, perhaps it could be thought of as a feminine force that enters into the masculine seeker (all seekers in the material whether male or female are masculine compared to the feminine versions of the Divine Spark). Providence thus could also perhaps be seen symbolically as Sleeping Beauty speaking to the prince.

Providence presents its information as an unseen voice and first begins by defining itself by saying *"I existed from the first, walked down every possible road, and became like my own human children."* Providence later indicates that she came into the Matrix realm three times. Then comes a critical comment, *"I am the remembering of the fullness. I walked into the place of greatest*

---

112 http://www.gnosis.org/naghamm/apocjn-davies.html , to follow along with the
    words in Coptic you can see https://marcion.sourceforge.net/nag-hammadi-
    library/apocryphon-of-john-nh2-en.html

darkness and on down. I entered the central part of the prison." These lines give more indication of our realm and what this voice is. Providence claims to have come into the simulation, which it refers to as the greatest darkness, *"I hid because of their evil. They did not recognize me."* Likely, the evil refers to the archons, but it can mean also that force within the material reality that follows the archon's directives. By saying she entered the central part of the prison stipulates two things. One is that the Matrix realm is a prison, and secondly that there is a central part of it. What this central part might be is not presented.

Providence being within the evil realm seems to have created problems for its stability, for twice the text claims that *"The foundations of chaos quaked."* It does not describe what the foundations of the chaos are, or why they seemed to be impacted by Providence's appearance. However, the text indicates that Providence has the power to cause this realm to "collapse" and can "destroy everything." On the first two trips, she does not do this, leaving to go back to her originating light. Why does she not want to cause the destruction of the Matrix on her first two entrances? These passages also indicate that Providence has the power to enter and leave the Matrix at will. She is not or seemingly cannot be trapped by it, yet still needs to act in ways to hide from the archons. Is she only able to enter and exit if she stays undetected? Alternatively, would there be some sort of alarm sounded to round up the Divine Sparks and move them to a new simulation that is harder for Providence to find, hence that is her reason to remain undetected? Again, much of the text is unexplained information. Perhaps these things were naturally more known with Gnostics at the time of writing. As they understood directly what these metaphors were pointing towards the details were not required.

The text mentions many times that Providence is light thus by entering darkness she is shining her light into it. This light is the Celestial Fire, the very light that was copied to become the false white light of Lucifer, the reason he is known as the "light bringer." Lucifer is bringing false into the Matrix, disguised as the original Fire from which he made the copy. This false symbolism has continued in torch symbol creations such as The Statue of Liberty (Columbia), or the torch of the Olympics. Today such symbols refer to the false white light of the Fallen Creator and not the light of Providence from the Pleroma.

On the third entrance of Providence into the Matrix, the hymn presents that she now feels it is meant to be the end of time (for the ruling of the archons and the system itself), thus the Divine Sparks to be freed. She makes a call for all the beings who can hear her voice that they should rise from their sleep. The text moves to a specific sleeping one who has heard this call and asks, *"Where has my hope come from. As I lie in the depths of this prison?"* There should be no further discussion that the simulated realm (or the experience of it) was considered a prison by the Gnostics, as it is mentioned specifically twice in this small hymn. Providence now induces herself as the thought of the Virgin Spirit. Thus, she is not Isis, Sarasvati, or The Magdalene per se, but the Deep Awareness that was present in those vehicles.

Providence then provides the path. *"Rise up! Awaken! Stay awake! Remember what you have heard. Trace back your roots to me.'* To trace back one's roots would be similar to Rose saying that the path is that one must retro verse their projected ray, to go backwards from the material realm of the Matrix to the Ultimate Source. To remember is to bring all of one's members together, which symbolically means all the bits of Truth that the Divine Spark can access. This is not a call for the character to re-member their life or experiences, but for the Deeper Truth to collect all can be known now that it is no longer in a coma. This statement made is similar to statements made in the Ancient Egyptian Pyramid Texts.

> *"O, raise thyself up; receive thy head, unite thy bones to thee, collect thy limbs, shake the earth (dust of the earth) from thy flesh. Receive thy bread which cannot mold, thy beer which cannot sour. Thou standest at the doors, which hold people back...The two doors of heaven are open for thee, that thou mayest go forth through them."*[113] - Pyramid Text 373-74

---

113 https://sacred-texts.com/egy/pyt/pyt19.htm

What is interesting in this one small section of the Pyramid Texts is the discussion to raise oneself up (get out of the coma) to bring the limbs together (re-member), that a gate of heaven is opened (a type of blocking force is removed) and that one has "no father or mother among mankind" (indicating that what one is comes from a place that has nothing to do with the material realm Matrix. I thought I would present this as a way of seeing that the Providence Hymn (and in fact the entire Apocryphon of John) may be an undated version of much earlier Ancient Egyptian presentations on these subjects.

The Providence text then discusses that the now awake one, hearing the call, gets their five seals sealed with light-water. Doing so the text claims that death will no longer have any power. The five seals are usually presented as a Gnostic baptismal right. A seal fastens or closes something completely. So what is being "sealed" here? A hole in the energetic structure? There is a version of the Gospel of Thomas that discusses there are five trees in paradise that never change or have their leaves fall off, and "whoever becomes acquainted with them will not experience death." Are the five seals to cover over the five senses? This would make sense that the connection to the Matrix via the body-mind is walled off, so that the only focus left would be a direct link to the Source. The Trimorphic Protennoia (another *Nag Hammadi* text) discusses that one who "*possesses the Five Seals...has stripped off <the> garments of ignorance and put on a shining Light. Moreover, nothing will appear to him that belongs to the Powers of the Archons. Within those of this sort, darkness will dissolve and ignorance will die. And the thought of the creature, which is scattered, will present a single appearance and dark Chaos will dissolve.*"[114] So from this text, these seals (whatever they are) will lead to any power the archons have to no longer be infiltrating the Spark or its vehicle (us in a body).

This Providence Hymn relates this sealing to happen with light-water. We know that the Cathars rejected water baptism as it related to the light of the Matrix and not the Fire of the Pleroma. Again, there is nothing bad or evil about water in the Matrix itself, but we can see that Lucifer has made water the "source" of

____

114 http://www.gnosis.org/naghamm/trimorph.html

existence within it. Water is not just required, but a key element of the make-up of bodies. I checked the original Coptic and the phrase (as it is presented to us) does have words similar for light and water. So why does the text want water to be used for the sealing, when one might think it is Fire. Then again, perhaps this is some sort of idea as Rose presented where one wants to use the mind, to go past the mind. To turn the mind back on itself. Can this be a call to "use" the Matrix in such a way as to go beyond the Matrix?

Providence ends her message by saying that she returns back to "the perfect realm," and that she "completed everything." What this short hymn has come to symbolize for me is that ancient texts presented that some force from outside of the Matrix, entered into this realm in order to pass along key information about the nature of the prison, the trapping mechanism, and how to extract oneself from it. I have previously mentioned how I have seen this same metaphor presented in various movies, such as with David and Jennifer entering the TV world to awaken the characters of *Pleasantville,* and Sylvia entering Truman's world to tell him the nature of his reality in the *Truman Show.* The point of this being, knowledge brought from the Pleroma into the Matrix does exist. Much of it has been usurped by The Fallen Creator, distorted, and twisted upside down. We have the job of unraveling this possible useful information, not taking it all at face value, but looking for the underlying original message beyond the distortion.

> *"I have lived on the lip of insanity; wanting to know reasons, knocking on a door. It opens. I have been knocking from the inside."*[115]
>
> Rumi

---

115 Found in Rumi, Translated by Coleman Barks *The Essential Rumi*

Chapter 9
EXIST TO EXIT

"Yesterday never happened.

Tomorrow never will.

Today does not exist."[116]

- Faith Mind Sutra

Why did I write this book? That is a very valid question. At first I worked on these notes as a type of clarification for myself, as my way to integrate various concepts that were not yet fully understood. But after a while I began to sense that these pages could be interesting for those who have read my previous books. Perhaps some of what is my process of understanding would be useful for another. So I had to start taking the notes to myself, and turn them into a presentation that could be read by others.

I decided that I could only write this for someone else if I got a sense of who I was writing for. Who would want to read such material? So I generated a picture in my mind. I can see people coming to this who have recognized they are caught up in a confusing reality, one built on suffering, one that we never consciously wished to enter. A place where we have been subject to the behind the scenes manipulations by archonic beings, at times toying with our existence for their own perverse pleasures (and

116 *Faith Mind Sutra* 27, found in Marshall, Bart *The Perennial Way* p.150

loosh harvesting), all the while interacting with a day by day deranged psychopathic material realm. The attacks from these unseen beings, be they at night in our dreams, as manipulated "coincidences" in our life, or just thoughts projected into our minds, are part of our worldly navigation. I saw that someone who would read this book had come to see that this reality is nothing like we have been told it is. The Matrix seems to not just be one giant challenge, but an attempt to pound us into submission to it. I too have been challenged all through my life, but it is not because I am in any way special or important, only because I am a human with a Divine Spark. That is reason enough to receive the attention from the cosmic "men in hats." I feel the readers and I have much in common.

Through it all I sense that the readers, like I, are working to find personal sanity in an insane world. We are looking for ways to find health, balance and clarity. Many of our attempts did not lead to what we were seeking, but that does not stop us. We took what we could find that was of value and moved further, looking for more ways to regain personal authority over our lives and thoughts. We could take solace from our own empathetic kindness that we shared with others, and appreciate the tireless work that others put in to be helpful; be they an elderly woman giving up hours of time a day to assist in the rehabilitation of abused animals, to a young man out planting trees in a cut down area (not because he is getting paid for it, just because he wanted to help bring back nature to the area), to a mother using some learned acupressure to lessen a pain in one of her children, or the time you or I bought a meal for the homeless person we passed on the street. These acts of empathy are the ways we combat the pressure of the narcissistic world surrounding us. We counter this reality via empathy, inner power and sanity. It is our way of realizing "they" might run reality, but "we" run ourselves.

But to Exit we must go further. Those that saw no loving god has been looking out for them, and no saviour is behind the next door waiting to pat us on the head for being good little girls and boys. The Matrix is a trap, one we no longer want to associate with, and thus a drive for Ultimate Liberation has been welling up inside, perhaps for years or decades. We feel complete Liberation from the Matrix is indeed possible, and we want that, no matter what it takes. Up until the last few years, such ideas were rare to find in mainstream spiritual traditions. They are becoming more prevalent as we move close to the "change point" of our simulacra.

To walk a pathway of Liberation is not what the archons want. They will put in play various "forces of adversity" that will test us mercilessly. Perhaps they even began with these blocks as soon as we were born. I had to endure horrible pain, operations and being close to death as a small baby. It didn't stop me it seems, perhaps slowed me down for a few decades, but here I am. My Divine Spark still stirred itself out of its slumber. I felt my readers were stirring their Sparks from their slumber. It all becomes a question of how strong is our Intent?

The more we continue on our pathway of Intent, the more we become like St. Anthony, resisting all threats and temptations thrown at us. We stay clear and grounded. We become masters of rejection, choosing instead: silence, empathy, integrity, sanity and detachment. The silence is not a silence of being somewhere with no outer sound, it means to have found the still point of what we Are within. The Empty Still center of Being. The detachment is not of giving up objects or experiences, but to see that the material realm is not the spiritual one. We gain a power to reject all attempts to manipulate and deceive us away from our Ultimate Intention. We see these attempts all for what they are, distractions against our Ultimate Aim. Our energy is for the Divine Spark, and thus she shares her power with us, we operate as her vehicle in the material.

At the same time we still act within reality as it is called for. We see what our character needs to do, or respond to, and that is acted upon. When completed, we no longer think about it. It seems like we are performing the same actions as previously, but now they are linked to a wisdom beyond the theater stage. We are still an actor on the stage of Earth, while now being in the audience watching the actor performing. We are a doer and non-doer at the same time.

REMINDERS

*"Only if you reject all the other paths,
can you find your own path."*[117]

\- UG Krishnamurti

A reminder that work needs to be done to Exit the Cave. It does not matter what Buddha did, Jesus did, or what Richard Rose did. What matters is what is the path required for your Divine's Spark's awakening, and then doing what is required for that to occur. Only you can figure out exactly what that will be. It is a journey you have to build, because it will be unique for you. You take what others did as a starting point, then modify it to fit your personal circumstances.

A great part of the work is to learn to fully trust yourself. You can not trust any outside authority, that includes me. You learn how to access the True part of you. Any answer that comes from an outside source must always be questioned, for it is someone else's answer. It is why I tend not to answer many questions directly, but point to how a person might be able to go about answering that question for themselves. Because once you have come to an answer from within, which is a realization, no outside source is needed to verify it. That is a part of the work for a while, learning how to differentiate between true messages from within, and continued distortion and lies. But when this True Part is connected to, the guru you have been looking for your entire life has been found.

Imagine that there are many doors of areas to research and examine. All of them (but one) will be interesting, fun, enticing and many you will seem drawn to study. There will be lots to experience and understand in those doors. But there is one door that a part of of you just does not want to go into, but that is the one that you have to go into if you want to really know who and what you are. If you are willing to do that, go into the place that

---

117 U G Krishnamurti, *Mind is a Myth*

everyone else will do just about anything to avoid, and no guarantees, your probability of overall success becomes high. If you do not go through that door, the probability of success is near zero.

I wanted to point to *The Faith Mind Sutra* that I began this chapter with. I feel this entire text sums up the clarity of the mood of Exiting the Cave nicely. The entire 27 stanza text is asking us to question every belief that we have, about everything. The text is a powerful presentation of how our basic mind has been structured, and since we spend 99% of our time perceiving reality with the mind, thus 99% of what we experience will be a false perception. The text is calling for us to "see" beyond all of the mental structures. It is a text that I read every day, for it is clear and concise and provides reminders for the "me" thing to not be too deep into duality at any moment. Reality is much more vast than our mind presents. It is the mind and its beliefs in language, duality, love, hate, fear and desire that have been the bars to the prison we had inhabited lifetime after lifetime.

But if reality can be eventually seen from the eyes of Emptiness. Now what? What can trap Emptiness or No-thing? The Celestial Fire is greater than anything in the Matrix. But as long as the deception of individual mind and reality is in place, the Spark stays in the coma, and we keep our focus and perception on a world of actions we have been conditioned to believe is important. Become the Fire, the power of the Pleroma, and then the message of Christ, Buddha, Krishna and all the other teachers are no longer messages. They become words from our Self to ourself, and thus become the building blocks to our own personal pathway Home.

Each of the books in the Cave series is a stepping stone. The first was to get you to step out of the belief that this is a wonderful reality. This to step out of the idea that you are an individual self. The next will be to step into the Stillness you have always been, but temporarily forgotten.

I don't have all the answers. Please take what is in the book and check it out for yourself. Use what you find of value for you, and keep developing your own personal pathway. Stay with the work of Self Definition, in whatever form and practices work for you. The process is challenging, the steps up the ladder confusing at times, and the various temptations for us to stop are many. But something greater awaits. Our Ultimate Intention is our overall guide. The mind and the individual self can never realize this, but You can.

Do you think you are going to Exit the Matrix?
Many believe it is so.
But without pure Self Definition,
How can you realize what can go?
False is the Matrix's make up,
It's all such a mess.
No-thing will Exit the Cave,
For what can contain Emptiness?
- Howdie Mickoski

Additional Material 1

Schopenhauer[118]

"If you want a safe compass to guide you through life, and to banish all doubt as to the right way of looking at it, you cannot do better than accustom yourself to regard this world as a penitentiary, a sort of a penal colony."[119] Arthur Schopenhauer

There is a branch of philosophy known as pessimism, and its poster boy might be the Dutch born, German speaking, Arthur Schopenhauer. The field of pessimism might be the most misunderstood of any branch of philosophy, simply because the main element to it (that life is inherent suffering) is so rare to be seen through by someone. Before I dig into the detail of this philosophical genius, perhaps an introduction as to what pessimistic philosophy is would be in order. Usually it is presented as pertaining to someone who focuses mainly on death, suffering, and meaninglessness. Yet this is not really a clear picture. A philosophical pessimists does not just have a psychological belief structure in things not turning out in their life, they are one who has seen the fabric of this reality as different that what is expected (via religion and spiritual promises), and begins to look for new ways to deal with a reality that they see as 100% opposite to what they have been told their entire life. There is no question that this philosophy has ties with standard Buddhism, which has its first of four noble truths to be Dukkha (this is a world of suffering).

---

118 Areas to find information on Schopenhauer include his works at Gutenberg.org , articles at einzelganger.co , the youtube channel weltgeist, and various biographies on the web.

119 Schopenhauer essay "On the Sufferings of the World."

The point of this chapter is not to show that Arthur Schopenhauer, early 19th century philosopher, was a genius (he was), that he was the father of modern psychology (he was) or even that he and I are similar in our views (in some cases we are, in other areas quite contrasting). This chapter is to present what might be called the origin of Exit the Cave type material after 1800, and to present that there are many areas of his writings that you might want to look into in more detail.

Most consider him to be German (as he lived in that country most of his life) but he was actually the son of a Dutch merchant born in the free city of Danzig (now Gdansk). In time Arthur would become fluent in German, French, Latin and English. His father died early (1805) likely from suicide, that Arthur blamed on his mother for showing no affection towards his father. This battle between son and mother would continue the rest of their lives. His mother became a well known novelist and also became a key salonist (intellectual meeting groups) in Germany (where Schopenhauer first met Goethe). She sent many letters to her son claiming that his philosophical works were useless, and him as being too moody and pessimistic, and specifically claimed that he was "annoying."[120] Thus it is no surprise that Schopenhauer developed a very strange ideology around women, all likely linked to the constant battles that he had during his life with his mother.

Schopenhauer was mostly unread in his day, and it was not until he published a series of essays later in life that he gained fame. You can read his life story yourself, about where he went to school, or his university battles with Hegel. This presentation is about his philosophy. At first I was a bit surprised that he wrote of the world as being a prison, but I did not see anyone mentioning that he was presenting Emptiness as a key understanding beyond the material realm. I wrote those ideas in my first draft of this chapter. Thankfully, just prior to publishing, I found that I had been inaccurate. He had indeed discussed Emptiness in his core 1844 text. That caused me to go back and do an even more complete overview of what he presented. And even I was surprised

---

120 https://www.thehumanfront.com/pocketsized-a-letter-from-your-mother/

by the depth that I found on this second more deep dive into his material.

He is most know for claiming that the world is a place of suffering, a prison, and for this reason he is labeled a philosophical pessimist. He wrote in one of his earlier works, "*In my 17th year, I was gripped by the misery of life, as Buddha had been in his youth when he saw sickness, old age, pain, and death. The truth was that this world could not have been the work of an all-loving being but rather that of a devil, who had brought creatures into existence in order to delight in their suffering.*"[121] Thus he has right from the start had a very Buddhist view of the world.

He never explained specifically what was in prison, only used the idea as a metaphor, but it led him to develop specific plans of action for one to suffer the least amount. Such an idea thus helped him to develop a close kinship to all others in this realm, including animals (he was one of the first advocates of animal rights). According to Schopenhauer: "*Since compassion for animals is intimately associated with goodness of character, and it may be confidently asserted that he who is cruel to living creatures cannot be a good man.*"[122] All animal rights and welfare groups in Europe come out of his presentations.

And in one of his unpublished works he gave a bit of an insight as to when the idea of the nature of this world began to show for him, "*In my 17th year, I was gripped by the misery of life, as Buddha had been in his youth when he saw sickness, old age, pain, and death. The truth was that this world could not have been the work of an all-loving being but rather that of a devil, who had brought creatures into existence in order to delight in their sufferings...At every stop, in great things and small, we are bound to experience that the world and life are certainly not arranged for the purpose of being happy. That's why the faces of almost all of the elderly people are deeply etched with disappointment.*"[123]

---

121 I think this quote is from *The World as Will and Representation,* found at https://www.faena.com/aleph/seeking-happiness-could-be-a-form-of-slavery
122 Schopenhauer, Arthur. *On the Basis of Morality* p 19
123 Quote found from Robert A. Gonzales "The Ambiguity of the Sacred in the Philosophy of Schopenhauer" pg 151 in Auslegung: A Journal of Philosophy (The

In his 1850 essay "On the Sufferings of the World," he presented that this world was built on pain and suffering, and as such, people should stop searching for happiness or pleasure, as such things are impossible here without understanding the mechanism behind the suffering which he labeled Will (I will get to this concept). Thus his original presentation upon seeing the suffering of reality was to find ways to reduce this constant suffering, not just for oneself, but for other beings we come across. His comparison of this world to a prison was partially based on that. Just like prison, no one "chooses" to be here. He never said we were tricked to being here, but I don't think if such an idea were presented to him he would have immediately rejected the possibility.

In his first major work *The World as Will and Representation* he presented that, "*if you led the most unrepentant optimist through the hospitals, military wards, and surgical theaters, through the prisons, torture chambers and slave stalls, through battlefields and places of judgment, and then open for him all the dark dwellings of misery that hide from cold curiosity, then he too would surely come to see the nature of this best of all possible worlds.*"[124] One of the best arguments for presenting the nature of this material realm.

When he did write of the creator of this realm, Schopenhauer held it up for being the creator of a suffering realm, "*There are two things which make it impossible to believe that this world is the successful work of an all-wise, all-good, and, at the same time, all-powerful Being; firstly, the misery which abounds in it everywhere; and secondly, the obvious imperfection of its highest product, man, who is a burlesque of what he should be.*" He also claimed that this creator must be getting great pleasure from all the insanity and suffering occurring, "*We are like lambs in a field, disporting themselves under the eye of the butcher, who chooses out first one and then another for his prey. So it is that in our good*

University of Kansas) file:///C:/Users/admin/Downloads/bitstream_22857.pdf and found in Schopenhauer's Nachlass, known as *Manuscript Remains* in English by E.F.J. Payne.
124 Schopenhauer *The World as Will and Representation*

days we are all unconscious of the evil Fate may have presently in store for us – sickness, poverty, mutilation, loss of sight or reason."[125] In essence he claims we are like an animal in a barn stuck there, waiting only for when the farmer will call the truck and take us to the slaughterhouse. At least this is how is tends to be presented in a simple fashion. He goes into much greater depth into where the origin of suffering lies.

Normally one sees that the search for pleasure and happiness, or their similar avenues of distraction (in drinking, consumerism, or sex) all to hide from the suffering we and the world experiences. He reminded that pain is always a more severe experience than pleasure, as he suggests the pain of the animal being eaten will greatly outweigh the pleasure or the animal that is doing the eating. Given that the search for pleasure and happiness could never succeed (because either we attain it for a while then lose it which will create more suffering, or we attain what we think is happiness only to find out that in the end it never brought us happiness at all), so Schopenhauer felt the antidote to it all was to find ways to reduce this suffering (firstly for himself, but also in others, animals, etc.). This a very Buddhist approaches to reality.

At the end of his essay he craftily stated that one should not say hello to someone with a phrase such as "hello fine sir" but instead by the phrase "hello fellow sufferer," thus constantly reminding one of the compassion and empathy needed to navigate a prison-hell world.

*

Similar to Richard Rose who once said, "*The longer I live the more I dislike this place,*"[126] so too did Schopenhauer have little good to say about life on Earth. But he describes the vicious cycle of the inner workings of the mind, information that possibly became re-catagorized by Sigmund Freud a half century later. Freud claimed that he never read Schopenhauer while he made his views of psychotherapy, yet when placed side by side, they are very similar around key elements. Freud's concepts for the Id and ego

---

125 Schopenhauer "On the Sufferings of the World"
126 Rose from John Kent

are almost the same as Schopenhauer's Will and Intellect. Both men also had sexuality as the core of their Id/Will. So powerful are Schopenhauer's presentations of the workings of both the conscious and unconscious mind, that Henri Ellenberger in his 1970 *The Discovery of the Unconscious* claimed Schopenhauer was "definitely among the ancestors of modern dynamic psychiatry," while Thomas Mann insinuated that Schopenhauer was "the father of all modern psychology."[127]

Schopenhauer identified a force that he labeled Will as the driving force behind all behavior, not just for humans but all creatures. The Will has the job of determining all desires and wants of the body, be they food, shelter, sex, importance, feelings. These underlying wants of the Will, which he also labeled as Will-To-Live, as "the unconscious source of bodily needs and wants, emotional impulses and desires, especially aggression and the sexual drive—the psychic force oriented to immediate gratification of impulse and desire."[128] This mirrors Freud's Id. It has its number one goal that the person survive, so that it can have a child, then help the child grow up, so it can have children and so on. Thus the sex drive, which we will come to next, is perhaps the most important of all the functions of Will.

The force that attempts to figure out how to satisfy what the Will is asking for, he labeled the Intellect. Generally this is rather weak (not just in humans but all creatures) and thus it is not fully able to satisfy all of the desires of the Will. Due to being mostly unconscious to what is going on in one's mind, most of all the energy spent in a day is just the actions of intellect looking for ways to satisfy the needs of the Will (first and foremost to survive and procreate). Granted when satisfying one of the (particular survival) needs, will create a short burst of short term pleasure (what dopamine was originally created to do), the pleasure is minimal and lasts for a very short period of time. Pain soon sets in as people try to figure out what they need to do to get another dose of

---

127 Connections with Freud can be found at http://www.the-wagnerian.com/2012/07/schopenhaur-freud-one-and-same.html

128 Schopenhauer Will information comes from the reading of his most famous work *The World as Will and Representation* and Freud Id ideas at https://en.wikipedia.org/wiki/Id,_ego_and_superego

this feeling, while others in the realization of "at the moment" no Will survival need requires to be fulfilled, they just lapse into a space of boredom.

A problem of the egoic Intellect is that it does not just search for ways to manifest the desires of the Will, it looks to fulfill those desires to excess, "We shall find that, in order to increase his pleasures, man has intentionally added to the number and pressure of his needs, which in their original state were not much more difficult to satisfy than those of the brute. *Hence luxury in all its forms; delicate food, the use of tobacco and opium, spirituous liquors, fine clothes, and the thousand and one things than he considers necessary to his existence,*" including "*ambition and the feeling of honor and shame; in plain words, what he thinks about the opinion other people have of him. Taking a thousand forms, often very strange ones, this becomes the goal of almost all the efforts he makes that are not rooted in physical pleasure or pain.*"[129] To him, this constant concern of what others think of us, and thus taking up valuable thinking time, and performing all sorts of actions designed to gain various objects and experiences in order to control these thoughts other people have of us was a key component in creating much of our own suffering.

There is a part of his work, one that rarely gets mentioned by those who study him, is about reaching what he called the Will-less state. He claims that getting to this place, where one you might say has seen through the desires of the Will (and even though unconscious) is in control of the Intellect as to no longer have have the body driving towards the fulfillment of any of them, produces a joy, but not something felt with normal satisfying of the Will. This is something different, and he described reaching this state as being the only valuable desire that one should really have.

The Will is the underlying principle behind everything that a human does, until they can attain the very challenging to reach Will-less state. Every single thing in reality has a Will which causes it to function as it does. Richard Rose might have labeled this feature The Umpire in his Jacob's Ladder analogy. The Will,

---

129 Schopenhauer "On the Sufferings of the World"

which is also known as the Love of Life, has as its greatest motive to be "sexual love." For without babies being born, the species (ie the next round of slaves for the system) would not be there, thus it is the number one focus of the Will.

Intellect is not separate from Will, and Schopenhauer even seems to suggest that it is the will that creates the Intellect in or to have a "success mechanism" in the material realm for its desires. Since the Will created Intellect, it is the driving guide behind all that it does. Another interesting question for us to ask just where our thoughts originate from. Because of this interlink between the two, Intellect is not as rational as most of philosophy presented, because it is the underlying and unseen Will that is really the force behind what the thoughts are. Intellect is taking the wants of the Will and scheming ways to make them manifest in the material realm. The big problem is that Intellect does not really know the complete wishes and plans of the Will, it is sort of in a "need to know basis." Thus the Intellect operates with the limited information and direction that it gets provided.

Why is his Will-Intellect discussion important? In his own way he is describing that one is normally behaving like a robot, as this unconscious and unseen Will is driving every action that the character undertakes. Intellect (what we normally describe as our standard awareness as well as the thoughts it is aware of) gets very little detail from the Will. Liken it to receiving basic text messages of what Will wants, but no underlying details why it wants what it wants. Intellect just has to take the want and figure out some way to make it manifest in material reality. That is why standard thoughts have very little depth usually, because they are operating with very little information.

He does describe a way past all of this, via what he calls and ascetic monk-like life, to be able to stop the commands of the Intellect enough so that a deeper more true awareness can finally get a glimpse at the workings of the Will, and begin to in a sense "cut off these wants" at the source. Doing so would create a Will-less or Desire-less state which Schopenhauer equated with the experience of true calm (as opposed to moments when external noise is low). Though he felt that so few people were prepared to do the level of work that would be required for this to occur, that he made his suggestion to find ways to reduce suffering in day to day life, as that was something everyone at any stage of the ladder could do.

Schopenhauer also had an interesting understanding of pleasure. He did not see it as a gaining of something "we like or want" but instead was the removal of something that was frustrating or annoying the wishes of the Will. Such ideas have led many today to see that he was a major influence on the upcoming field of psychiatry. The very interesting article by Wagnerian.com presents the links between Schopenhauer and Freud's ideas. The article suggest some of these areas are: the idea that madness (psychosis) originates with the repression of traumas, that the problem lies in the memory which takes the event and creates a fiction around it, thus through working with healing the memory one can heal the psychosis (my guess is that Schopenhauer would have valued recapitulation to help this healing process). This repression and placing away of what is really going on in our subconscious was a main reason for the inner problems one was facing. Since it is Intellect that has been making a fiction to hide the pains the Will has suffered, Schopenhauer suggested that the healing process must start with the Intellect (mind) so that a better doorway to deeper seeing and awareness of these traumas can emerge. So much of this is could be called a Freudian mindset.[130]

He was one of the few philosophers of the 1800s to discuss sex, and he does have some unique and odd ideas around this subject and women. It is such a complex area that I will leave the majority of that discussion for a future book, but to simplify his message: sex is not evil, just another part of life, but one should only engage in the practice if they can be sure that they will not create more children from it. To him, the sex urge was the most powerful and declared the "genitals were the focus of the Will." Sex was more important for the Will than even eating, as it was the

---

130 http://www.the-wagnerian.com/2012/07/schopenhaur-freud-one-and-same.html

force that would get more babies born, so that the slave energy system could keep running.[131]

That being said he did seem to indicate that if one could not get this inner pressure from the Will under control it would turn into a "malevolent demon" because it would take so much of one's time and energy. These two quotes sum up his views very well,

> *"It is the ultimate goal of almost all human effort; it has an unfavorable influence on the most important affairs, interrupts every hour the most serious occupations, and sometimes perplexes for a while even the greatest minds. It does not hesitate to intrude with its trash, and to interfere with the negotiations of statesmen and the investigations of the learned. It knows how to slip its love-notes and ringlets even into ministerial portfolios and philosophical manuscripts. Every day it brews and hatches the worst and most perplexing quarrels and disputes, destroys the most valuable relationships, and breaks the strongest bonds. It demands the sacrifice sometimes of life or health, sometimes of wealth, position and happiness...the ultimate aim of all love affairs, whether played in a sock or busking, is actually more important than the other aims in a man's life; and therefore it is quite worthy of the profound seriousness with which everyone pursues it. What is decided by it is nothing less than the composition of the next generation."[132]*

I do want to say that he also presented a few very odd views on this subject. There will always be distortion in any philosophic

131 Schopenhauer *World as Will and Representation* p. 514, 533
   https://antilogicalism.com/wp-content/uploads/2017/07/schopenhauer-the-world-as-will-and-representation-v2.pdf
132 Schopenhauer *World as Will and Representation* p. 533
   https://antilogicalism.com/wp-content/uploads/2017/07/schopenhauer-the-world-as-will-and-representation-v2.pdf

area because any message is being delivered through a body-mind instrument that can never be "pure." I mention this should you want to look into this area of material of his and make judgments on it for yourself.

*

There is far more in his philosophy, from why suicide is not helpful (as it is a problem of the Will/ego not the body life), the reasons to not have children, the need for good health, views on art and beauty, a dislike of noise, and to not care what others think of you. You can examine all of this in more detail if you choose to.[133] He was a big fan of the small 1647 book *The Art of Worldly Wisdom* of how to live aphorisms by Spanish poet Balasar Gracian. This the most brief of an overview of what is a massive tome of information.

Good health was at the top of his list for dealing with an insane world. This was way more important than any fame or wealth we could come across as he wrote that, "The healthy bum is happier than a sick king." For him when it came to money, he recommended that one should only strive for enough money to allow them some time and space to do the things they really want to do, but any striving for more than that will just in time increase suffering. As is the need to become happy with who we really are, and enjoy that no matter what others might think of us. He also spoke of cheerfulness, and the need to just have good spirits for no reason than just to have them. It is quite a tool. Cheer fullness is a cheap and easy way to have more moments out of misery. The pursuit of happiness or objects or views of others will just chase this natural cheerfulness away.

He saw art and beauty as something important, as the best artists who create beauty in their art (he would have hated all modern art) could be used (as it can bring in a deep contemplation and enjoyment). He very much disliked noise, wrote an entire essay on it, and suggested that if someone was not bothered by

---

133 Much of his "how to live" philosophy can be found in his book *Councils and Maxims* https://www.gutenberg.org/cache/epub/10715/pg10715-images.html

noise, they must in fact be stupid. Real thinking can only occur when noise has been reduced to near zero. He also felt that those who were people of high intellect needed to withdraw from society as the best strategy is to not have to deal with all of the mess of it, for to stay around the masses would just cause one's talents to be dragged down by the rest. Yet when one did need to go into the world of people, they were to play dumb, for people will always feel threatened and dislike those that they deem smarter than them. "It is an exceedingly rash thing to let any one see that you are decidedly superior to him in this respect, and to let other people see it too, because he will then thirst for vengeance."[134] His basic principle for dealing with human society, was be in it as little as possible. Do you what you must do in it, with as much anonymity as possible, then get the hell out again. This is pretty much the ideas of Controlled Folly over one hundred years before there was a Castaneda.

One last element of his philosophy I will share is that he thought (even in the 1800s), that everything education was doing was backwards. He felt one should first have an experience, and then go into books and ideas. Education he claimed puts the idea first, but produces or wants no experience to verify or deny it. The idea has to be accepted as true because a teacher of book said it was. Thus to Schopenhauer anyone whose knowledge came only from books and not the real world, would lack common sense and not really know how to think, only listen and agree with what someone else tells them. That is a good summation of our current state of the modern world.

Along these lines he also suggested to read less, not more. Thus one should only choose to read the best authors and best books, and read those several times to get the complete depth they offer. Thus to learn to quickly find which possible book might fall in the bad category, and save one's time by not even opening the cover. He also then advised that one needed to take time to then actually think about what one reads, or the reading would have been of little value. Thus his belief that any scholar whose

---

134 Schopenhauer *Councils and Maxims* section 34, Why it pays to play dumb
    https://www.youtube.com/watch?v=uI5LsMalZ7M

supposed knowledge comes only from books, would never have had time to really go within and come up with their own ideas, their own philosophy, their own way of presenting ideas. Schopenhauer, if he were alive today, would have hated video sites like Youtube, where millions of videos just get plastered to an overwhelmed audience, and all generally having no real purpose except to entertain, distract, or for the maker of it to ramble incoherently for an hour.

*

In his famous multi-volume work *The World as Will and Representation,* Schopenhauer does touch briefly on Emptiness in his fourth book of the first volume. He discusses that this state is where one can be led to if they can learn to reject the wishes of the Will (ego). The Will-less state is found from the concept of Nothing. The last three long paragraphs of the fourth book (which I recommend you read at the end footnote of this paragraph) is a detailed description of the value of becoming "nothing." Some excerpts are below,

He begins his discussion by how he defines nothing, and for him it is the negation of something. Thus nothing and something are a tandem. Nothing presupposes a something that it is the antithesis of. Right away this makes me wonder if Schopenhauer had an actual realization of Emptiness (which my guess is he did not) or only gained an intellectual understanding of it from reading mostly Asian texts (likely) which means what Nothing is or is not, will only be presented from an intellectual as opposed to an experimental level. Yet for him the entire world only exists because of Will. As long as the Will is still present, something is present. He would suggest that when Will is abolished, so too for all intents and purposes is the world of objects. "Before us there is only nothingness. But that which resists this passing into nothing, our nature, is indeed just the will to live, which we ourselves are, as it is our world. That we abhor

235

annihilation so greatly, is simply another expression of the fact that we so strenuously will life, and are nothing but this will, and know nothing besides it." To continue beyond this Will he suggests that the result of this would be the state of being Will-less, having the Will no longer being the driving factor in one's life, " *Yet this (the discussed state is the only consideration which can afford us lasting consolation, when, on the one hand, we have recognized incurable suffering and endless misery as essential to the manifestation of will, the world; and, on the other hand, see the world pass away with the abolition of will, and retain before us only empty nothingness."*[135]

To reach this state beyond the Will is not an easy prospect, and thus is why he recommended the ascetic monk-like practices of Eastern philosophy such as Buddhism and Advaita, as well as Christian monastic (Hesychian practices) of Europe, thus be able to go past their base unconscious desires. The ascetic stops following the normal ways to live, in a sense he or she turns 180 degrees to no longer live for any desires or goals to be filled in the future, nor to deal with the layers of their past, but to be still both within and without. He realized that few would be able to follow on such a detailed, structured, and focused life hence his rules for the average people to help make their existence in the prison realm a bit more manageable. He seemed to indicate that standard religious practices would only strengthen the Will, not reduce it.

He sums up his ideas regarding reaching the Will-less state, via the avenue of nothingness by the following passage,

> "Rather do we freely acknowledge that what remains after the entire abolition of will is for all those who are still full of will certainly nothing; but, conversely, to those in whom the will has turned and has denied itself, this our world, which is so real, with all its suns and milky-ways—is nothing."[136]

---

135 Schopenhauer *On Will and Representation* vol 1 pg 525

136 Schopenhauer *On Will and Representation* vol 1 pg 526 and in his own footnote compares this state to the Pranja of Buddhism where subject and object are no more

There is much to like in what Schopenhauer states, but it still comes to me that the areas of Will-less, Nothingness and the like are less direct realizations he held, as opposed to deep feeling and intuition where those texts were leading. I do not know for sure, but needless to say the subject of how he understood Emptiness is something I would have very much liked to have asked him.

Additional Material 2

Sleeping Beauty

I have mentioned the tale Sleeping Beauty a few times through this work. Now I would like to give a short overview of why the tale is important for those with a focus on Exiting the Cave.

When I was writing about fairy tales in 2004 for my book *The Power of Then,* I looked into this tale but could not figure much out about it. Unlike Little Red Riding Hood, Cinderella or Iron John, where I found very clear alchemic and Hermetic symbolism, in Sleeping Beauty I was mostly baffled. There was little in the tale to explain why it had stayed so popular in the public. It took until my deep dive into Gnostic texts to begin to see that Sleeping Beauty was different from the others. This was not a tale about growth or knowledge or the Matrix, or the masculine and feminine: it is a tale specifically about the awakening of the Divine Spark. Only with that understanding did the tale make sense.

Most of what is known today about his tale comes from various European versions, through the 1950s Disney movie, of a girl with various names (Brunhilde, Briar Rose, Talia, and Aurora) who is put to sleep by a magic spell/curse, then awakened by the kiss of a prince. When one understands that it is not just any prince who awakens the princess, but a prince who has done his inner work, the tale again gets clear-er. The prince is the seeking tool within the Matrix, while Sleeping Beauty is the Divine Spark in the coma at the edge of this reality.

The standard tale[137] comes from a few key sources, specifically in French by Charles Perrault and in German by Brothers Grimm. The original tale was titled Sleeping Beauty of the Woods. There was no castle, she was asleep in a deep dark woodland, representing the darkest regions of the Matrix where one encounters Emptiness. I will discuss this again in the final chapter, the Divine Spark is the full side of Emptiness and No-Self is the empty side of Emptiness. The oldest mention of the tale is found in the French 14th century Perceforest. That the tale shows its first origins in France is important, for it links with the Grail romances (which is also about the Divine Spark) and also to the mystery of Rennes Le Chateau.

In what became the more standard version, there is a princess (sometimes un-named) who has an evil witch or fairy unhappy that she has so much attention placed on her at birth. The fairy puts a curse on the young woman that she will die before the age of 16 by a prick on her finger from an item often flax, or a spindle). Sometimes another fairy is close by to lessen the curse to just a long sleep instead of death. Can this first part of the story indicate that when the Divine Fire entered this realm, the Fallen Creator wanted it to be dead, but some other "force" lessened the Matrix attack to only a coma, a coma that the Divine Spark can come out of? What the tale discusses is that it is not the Spark itself that gets it out of the coma, it requires some "in the world" action to do that. The action of course would be performed, in the story by a prince, in our reality by the seeking part of the character that the Spark (via the soul) is linked with,

Even though her parents remove all of the "dangerous" items from the kingdom, one still exists and of course she pricks her finger on it, sending here into a deep sleep. The curse was meant to kill her, but due to different reasons in each tale, instead she falls into a deep 100 year sleep. Many princes attempt to reach her (who all die), with only one being successful. The tale we tend to know she is awakened by a kiss, but in many early versions she was raped by the finding King-prince, to whom she awakens and

---

137 Information on the story of Sleeping Beauty found at
   https://www.supersummary.com/sleeping-beauty/summary/, and
   https://en.wikipedia.org/wiki/Sleeping_Beauty

has twins (a boy and a girl). The boy is named Day, while the girl is named Aurora (as in Borealis, that which lights up the night sky. While the original is harsh, we are seeing in this section of the tale via the rape, not the awakening of the Spark, but the splitting of the Spark by the Demiurge. Lucifer is the rapist king of the Spark, who splits it in two (a masculine and feminine half). Thus the boy half (Day), becomes the seeking prince, while Aurora becomes the still in a coma feminine half that must be awakened. Their combination (that is presented in various ways near the end of the tale) indicates a Spark that is now united and on its way towards the Celestial Fire, which an Old Norse version of the tale brings out more clearly.[138] The end of the tales tend to indicate that the entire group live their lives "happily ever after."

What does happily ever after mean? Most have come to take as some sort of extended romantic marriage and family bliss, a concept that is programmed into young girl's through the modern tales. This foundational concept is one of the main reasons for so many divorced marriages. They are expecting "happily ever after" and what they get is daily challenge and work. The tales never promised that. What the tales suggest with the happy idea has nothing to do with the character, with the people in the Matrix world. An Awake Spark will live happily ever after, as they are extricating themselves from the Matrix and moving to their place of origin. Even then is not what one would come to believe, some place where one can be rid of their suffering. Happily ever after will mean the Divine Spark on going forward will have its energy and Awareness connected to ITSELF not "you." You remain as a dream character playing out their assigned role in the Matrix, while the Divine Spark gets closer and closer to the complete dissolving from the Matrix entirely.

That is the overview, but a few additional insights to consider, in mostly point form to keep this chapter "moving

---

138 Other elements of the longer version of the tale has he back with the King and her children, but another woman in the court (often the King's mother) dislikes the princess and her children and asks the cook to kill the children and serve them as food to the King. The cook hides the children and serves livestock or lamb. When she demands the princess be cooked and eaten, the woman's true nature is seen, and she is the one put to death, where afterwards everyone lives happily ever after.

along." The prince braves the tall trees, brambles and thorns which part at his approach, and enters the castle. These are the tests of Self Definition and of gaining a clear seeing of the Matrix. This is hard work, and most will at some point just turn around and give the whole endevour up. Instead of seeing other princes as having died on their journey, it is more realistic to see that the work got too difficult and they simply turned around and returned to normal life. That is very common actually.

In some of the Middle Ages versions, the prince never touches or kisses the princess at all, just falls to his knees due to the "radiant beauty before him." I know a few people who met their Divine Spark might put the experience of it in similar terms. The prince's acceptance of the overwhelming perfection of the Spark is what causes the Spell to be broken. The idea of beauty of the Spark. In a sense when one sees beauty any place in the material realm, they can see it as a reflection of the beauty of their own Spark. This is another reason that the Matrix wants to stop the focus on beautiful things (be they artwork, architecture or people) and put the focus on liking the things that contain no beauty (modern art or architecture is a prime example). There is a reason the ancient world created beautiful objects, be they statues or paintings. They wanted the overwhelming beauty of the artwork to touch the experience deep within and open up the direct connection to their own Spark. There is thus nothing wrong with the admiration of a beautiful person as well, not to own or possess them as an object, just as another pointer placed into the world to use as a mirror within. This includes mostly the people we deep as "beautiful within" for they are the closest mirror to the Spark, and why the Matrix works so hard to get the average person focused on people who are anything but beautiful within. There is a reason for it all.

The Brothers Grimm gives the princess the name, Little Briar Rose, linking the name to the alchemic rose which can be a symbol of the philosopher's stone.

Modern day feminists tend to dislike the tale for making women seem passive and focused only on beauty, perfectness, and becoming a housewife for the prince/king. They do not understand that this is not a tale about girls, femininity, or this world. It is about the Divine Spark. Hence the tale can still be right in front of everyone's noses, yet no one sees it.

The Norse version is titled Sigrdrifumal, one of the Norse Edda poems.[139] This version has a prince named Sigurd, awakening the Valkyrie Brynhild, also called Sigrdrifa ("driver to victory"). That the two are named the same is a clue that the feminine half of the Spark in the coma, and the male seeking half (at the doorway of the Matrix) are one and the same spark, only split.

This tale begins with Sigurd riding up a tall mountain when he saw "a great light, as if a fire were burning, which blazed up the sky." Following that there was a "skialdborg" (a series of warriors in a protective formation with their shields raised). He entered and saw a fully armed soldier on the ground asleep. When he took off the soldier's helmet he saw that it was a woman. Sigurd used his sword to break the armor (symbolizing the curse or poison of the coma sleep on the Spark) to free her from it which caused her to sit up awakened. She makes an interesting comment "Long have I slept, long been with sleep oppressed, long are mortals' sufferings! Odin is the cause that I have been unable to cast off torpor (lethargy/coma)." Here we see that her suffering has also meant the suffering of mortals (any being in the Matrix living with a Divine Spark trapped in the poisoned armor). She claims Odin is the cause (representing Lucifer/Fallen Creator, though the text claims there was a battle between kings that Odin has in a sense bet on one side to win). This is a bit of misdirection, caused likely by Lucifer himself by rewriting some of it, to hide himself as the obvious origin for the sleeping woman's coma.[140]

---

139 Found at https://en.wikipedia.org/wiki/Sigrdr%C3%ADfum%C3%A1l
140 Tale quotes found at
  https://web.archive.org/web/20160819144557/http://www.northvegr.org/the
  %20eddas/the%20poetic%20edda%20%20-%20thorpe%20translation/sigrdrifumal
  %20-%20the%20lay%20of%20sigrdrifa%20page%201.htm, and https://sacred-
  texts.com/neu/poe/poe25.htm

She claimed to have made a promise that she would never be married to a man who knew the meaning of fear, in a sense saying that the seeker of Truth, Spark and Self must be fearless. She then gave him a drinking horn filed with mead, acting like a memory aid which would be removing the memory wipe given by the archons. She then goes through most of the rest of the story giving rune magic to Sigurd. This would be sharing lessons on how to navigate through the Matrix in the best way possible after now being connected to an awakened Divine Spark.

*

Again I find it so interesting how many elements of my research for this book tend to connect back to the mystery at Rennes Le Chateau. Sleeping Beauty is another of those. She is found in the third section of the very odd document called *The Serpent Rouge* (Red Serpent). It is divided into 13 sections (one for each of what is claimed the original 13 signs of the zodiac). In the third section for Aries it is written, "*During my testing pilgrimage I tried to clear a path with the sword crossing the inextricable vegetation of the woods, I wanted to reach the residence of the sleeping BEAUTY in whom certain poets saw the QUEEN of a past realm. In desperation of finding my way again the parchments of this Friend were for me, the thread of Ariadne.*"[141]

Without going into the depth of this mystery, or this odd document (which I will do in an upcoming book) the speaker of this stanza is related to the prince, who is clearing a path through the thick vegetation around the castle where Sleeping Beauty is found. Symbolically they are getting their "house in order." In the text she is called the "queen of a past realm," this past realm likely a mention of the Pleroma. The short stanza ends with the idea of walking the labyrinth, as it is Ariadne's thread which is the guiding force. I bring this up because these mysteries: Cathars, Holy Grail, Knight's Templar, Rennes Le Chateau, Cathedrals of St. Sulpice and Chartres, all interlink.

---

141 http://www.connectotel.com/rennes/serpmwch.html

Additional Material 3

A Time Loop?

"Your lives are all fabrications within a simulation that continues to repeat over and over. It is likened unto a never-ending story. And yet only the awakened can begin to recall the constant torment the soul has gone through."[142] John Panella

One who gave an interesting overview regarding the end of this current reality was John Panella. Beyond the possibilities for the end of our simulation of Exiting completely, or going into the new 5-d simulation, John adds a third possibility. That being a time loop for the current reality we are in. In his theory, this simulation we are currently experiencing will not specifically end, just recycle back into itself to a certain time in the past, where all the experiences will again repeat. I wrote about time loops in *Falling For Truth,* and still very much agree with the idea that reincarnation is much more a sense of living the same life (or a few lives) over and over rather than hundreds of various lives through long stretches of history.

Panella presents a specific time framework for this time loop, that being a 1000-year cycle, that was purposely put into place by the archons when this simulation ended the "first time." His theory links to the 2160 year precessional age clock, but he claims

---

142 Panella, John *Time Loop Chronicles* pg 199. He wrote several books on a variety of subjects around a reincarnation trap, simulation theory and time loops.

that the cycle was tampered with and uses a half cycle (which would be 1080 years) to keep this simulation into a looping half of the last half of the Piscean Age. This part of what we call history is thus the only element that has any realness or even any memory to it (given potentially thousands of these resets), and so to him everything beyond 1080 years is simply lost to memory and unable to be found.

I was looking over my Panella notes on this topic, and I began looking at his half-precessional idea. Therefore, I began wondering what dates I could find if I looked for various "half dates" in the cycle, to see if various key dates would match history. I did this via looking at split years, using 1080 as a base line, then begin dividing it and looking to correlations to 540 years, 270 years and so on. It gets a bit tough after the 135 year split "as the halves are no longer perfect round numbers), but this comes close.

Panella suggests that this loop began in the year 2027, which when I did the match to check the base line half years, tends to miss many key historical dates. However, if I use the year 2032 as the starting date, 1080 years ago would be 952 AD. Thus 540 years added would be 1492, 270 years would be 1764, 135 years would be 1897...after this the divisions get a bit off center, but if we take the next split to be 66 would be 1963, next 33 would be 1996, next at 16 would be 2012, next at 8 would be 2020, next at 4 would be 2024, next at 2 would be 2026, next at 1 which would be 2027...that would be the end (save perhaps for faster and faster halving of time as suggested in the novel *Replay* by Ken Grimwood). Therefore, what is interesting to me was that his 2027 date and my start date of 2032 for going back in the loop both fit perfectly into the cycle.

The dates are interesting. 952 AD is a time period has so little corroborating evidence of anything, but it does relate to the exact period of the supposed end of the Vikings in Scandinavia, yet is the same time period that the Normans (Viking) conquer France. Something just does not match with these historical events. The Vikings are not strong enough to hold Norway, but they can take over France? The year 1492 is the famous date given for the voyage of Columbus to the "New World," which was just the beginning of a European take over a continent. The year 1764 was right at the end of the Seven Years War in Europe and North America, while 1897 was in the midst of the time of the World Fairs. The next year lands perfectly on 1963 and the "assassination" of Kennedy. 1996 is the year of the Atlanta Olympics, but more odd might have been a website, that later became a book called the World Fair of the Internet (where a symbolic online Fair about the Internet), was created. The next year on the scale is 2012 (the constantly presented Maya calendar date), 2020 was the start of the new "reset" playbook that got rolled out, 2024 (which we are in now, is still not ended but has had many possible major direction pointers). The next date would be 2026, with 2027 the possible end of the simulation and the merging of the AI to the human. The dates when laid out seem to connect with world history clearly.

Then we look at the half points between the dates. For example, the half point of 952 and 1492 is 1222, which is right in the time line of the Cathars. The next half year becomes 1627 (the year of the creation of the St. Sacrament in Paris along with the first Et in Arcadia Ego painting by Nicholas Poussin's, linking to both the previous half point of the Cathars and to the story of Rennes Le Chateau.

There might be a lot to what Panella was sharing with his idea of a 1,000 year time loop. I present this as this as a possibility for your further examination.

Additional Material 4

THE PLATO DECEPTION

So how many wisdom seekers and philosophers attack Plato? Not many right. Karl Popper did in the 1950s, but it is rare. I had some serious questions about Plato when it came to re-reading his cave analogy, and most importantly, what it ignores. That is when I first began to wonder if Plato was a fraud, in the sense he was promoting one thing, but history was presenting a different message. Secondly, did Plato even exist? Like most of what we call history, in that regard we can never know. But what can be done is look at the writing that is claimed to be of this Greek philosopher which has shaped much of the last 2000 years of Western Society. It might be nothing but misdirection, only more concepts to strengthen the ruling elite and hide the depth of the enslavement of people to the Matrix. Plato's *Republic* may have even been the first book to call for totalitarian control of the population. It is in this text that one finds the "allegory of the cave." Plato was also the first, in his book *Timaeus,* to use the word Demiurge. Demiurge is a Greek word for craftsman, but also sometimes a slave, used by Plato to mean the one who crafted reality. On looking into this writing closer it became clear that Plato was presenting that his Demiurge was Good.

A fundamental flaw of Plato and Pythagoras (and all the so-called great early wisdom presenters) was seeing that the creator of this realm was somehow good, caring, and loving. The problem is no one is able to reconcile the so called loving creator with the insane mess of the reality experience. *Timaeus* describes the Demiurge as "unreservedly benevolent, and so it desires a world as good as possible." The world must be good because of the belief that the Demiurge is good, and ends the questioning. Actually, there is no subject that is more important to continue to ask questions about.[143]

Carl O'Brien presented that to Plato, "Demiurgy can be described as a world-generation via the ordering of per-existent matter by an entity." The Demiurge creates order, harmonizes the four elements, and shapes the cosmos into a sphere and gives it a circular motion. To construct a soul, the Demiurge produces three essences (Being, sameness and otherness). He uses various mathematical combinations, such as 1, 2, 4, 8 or 1, 3, 9, 27...thus seems to equated by doubling or tripling (a similar way that a computer does its mathematical calculations). Plato claims that it is this ordering of the pre-existent mass that allows it to be become a living being.[144] Some have suggested that Plato is not using the word Demiurge to refer to the actual creator of this world, but the being that did the creator's fashioning of the realm into matter. As such this word being referred to links to the Greek God Hephaestus. And there are many similarities between the these two presentations.[145]

Plato also presents that this Demiurge, after making the living universe, then made lesser gods which are called such things as stars, planets, and gods. This description of creation is similar in layout to how the Gnositcs presented it, except that for them they saw the creator as the Fallen Yaldabaoth, and the first creations he made were minions (demonic archons) to help in his creation. But for Plato, since the Demiurge is our friend, these archons become angles in his mind. Thus when one examines both Timaeus and *Republic* as a whole, it can become a possible conclusion that the Cave analogy was likely a type of misdirection.

---

143 O'Brien, Carl S, *The Demiurge in Ancient Thought* pg 17
144 O'Brien pg 21, 29-30
145 As R Blackhurst suggests in a 2003 article "The Mythological and Ritualistic Background of Plato's Timaeus"

The fashioning of man is presented as somewhat more complex. The Demiurge provided man only with the higher, immortal part of the soul. While Plato claimed that the soul's inferior (mortal part), as well as the human body, are the creation of the inferior gods (so lower archons). All souls individual destinies are to be determined by either their either following or neglect of piety and righteousness. In a sense an early idea of karma.

Plato described the highest aspect of the creator as the One or Monad. This One is above the Demiurge. The question to ask is, is Plato's One the Father of the Gnostics outside of the Matrix or is he the Fallen Creator, and Plato's Demiurge takes the role of first archon, the first created "worker" for Lucifer? Interesting that Neo is described as the One in the Matrix. Are the writers of the movie insinuating not that Neo is a saviour but the Fallen Creator?

Emil Cioran wrote the essay "The Evil Demiurge" in 1969. Many claim that article was a Gnostic interpretation, but to my eyes it is that is more of a Schopenhauer look at the idea of an evil creator creating a world of suffering.[146] Cioran claimed, that there likely is a good God, but being good would mean he is impotent because *"Goodness does not create: it lacks the imagination needed to fashion a world, even a slapdash one... The good god was decidedly not equipped to create...he is the prototype of inefficacy: he can't help anyone."* To Cioran, it must be evil god that does any creating, with all of manifestation coming out of himself as if via Will. This is similar to the myth of how the Ancient Egyptians described the first creation coming from Atum masturbating out of himself the first beings. I find this interesting that in the Gnostic myths the first to attempt to create without her opposite gender consort Sophia, and this led to the creation of Yaldabaoth (Demiurge in this context) who would be Atum to the Egyptians. Thus Atum follows the same mistake by creating without a female consort. It could also be a way of explaining a type of artificial AI idea of creation without a computer metaphor.

146All Cioran quotes in this section can be found in
   https://coronzon.com/pdf/cioran/The_Evil_Demiurge_Cioran.pdf,
   [Translated by Frederick Brown]

This question of if the world is just the ideas of evil creator was presented by Cioran as, *"How can we not presume that existence was fouled at its source...? He who does not feel compelled to entertain this hypothesis at least once a day will have sleep-walked through life."* Since all in existence (duality) has come out of this evil creator, it then to Cioran's eyes would have to mean that everything can only be encompassed by evil. There can be nothing good in any of it. And this becomes the ultimate question around creation. What was the Intention of this creator, because based on the Intention, can we understand why reality is as it is. Plato attempts to step around this by claiming, that while the Demiurge is benevolent, *"The world remains imperfect, however, because the Demiurge created the world out of a chaotic, indeterminate non-being."*[147]

*

It is Plato's works that are claimed to be the foundation of a series of 2nd and 3rd century philosophers know as Neo Platonists. they kept the term of the Demiurge, but made it more into a second part of the creator that they linked with the ideas of nous (thought). To a Gnostic, nous was something much different than regular thought, what we might call Divine Knowing or Silent Knowing.

The main proponent of this period was Plotinus (who interestingly has the anagram of Plato to start his name). Plotinus led some strong attacks against the Gnostics of the day writing. A.H. Lawrence presented, *"The Neoplatonic philosopher Plotinus addressed within his works Gnosticism's conception of the Demiurge, which he saw as un-Hellenic and blasphemous to the Demiurge of Plato."* A key underlying reasons for Plotinus' attacks against the Gnostic was because they were describing the creator of matter as evil. *"Plotinus saw the teachings of the Gnostics to be nontraditional, irrational and immoral and perverted the true traditional Platonic doctrine. Worst of all, they despise and hate the material universe and deny its goodness and the goodness of its*

---

147 https://platoindepth.wordpress.com/about-plato/the-demiurge/

maker."[148] One of the things Plotinus was doing in his writing was to make the presentation that to not believe Plato made you non-intellectual or not trustworthy. Several times in his writings he presented that only Plato can be used for the determination of what is true. This is a rather dangerous, to say that only one authority (a figure that he has never met, nor whose students he has not met as they would all be dead by his time period) yet holds up whatever is in a book attributed to him is automatic unquestionable fact. Believe Plato or you are wrong is the message. This is not the place to get into depth with Plotinus and the other Neo Platonists, but you can look up ideas as to how they viewed such ideas as the World Soul (Anima Mundi), Emanation and other terms that attempt to explain why the Demiurge is a good figure. All in all it seems to be another suggested attempt at trying to explain away the obvious world of suffering without any real explanations.

*

Plato had his philosophical detractors. Neitzsche wrote in *Twilight of the Idols, "Do not let anyone suggest Plato to me. In regard to Plato I am a thorough skeptic, and have never been able to agree to the admiration of Plato the artist, which is traditional among scholars."*[149] Karl Popper[150] directly blamed Plato for the rise of totalitarianism in the 20th century. To him, Plato was the Origin of both Hitler and Stalin. This is the hardest part for the average person to realize, that Plato was not writing a philosophic text about freedom, individualism, or Truth, but was writing about how to have an idealized city state. This state was to be led by a group whose job it was to openly lie to the public, with the purpose of controlling the population, so that a societal order could be produced and maintained. This is why the Demiurge had to be presented as good, and who brought in a cosmic order, because the order of the state is going to be linked to the creation of the world. The Demiurge is good, order is good, so it is OK for the state to take away people's freedoms. The concepts Plato is writing on seem not to free anyone, but enslave them even deeper into the

---

148 A. H. Lawrence, *Introduction to Against the Gnostics in Plotinus' Enneads*, pages 220–222

149 https://www.rasmusen.org/blog1/nietzsche-and-plato/

150 Austrian 20th century philosopher can be found at https://en.wikipedia.org/wiki/Karl_Popper

251

material mud. I know this twist is amazing to contemplate until actually reading what he is attributed to him. Again, I do not even know if Plato existed, and if so, what is claimed to be said by him is what he really said. What we do have to examine is that this Greek figure is placed at the top of the intelligence totem pole for several thousand years, thus what gets attributed to him is expected to be followed as "the way one should do things."

Plato's writings suggest that society should be divided into three groups: producers, military and rulers. The rulers need to implement what is termed a "noble lie" to keep everyone to blindly follow the caste system that they set up. The lie he suggested was to tell people that were born at a particular level (labeled as having either gold, silver or lead within their soul, and that metal will determine one's life role. So, can you guess who had the 'gold ruler essence'? Correct, it was Plato and the others he would deem the elite. The military group is self explanatory. The producers (iron group) included everyone else on all other levels (doctors, farmers, craftsmen, judges, artists and merchants). Everyone who was not a soldier or ruler. Thus even those who think of themselves as the elite (doctors, entertainers and the like) are still just a part of the producer-lead class in Plato's set up. Actually these ideas are identical to the way Huxley had set up his totalitarian society in *Brave New World*.

The golden rulers he presented as philosopher-kings. Ideally Socrates suggests that these rulers (of which could include women) are there because they are wise, virtuous and selfless. To combat corruption, Socrates suggests that the rulers would live simply and communally. However only those "born" into this class can be allowed to rule, and as such rulers should only mate with rulers, what we today would call "bloodline breeding." Plato however was critical of these ideas of Socrates, and instead discussed systems to be in place to stop all "political and social change and turn philosophy into an enforcer, rather than a challenger, of authority, while establishing a hierarchical system in which the freedom and rights of the individual would be sacrificed to the collective needs of society." He also claimed that democracy was a problem "due to its excessive freedom." [151]

Hi attempt around the "democracy problem" was to indicate that a problem with democracy is that this structure tends to bring dictators and tyrants to power. And others may claim that his reasoning for this type of "controlled philosopher elite" was to keep a state in a high moral standard and stop the population from splitting into two factions that oppose each other rather than support each other. But there were more concerns when reading his work.

As I dug more into this I found that it seems to be Plato who first devised the metaphor of the state as a ship in book six of the *Republic.* A reminder that this is the same text where one finds the Cave analogy. If you notice, modern law has been set up as "maritime law" not civil law, and that the language of law is full of ship and water references. Key English words in daily use often end in ship: leadership, worship, friendship, citizenship, scholarship, or ownership. Even the word used for entering this reality, "birth," is also the cargo hold of a ship.

Plato's perfect society is presented as a type of ship that, of course, only the ruler Kings can captain. You will surprised how often you find the metaphor of a "ship at state" to be found when discussing government actions. Part of the reason for this Plato claimed is that all the regular sailors (producers) are ignorant and unable to have any real direction themselves, so needs a noble captain to guide them. In one sense there is a bit of truth to this metaphor, the problem is back a few paragraphs, where it is deemed that lies are needed because they are for the "Greater Good." And how many times between 2020 and 2024 has some government official proclaimed the next attempt to trample another human freedom was required for the "Greater Good." Plato's ideas are still living on in our reality.

---

151 Internet Encyclopedia of Philosophy and its Authors, https://iep.utm.edu/popp-pol/, "Plato Political Philosophy" https://iep.utm.edu/platopol/#H1

The reason for this presentation is that everyone needs to take a long look at whoever they have chosen to be foundational "trust figures" for understanding reality. Plato is but one example. His work is constantly presented as the pinnacle of understanding the nature of our world. But with so many discrepancies, not only in the Cave analogy, but his whole work, this all needs to be questioned.

Additional Material 5

Anthony in the Desert?

There was an interesting twist that I found while researching St. Anthony.[152] According to the one who first chronicled his life, Athanasius, Anthony first chose to live in semi-exile in the Nitrian Desert west of Alexandria. After several years there, he decided to withdraw from society completely and went to live in an old Roman fortress near the desert mountain called Pisper, supposedly now with the name Der-el-Memun. There is almost no information on this mountain, only that is opposite Arsinoe (in the Faiyum), but another source placed the mountain in the Giza District. The problem is that Faiyum is not in the Giza District. In looking around, I could not find this mountain currently presented anywhere in Egypt. What if there was no actual mountain? What might it have been a symbol of?

If it was a symbol for Giza, as the Wikipedia page suggests, that would put Anthony right in the heart of pyramid territory. Was he in a fortress, or inside one of the main pyramids of Giza? Was the level of temptation so great because he was having long meditations inside the main chambers of the pyramids? The stories of the few who have shared their experience of overnight stays inside of the King's Chamber of the Great Pyramid are similar to the stories of the temptations of Anthony. If instead this mountain is supposed to be near Arsinoe in the Faiyum, it is very close to the famous labyrinth at Harawa. Could the stories of meeting and dealing with the Minotaur in Greek Mythology be linked to, or even be the same as the Anthony story? Either way,

---

152 Anthony info at https://en.wikipedia.org/wiki/Dayr_al-Maym%C5%ABn,
    https://en.wikipedia.org/wiki/Anthony_the_Great,
    https://www.trismegistos.org/fayum/fayum2/map.php?geo_id=325

his so-called exile might not have been to be alone in the desert, as much as into an Ancient Egyptian structure, which he used energetically to deepen his inner process. This very much makes me wonder about the exile these early Desert Fathers were taking. Most were from Egypt. Was the moving to the desert to get away from human society and noise, or was it to put themselves on Ancient Egyptian power spots, and allow the ancient energy to impact their inner work?

I can say for myself personally, that though I have spent time in various sites all over the world: from stone circles in England and Scandinavia, Toltec and Mayan sites in Mexico, cathedrals in Europe, nothing has matched the intensity or depth of experiences that happened to me in various pyramids of Ancient Egypt. I found one specific spot on the Giza Plateau that seemed "made" for recapitulation. Perhaps this is the underlying message in the work of the Desert Fathers. It is not so much the exile away from regular civilization per se that was important; it is that one takes themselves and their practices to an ancient power spot. Moreover, not for a few hours or months, but a year or two. A

As an aside, one of the most surprising weeks I had from the standpoint of "messages beyond the Matrix" came from spending 12 hours a day for over a week at a set of stone circles in Southern Norway. Not only does one require a place of quiet and stillness where one can go deep within without distraction, but to so at a site of ancient power is what magnifies the process. That might be the underlying message in the stories of the Desert Fathers and Mothers.

I want to add a part as well for future research, that being the rarely mentioned link of the story of Anthony and the story of Rennes Le Chateau and the mystery of this small Southern French village. Two paintings mentioned in some very odd 1960s documents.[153] One was Poussin's *ET in Arcadia Ego*. When one realizes that in this context Arcadia is not heaven or nirvana, but

---

153 The story is presented in some detail in a 11 part series on my Youtube channel.
  The validity of these parchments are up for question, but they do offer clues to the
  overall mystery

the Pleroma, the painting begins to make more sense as to why the key figure of the four in the painting is the shepherdess (Divine Spark, Sleeping Beauty). The second parchment clue was the phrase "Teniers no temptation." Teniers were father and son painters (known to history as Older and Younger) and each painted several versions of Anthony being tempted. The parchments seems to be referring to one specifically, but which one? Henry Lincoln found a painting by Teniers the Younger, which had been incorrectly labeled, at Shugbourough Hall in England (where one also finds a reversed *Et in Arcadia Ego* relief). The painting turned out to be *St. Paul and St. Anthony in the Desert,* one of the few paintings were Anthony is not being tempted. I won't go into all the symbolic detail in the painting, I will save that for my upcoming book on Southern France, but the painting of Paul and Anthony is a depiction of life after fully entering Emptiness and awakening the Divine Spark. This painting is showing the reality after Anthony had rejected everything that the Matrix simulation could throw at him, and had reached his Intended goal. You are looking not at a painting of detachment, as a practice that someone is doing, but rather a living reality from having seen though every deception, lie and error of the Matrix and self, and is now abiding in the Oneness of the Celestial Fire.

There is one final connection of Anthony to the mystery of Southern France. The date of January 17 turns up repeatedly in its history of deaths, ceremonies and odd events. Rarely mentioned is that St. Anthony's death was on January 17. Another desert father interestingly is also venerated on January 17, is Pachomius the Great, another exile who lived at the time of Anthony (and who claimed to use him as a model). Pachomius first lived near Luxor but later moved north and set up a type of hermit sanctuary near Nag Hammadi (yes that Nag Hammadi, right at the time Gnostics were living and teaching in the area).[154]

---

154 https://en.wikipedia.org/wiki/Pachomius_the_Great

Additional Material 6

Commitment

A key foundation for any pathway is commitment. It can also be called Ultimate Intent or having a clear vector. I discuss some of this in chapter three of *Falling for Truth*, but the topic deserves a reminder here. Without commitment within our reality, not much is going to happen. No matter how big or small the want, the focus we put towards it makes the possibility of reaching it or manifesting it possible. Of course in a book like this we are discussing what might be said the Ultimate direction of energy, and thus commitment becomes a magical force when applied to the fullest. In the sense of Knowing Oneself, Finding Truth or Exiting the Matrix, there can be no secondary commitment.

I had not come across Richard Rose's material until eight or nine years after I had my Egypt TV experience, but when I read the sections he wrote on commitment I understood the concept immediately because it was something that I had been doing after deciding that the study of Ancient Egypt was my one and only focus. I felt that there was a message for me waiting in the Egyptian Pyramids, I knew I was going there at some point in the future, and everything in my current life up was simply preparing me for that experience. So anytime a decision on anything would occur in the course of the day, there became one simple question I could ask myself, would this activity, person or event take me closer to being ready for my trip to Egypt or not? Everything became quite simple. It either fit into my overall deepest direction, or it did not.

Richard Rose described Ultimate Commitment by the phrase of having a vector. A vector is a principle in physics meaning a strong force moving in a specific direction. It can be anything that we think we really want. If someone wants ten million dollars, a gold medal, to be a great parent, or know what God or Self is, then one has to be focused enough in intent to create that direction, and then disciplined enough to follow the course required. And that means you have to know yourself well, to what that one main drive for you really is. You can't have ten different commitments and think you have the energy for all of them, there has to be one that is going to be your focus and it is where you will put at least 50% of your total energy expenditure.

Now before I go farther on this subject, I do have to add that commitment and hard work is only one half of the path to Ultimate Achievement (well reaching any goal). That the other side includes the ideas of between-ness, which is a knowing of when to step back and stop. Certain times call for a pause, literally as the other side of commitment is non-action. The move together like the swinging hand of a grandfather clock.

For Rose making an Ultimate Commitment was a holy act, it is what opened the doors to all sorts of power. Rose fully believed that once any major commitment is made, it brings in a secondary layer of help. I do not think this is coming from angels, spirit guides, Jesus or anything else, but comes from the depth of that which we are. This manifests as pointers, direction turns, magical occurrences, and even the ability to make slight changes to the material Matrix. This is not a goal in itself but are secondary results of the vector once established. Thus to Rose prayer is not something that was thought of as asking some higher deity for help or materiel goodies. True prayer was an honest vector (meaning a vector that merged with our deepest wishes) and then lived out fully day by day, moment by moment. That is how one's life becomes a prayer, we turn our life into the direction of our vector. The Divine Spark is responding to the deepest intent of the character/vehicle it is connected with.

The commitment we make, and the parts of it that we decide to put into our day to day live become what is important. I was with Mr. Park when the 2001 event happened event happened. During the day, many of those of us at the house were rather concerned about the world situation at that point. Four or five of us went into his room to ask him a key question, with what just happened in New York and the possible start of World War 3, what should we do? His reply was simple, "do your exercises." Then he sort of shewed us out of his room like mosquitoes.

We went to the living room area and discussed the message. By exercises he meant the practices that we were all doing on any given day. The point of course, just because the world changes around you is no reason to stop doing one's exercises. In a sense he was asking us, decide on what is the most important thing in your life? What is our vector (which for us these daily exercises were a part of). So that afternoon and evening we just went back to exactly what we had been doing the previous day. That continued with no reason for it to change, unless we chose to stop or change the exercises for personal reasons, not because of something the outer world was doing. Our inner world, and our commitment to knowing was what was important. And as such the way our day to day world was being structured was to reflect that inner direction.

Additional Material 7

The Vision[155]

There is another viewpoint to this realm and why we are the way we are. I have only alluded to it at this point in the book, but will share that view now. I had this vision in 2009. My vision was that it was not the Demiurge that made us, but nature, in order to help us find an escape route from the Demiurge. The vision indicates that the Demiurge made the world, but nature made us, and this is the reason his archons and in-world minions are trying so hard to stop us and slow us down.

Looking back on the experience, what was quite co-incidental, was that to "have this vision," in my dream journey I went into a "cave." What is also very interesting was how I felt when I exited, refreshed and renewed. I have left the vision as is, but have included double brackets around an added idea that gives another viewpoint on what the original vision may have been pointing towards. This vision claims all of nature is trapped, but it did not tell me how it had been created, what the original trap for it had been, nor how souls animate humans.

In late 2009, an inner alchemic fire started to burn inside. Hidden parts of my own egoic structures I thought were long gone, had come to the surface, bringing much pain and confusion, matched by the fire inside that would not go out. Demons and dark forces began to up their attacks. On one hand I wondered why? Why attack a man in trouble, you attack when someone needs to be stopped? I dealt with it, night after night of one hour of sleep and little interest in eating. Suffering inside over my own mistakes, and my own lack of belief in all the gifts I had been

---

155 The section originally appeared in (originally appeared in *Exit the Cave, Ending the Reincarnation Trap*)

shown. I spent a weekend with a Native Medicine Man, Jerry, and in the course of that weekend this "old" vision appeared to me. By old I felt this was what came to early humans 100,000 years ago to explain who we were, where we came from, and what it means.

"Before the first humans were born, there were rocks, trees, plants, animals, water. One day they realized that for all their seemed freedom and peace, they were trapped in a type of loop. They saw what was needed to be done for all of them to gain their freedom, but they themselves (nature) could not accomplish that act. They had a meeting of what to do about it.

They asked Mother Sophia for help. She allowed nature to create a new being to help them do what they could not. Nature created humans as the active force to open the freedom door for it, and to assist us, nature would be our guide. Nature created humans out of all the parts of itself: one plant, one rock, one drop of water, one gust of air, and one animal all combined their forces. The animal part that came for each individual human is now called the "power" or "totem" animal, because it is the easiest part to reach of the nature forces that created us. All humans were created at the same time, but were only brought into the manifested world as needed. And then they asked us to do the things that needed to be done for them.

That is why nature allows us to use it. Because we are a part of nature, we are here to do a job for nature, it was they who asked us to be here and created us. It is why trees allow themselves to be cut down for warmth or a deer allows itself to be killed for meat. They do so as a sacrifice for us, so that humans can keep going to fulfill the very role we were created for. If we can complete that, then not just all humans, but all of nature as well, will be free. The loop will end. Nature can take humans with guidance to that doorway, but needs the humans to walk through it.

When nature first understood these things, they also saw that there was a dark force in place that kept everything locked in an odd continuing loop of time. At first this darkness did not need to do much, because there was little that nature could do itself to end it, because nature was set up as a loop "circle of life," ((food chain)). It could not end the loop without ending itself. That is why nature created humans. And this dark force instantly recognized that humans were a danger for the entire system. The dark force created a counter-force out of itself that had the only job of making sure humans could not complete their task. ((You could see this as an army of Matrix Mr. Smiths)). Because if humans succeeded, all of nature would be free, and the dark force would have nowhere to go. The dark force is dependent on the vortex loop.

It is why this dark force attacks humans so hard, but rarely attacks nature directly. Nature set up power spots, places of strong energy where humans can go to and have open communication with the spirits of nature- and with the spirits that live in the realm above nature. Early humans built temples and structures here to make this communication, or to amplify the power of what was shown to them. The dark force saw this, so spent much of its time attempting to gain control of these power spots, that are the direct openings of communication between nature and humans. As more of these spots were taken over by the dark forces, nature passed on a new way to communicate that while not as clear and perfect (like a semi-garbled phone line) it was a line the dark forces could not cut. They gave humans ceremony, and power tools that would in a sense create a small power opening where the ceremony was performed.

As humans learned more, and gained more understanding of what this place is and what our job is, the dark forces needed to up the attacks even more, and manifested a "computer generated force" of supreme attack inside the dream state. Part of their job was to do everything to block the ceremonies given to humans, and thus began their own counter ((inverse)) ceremonies "satanic ritual, subliminal conditioning and mind control." One of their most amazing attempts to stop humans was to give us a parasite, the egoic mind. This virus spread until few could even realize there was a time when it was not here, and no one questions the egoic mind's origin. Yet every spiritual work in history talks of the dangers of our own mind. Why should our mind be dangerous if it is ours? And that is the point they miss. It is not ours; it is the blocking mechanism of those dark forces. ((These dark forces over time have gotten humans to forget more and more why we are here. Many humans even spend their time destroying and harming nature and its creatures, the very things that gave us our original life)).

Nature knows the way out. They know where the doorway is and what to do. They want to take us to that door. But they also know that first the parasite-virus (egoic mind) must be removed. And this is far more of a challenge than anyone understands it to be. Only when that parasite is completely gone, can nature be back in direct conversation with us, guiding us, and showing us what needs to be done. Nature can pass on messages, provide energy, open blocks, but we will have to do the rest. Nature is not in any way separate from us, we come directly from it. There is a reason the creation myth has humans made out of the clay of the Earth. It is symbolic to say our creator is nature itself, the Earth allowed the creation by nature to be. Earth is not our mother, but our GRANDMOTHER. It is why in the old writings nature was not just female, but also male, it encapsulates all.

The entire structure of the earliest human wisdom, mythology, texts and tales were passed on for generations, and at its core is about this creation, the wants of nature for us, and the dark forces that are attempting to stop that from happening. When we reach back to this place within and without, we will know exactly what we are asked to do, and then we either do it and end the loop once and for all. If we do not, the loop will reset, and everything starts all over again.

This is the vision that was presented to me in the cave. Thank you."

*

What also makes this vision so interesting is that we are not trapped by the Demiurge directly, we are trapped because we originate from that which is already trapped "nature." But within humans is a special part that would allow, not just our exit, but that for all of nature, in fact the entire realm. My vision is thus very different from the creation myths of the Gnostics and Cathars, who believed that humans souls were tricked into coming into matter. It

makes quite a change to think we might be a "non-individual" soul
as we normally think of it, but instead tied to the souls of nature.
Perhaps each human who ends the reincarnation cycle takes some
of nature along with it, when we leave.

BIBLIOGRAPHY

Anagnostou, Angeliki. *Can You Stand The Truth? The Chronicle of Man's Imprisonment* (Kalogera 2012)

Caplan, Mariana. *Halfway Up the Mountain* (Hohm Press 2015)

Carse, David. *Perfect Brilliant Stillness* (Paragate Publishing 2005)

Cartwright, David E. *Schopenhauer: a Biography* (Cambridge University Press 2015)

Castaneda, Carlos. *A Separate Reality* (Washington Square Press, 1991)

Cioran, Emil. "The Evil Demiurge" (*Hudson Review* vol 20, no2 1967)

Climacus, John (trans by Archimandrite Lazarus Moore). *The Ladder of Divine Ascent* (Harper and Brothers 1959)

Eliade, Mircea. *Shamanism, Archaic Techniques of Ecstasy* (Routledge and Kegan Paul Ltd 1970)

Gold, David, Marshall, Bart. *After the Absolute* (Realface Press, 2023)

Grimwood, Ken. *Replay* (William Morrow Paperbacks 1998)

Kent, John. *A Path to Reality Through the Self* (PHD thesis) available to read at https://www.searchwithin.org/johnkent/index.html

Kushi, Norio. Awake at the Wheel (TAT Foundation Press, 2018)

Johnson, Julian. *Path of Masters* (Radha Soami Satsang Beas, 1939)

Marshall, Bart. *The Perennial Way* (TAT Foundation Press, 2009)

-------------- *Becoming Vulnerable to Grace* (Realface Press, 2021)

McGowan, David. *Weird Secrets Inside the Canyon* (Headpress 2014)

Monroe, Robert. *Ultimate Journey* (Harmony Books 1994)

O'Brien, Carl Sean. *The Demiurge in Ancient Thought* (Cambridge University Press, 2018)

Palamas, St. Gregory, translated by Robin Amis. *Holy Hesychia: The Stillness That Knows God* (Pleroma Publishing 2016)

Palmer GEH (translator). *Philokalkia* (SD Books 1983)

Panella, John. *Time Loop Chronicles vol 1* (Create Space 2017)

Renz, Karl. *The Myth of Enlightenment* (Inner Directions, 2005)

Schopenhauer, Arthur. *On the Sufferings of the World, On the Basis of Morality,* and *On the Will and Representation* (original works found at project Gutenberg, gutenberg.org)

Segal, Suzanne. *Collision With the Infinite* (Blue Dover Press 1996)

West, John Anthony. *Serpent in the Sky : The High Wisdom of Ancient Egypt* (Quest Books 1979)

Wortley, John. *The Anonymous Sayings of the Desert Fathers* (Cambridge University Press 2013)

About the Author

Howdie Mickoski is an author and researcher focusing on philosophy and history. He shares his opinions on reality and hopes they are of value to people as they look within to find their own answers.

howdiemickoski.com/

howdiemickoski.locals.com/

Other books:

Exit the Cave Book 1: Ending the reincarnation trap

Exposing the Expositions: 1851-1915 revised

Falling For Truth: A spiritual death and awakening

The Power of Then: Revealing Egypt's lost wisdom

Hockey's Origin Unmasked